BATTLE THE FLAMES

David Needham

Dedication

This book is dedicated to the men and women of the Local Authority Fire Brigades, the Auxiliary Fire Service, the National Fire Service, the Air Raid Precautions Services and the Civil Defence Organisation.

Their service to the people of Nottinghamshire and throughout the United Kingdom was a shining example of selflessness, courage and determination.

Above: The Fourth Arm'. A statuette commissioned to commemorate the Civil Defence services who were considered to be the Fourth Arm of the United Kingdom Forces

Published by

The Horizon Press
The Oaks, Moor Farm Road West, Ashbourne, DE6 1HD
Tel: (01335) 347349 Fax: (01335) 347303

1st Edition

ISBN: 1 978-1-84306-486-2

© **David Needham 2009**

Acknowledgements

Alsop, Iris
Barratt, Jennifer
Bartles, Charlie
Boots PLC
Broughton, Bill
Brown, Ray
Burton (nee Singleton)
Carrott, Monica (nee Emery)
Caunt, Albert
Cawthorne, Anne
Cawthorne, Ted
Chadwick, Sam
Chadwick, William
Chamberlain, Bernard
Chamberlain, George
Chapman, Nigel
Clay, Frank
Cooke, Janet(nee Sayer)
Dobbs, Albert
Dunkerly, Jill
Dunkerley, Jim
Elliott, Keith
Freer, Pat
Grundy, Richard
Hammond, Andy (NSK Europe Ltd.)
Hatherley, George
Haynes, Rose (nee Carlisle)
His Majesty's Stationery Office
Hodson, George
Hogg, Doris (nee Bennett)
Iqbal, Zaf
Joyce, Margaret

Kummer, Fred
London Fire Brigade
Magginnis, Carolyn (Nottingham Evening Post)
Maslin, Bob
McKenzie, Clifford
Miller, Reg
Mitchell, Stan
Musgrove, Irene
Naylor, Geoff
Needham, Gordon
Newark Advertiser
Newark Library, local studies section
Newark Museum
Nix, Leslie
Nottingham Central Library, local studies section
Nottingham Co-operative Society
Nottingham Evening Post
Nottingham Guardian Journal
Nottinghamshire Archives
Nottinghamshire Fire & Rescue Service
NSK Europe Ltd (previously Ransome & Marles)
Parker, June (nee Parkin)
Parkes, David
Parrott, David
Patrick, Patricia
Porkett, Alf
Raybould, Chris
Revill, Nancy
Roe, Harry
Rose, Victor
Rossia, Anna
Ritchie, Dorothy (Nottingham Central Library)

Sallis, Jean
Sayer, Marjorie (nee Bailey)
Sewell, Dolly
Sharpe, Edgar
Shaw, Bill
Shelton, Charlie
Shipley, Coris
Shipley, Fred
Smedley, David (Nottinghamshire Fire & Rescue Service)
Spendlove, Glyn
Springthorpe, Joe
Spyby, Arthur
Stanton, Arthur
Strickson, Henry
Swain, Sam
Tinley, Joyce
Theaker, Arthur
Varley, Iris
Wadsworth, Les
Wakelin, Dorothy (nee Heald)
Walls, John
Warner, Tim (Newark Library)
Webster, Grace
Whitworth, John
Wilkin, Colin
Wilson, Ida
Wolf, Roy
Woods, Murie
Wright, Pauline

Printed by: CPI, Anthony Rowe, Chippenham   **Design:** Mark Titterton   **Edited by:** Ian Howe

Front cover: Left: Trivett's factory in Nottingham's Lace Market. Burnt out after an air raid on 8th/9th May 1941
Right top: Fire crews of Fire Force 8 (Nottinghamshire), the National Fire Service, direct cooling jets onto a gasometer during
an exercise. Middle: St John's Church, Leenside, Nottingham burnt out after an air raid on 8th/9th May 1941
Bottom: Fire Crews of Nottingham's Auxiliary Fire Service provide a 'water curtain' to protect buildings during a national
exercise held on 4th May 1940

Back cover: Top:Firemen of Fire Force 8, the National Fire Service, at a training exercise where foam has been used on
gasometers in Radford. Bottom: Air raid damage -The Moot Hall

Contents

Introduction

If the Battle of Britain was won by "The Few", the Battle of the Flames was won by the many. The many who were for the most part ordinary people whose jobs did not involve them in battling against fires, or saving lives. They learned new roles and quickly became the army that defended the United Kingdom and its people in the face of total war, the likes of which the world had not seen before.

It was through their hard work, bravery and devotion to duty that the battle against flames and explosives on the home front was won. From there, the armed forces of the United Kingdom and its allies were able to step forward in liberation.

This book began life as an article for the journal of the Nottinghamshire Fire and Rescue Service in 1990. Through talking to wartime veterans of the Fire Service and the Air Raid Precautions Service, it became apparent that the story they had to tell of what had happened during those years was so compelling that it seemed essential to record it for posterity.

Frank Clay was one of the firemen who told me what he had seen and what he and others had done during the war and he commented afterwards, *"I feel relieved that I have told you all this because I know that you will write it down so that it will not be forgotten."* It felt a great burden to be entrusted with such a task, but it was also a privilege that so many people shared with me their hopes and fears and innermost thoughts from those war years.

This is the story of the people of Nottinghamshire and the aerial war waged against them.

Personal acknowledgements

In addition to the acknowledgements at the back of this book I want to personally express my appreciation to those who have given their time to help me piece together the information for this book many of whom have since passed away.

I also want to thank Miriam, Catherine and Louise for encouraging me to tell the story contained in this book and having the patience to allow me to complete it. Particular thanks go to Catherine for proof reading chapters and checking photographs.

1. Air Raid Precautions

". . . In war, whichever side may call itself the victor, there are no winners, but all are losers . . ."

Neville Chamberlain
3rd July 1938

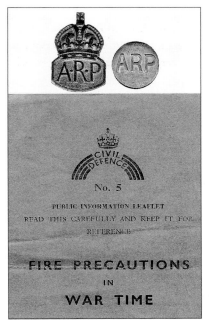

Above: Air Raid Precautions badge and an ARP Warden's uniform button Below: Fire precautions in wartime booklet

Nottinghamshire's air raid precautions were under way long before war broke out and Captain Athelston Popkess, the Chief Constable of Nottingham City Police, was appointed as Air Raid Precautions Controller for the city. He had observed the effects of air raids on cities during the 1936–39 Spanish Civil War.

As early as 1933 the Fire Service had considered the problem of large numbers of fires caused by bombing. They were under no illusions as to the effect of a concerted incendiary raid or the use of high-explosive bombs on any major town or city in Britain. The slaughter of 2,000 civilians during air raids on Guernica in Spain, carried out by Germany's Luftwaffe, showed what modern bombing techniques could do. Most of the Guernica casualties had been caused by the massive fires that had burned out of control and the lessons learned by the Luftwaffe during the three years of the Spanish Civil War were put to use when they began their bombing campaigns against enemies during the Second World War. The Air Raid Precautions Act 1937 compelled local authorities to prepare civil defence schemes that would enable them to deal effectively with the results of enemy air attacks. The Home Office issued a thirty-six-page booklet in 1938 which cost 1d and was entitled *"The protection of your home against air raids"*. It gave advice on the air raid warning system, respirators, choosing refuge rooms and the items required in them. The booklet explained how to prepare the refuge room against gas attack, how to use materials to make an effective blackout for the home, and gave useful hints on first aid.

The "Precautions against Fire" section of the booklet left people in no doubt that they would have to do everything they could themselves to save their own property when raids took place.

"An air attack may include the use of large numbers of incendiary bombs. So many fires might be caused that the fire brigades could not deal with them all and every citizen must be prepared to help. Do these things the moment you receive official warning that war threatens:

1.) Clear the loft, attic or top floor of all flammable material, paper, litter, lumber etc., to lessen the danger of fire and to prevent the fire from spreading.

2.) If the materials are available, protect the floor of the loft, attic or top floor in one of the following ways: with sheets of corrugated iron or plain sheet iron (22 gauge or thicker), or asbestos wallboard, or with two inches of sand if the floor will bear the weight.

3.) It is advisable to coat all the woodwork in the attic or roof with limewash, to delay its catching fire.

4.) For controlling an incendiary bomb, have on an upper floor a bucket or box of dry sand or earth, together with a shovel fitted with a long handle.

5.) Water is the best means of putting out a fire but the mains may be damaged in an air raid or the flow restricted by fire fighting operations. So, make sure you have some water ready in buckets about the house. A simple appliance for households is the stirrup pump for use with an ordinary bucket. It has thirty feet of hose and a special nozzle which can be adjusted to deliver a jet for dealing with fires or a spray for use on an incendiary bomb."

Two items which formed part of the personal protection for civilians in the event of war were respirators, or gas masks as they were known to the public, and an air raid shelter.

Anderson Shelters were designed in 1938 in response to a request from the Home Office for a design that could be mass-produced relatively cheaply. It comprised sections of curved and straight corrugated iron that were assembled on site. The shelter was intended to be partially embedded in the ground and then covered with a bank of soil on the parts of the sides and top that remained above ground. This provided additional protection from the blast of bombs and debris thrown through the air by explosions. Six people could be accommodated in an Anderson Shelter and each householder was required to equip it in such a way that the family could shelter

Above: Inside an Anderson Shelter

in it for many hours. Some householders built bunks to go into the shelter and achieved a level of relative comfort. Other householders ended up with a damp, cold, inhospitable structure that flooded every time it rained because it was situated on low-lying ground. Anderson Shelters were issued free to households where the weekly income was less than £4.0s.0d.

Where it was not possible to erect an Anderson Shelter because there was no garden, then the basement of the property, if it had one, would be strengthened for use as a shelter.

Another answer to the problem of providing personal protection during an air raid was the Morrison Shelter. This shelter was named after Herbert Morrison, the Minister of Home Security, and it was issued to families who had someone who was disabled or had a long-term illness and could not be expected to seek refuge in an outdoor shelter. The Morrison Shelter was a steel shell in the form of a table with a cage around the underside. The family had to crawl underneath this protective structure situated inside the house and take shelter there.

An ARP warden tackling an incendiary bomb Right: A 1kg magnesium incendiary bomb (Photographs courtesy of Nottingham City Fire Brigade archives)

Street shelters built of brick were also provided and these could accommodate 20 to 40 people. In some parts of the country, the construction of large numbers of brick shelters was seen as a quick way to make money out of the government and builders used cheap mortar in the construction. The mortar had too much lime in it and as a consequence of this, the first serious blast that it had to withstand brought it crashing down on to the occupants with serious results. Fortunately there were no recorded instances of this occurring in Nottingham.

There were 288 public shelters in Nottingham which provided accommodation for 33,200 persons. Caves in the Nottingham Sandstone accounted for 72 of the shelters, with a capacity of 7,754 persons, and 110 basements gave another 13,581 places. The remaining 11,865 places were provided by surface shelters and trenches. Anderson shelters were distributed to 24,200 families on city housing estates and 2,280 other people had their shelter arrangements provided for by a brick-built surface shelter being constructed in a back yard. The basements of 6,400 houses were strengthened and 1,402 communal surface shelters built, and Morrison shelters were issued in 1,225 cases that qualified for them.

The authorities expected citizens to volunteer for Air Raid Precautions (ARP) Services. Volunteers were required for air raid wardens, the auxiliary fire service, communications services, decontamination squads, demolition parties, rescue parties, medical duties and the medical transport corps. There was also a request for people to lend vehicles for use by one of the branches of civil defence.

The country was divided into twelve civil defence regions and Nottinghamshire was in region number 3 along with Lincolnshire, Leicestershire, Derbyshire, Rutland and Northamptonshire. The headquarters for number 3 region was at Mapperley Hall in Lucknow Drive, Mapperley Park, Nottingham and Lord Trent was appointed as the ARP controller for the region.

The city was divided into five civil defence divisions: City, Bulwell, Hyson Green, Leenside and Radford. Each division had a control and reporting centre that would deal with information concerning air raids. It would co-ordinate all the measures that were taken to deal with air raid damage. The main Nottingham ARP control and reporting centre was situated in the basement underneath the Central Fire Station in Shakespeare Street. The fire brigade control and the police control were also in rooms off the corridors beneath the station. No doubt this seemed to be advantageous when the arrangements were made, but the decision to have three key control rooms within the same basement area was complete folly and only serves to show the lack of understanding on the part of the ARP controller who approved the arrangements. One large-calibre high-explosive bomb could have destroyed all three control rooms in one go.

The county was also subdivided and this was done simply by district council areas. This meant that there were 21 ARP reporting centres stretching from Bingham and West Bridgford in the south through to Mansfield, Worksop and Retford in the north. To the east of the county was the reporting centre at Newark and one at Southwell, whilst Kirkby and Eastwood each had a reporting centre to the west.

Left Top: The Shire Hall on High Pavement where the County ARP control room was situated in the basement

Bottom: Central Fire Station on Shakespeare Street – The City ARP control, Fire Brigade control and Police control were all situated in the basement of this building

County ARP Control

City ARP Control

Left: View across the city centre showing how close the city and county ARP control rooms were

The ARP control and reporting centre for the county was in the basement of the Shire Hall on High Pavement in Nottingham. To have the county control situated within Nottingham City was another foolhardy decision as a concentrated air attack could have led to both the city and county controls being put out of action. The two locations in the city centre were just seconds apart in terms of flying time and it is not unrealistic to suggest that a single aircraft releasing its bombs could have destroyed the city and county ARP controls and at the same time destroyed the fire service and police control rooms for the city. This would have been a catastrophic blow from which there could have been no recovery during the raid and in fact it would have taken weeks to replace the infrastructure destroyed. Arguably this went beyond being foolhardy and bordered on serious professional misjudgement. It calls into question what those making the decisions about the locations of these control rooms were basing their decisions upon given that the effects of bombing on built-up areas was already known. The authorities were extremely lucky, as events were later to show when the building housing the county control was set on fire by an incendiary bomb and, at the same time, the city control was within 20 yards of a direct hit by a high-explosive bomb.

The control and reporting centres were embodied within the air raid warden service and were staffed continuously by a core of paid full-time personnel. The full-time staff were augmented by volunteers on a nightly rota basis and by yet more volunteers when the air raid sirens gave the alert.

The whole-time staff consisted of 107 women and 27 men. There were 180 part-time volunteers, 144 of these being women, who were telephonists. The reporting centres had a crucial role to play and their chain of command went right up to the war room in London. The air raid warden service for Nottingham was under the direct command of the Commandant at Goldsmith Chambers in Goldsmith Street, Nottingham. There were 177 warden posts, of which 125 were made of concrete, and a further 52 warden posts were situated in buildings or basements which had been specially adapted for the purpose.

The warden posts were equipped with telephones and electric lighting, an electric radiator, gas boiling ring, chairs and bunk beds. They also had first aid equipment, a stretcher and a stirrup pump and bucket. Although the picture painted is one of comparative comfort, this should be tempered by the fact that only 102 of the posts had *"sanitary annexes"*. Of course the question that comes to mind is – what did they do at the other 75 posts?

A great many volunteers were needed for the warden service and Nottingham people responded magnificently; 2,294 men and 700 women became part-time wardens. In addition, 335 paid whole-time wardens were recruited; they consisted of 258 men and 77 women. Elsewhere in the county, people were no less unstinting. West Bridgford recruited 200 wardens, Bingham had 191, Beeston 529, Arnold 196 and Carlton 340 wardens. Basford was very well provided for as they recruited 1,054 wardens.

The air raid wardens were said to be the *"eyes and ears"* of the civil defence organisation and great reliance was placed upon their being local people. They would know the area that they covered extremely well, and they would know who lived where and when they were at home or at work. They would know who could be relied upon to help in an emergency and also those in their community who would need help. The wardens were actually required as part of their duties to keep up-to-date information about the number of persons residing in their sector and where they normally sheltered. This information was for the use of ARP Incident Officers.

ARP Incident Officers were air raid wardens who had been selected to undergo additional training to enable them to take charge of all civil defence matters at an incident with the exception of firefighting. The reason for this was that firefighting was a specialised element of civil defence work and the fire service already had a command structure that was well trained; each fire crew knew the area in which they operated, including specific industrial risks. There was nothing to be gained by duplicating this structure.

At incidents requiring the attendance of the ARP services, the police were tasked with controlling an outer cordon around the incident and would be responsible for controlling traffic and public order. Inside this ring, the ARP Incident Officer would liaise between the various elements of the ARP service and ensure the smooth running of their operations. The fire officer would direct firefighting operations and liaise with the ARP Incident Officer. The concept was simple and effective when operated by officers with a professional common-sense approach.

Many Chief Constables were not satisfied with these arrangements and agitated until some senior police officers were also trained as incident officers. The reason for this became apparent once ARP incidents occurred during the war as many of these senior police officers went out of their way to try to prevent ARP incident officers taking charge at incidents. Some police officers put their egos before the interests of the public and ordered ARP incident officers away from the scene of operations. This was an abuse of authority and only served to make the ARP services aggrieved at the police involving themselves in areas of work they knew little or nothing about. The ARP officers reasoned,

". . . surely the police have enough other work to do at an incident without taking over the command of operations that they have no experience of."

The various sections of the ARP service all had their own commandant who was answerable to the ARP Controller, who was in turn answerable to the Regional ARP Controller. The medical services were under the command of Dr Vernon Taylor, whose headquarters was at 118 Mansfield Road in Nottingham. This service comprised of first aid parties, first aid posts, casualty depots, cars for first aid parties and also ambulances. They had nine depots within the five divisions of Nottingham and were responsible for casualties from the time they were picked up until they were handed over at a hospital or a mortuary.

There were 93 first aid parties in Nottingham, consisting of 355 whole-time men and 244 part-time men. They were equipped with 38 cars for transport and a further 10 cars for evacuating

Issued by the Ministry of Health and the Department of Health for Scotland.

FIRST AID IN BRIEF

Read this carefully several times, then carry it in your pocket or bag

AFTER AN AIR ATTACK First Aid Parties will reach the wounded within a few minutes. Even such a short time counts. The man or woman on the spot can save lives by immediate and proper action.

Be prepared to see severe wounds. Be courageous and keep your head. Keep your mind on your duty to your injured fellow man.

Everyone in these days of danger should carry several clean handkerchiefs or small towels. These can be used as bandages, and their inner laundered surfaces are quite suitable for application to open wounds as a first dressing. Unless a patient is in a highly dangerous place you should treat him where he lies. To lift or drag the wounded can do serious damage. Your general rule is that the moving and transport should be left to trained parties. **The first and most important duty of the civilian helper who first reaches a casualty is to stop bleeding.**

When you cut a limb you naturally grab it firmly with the fingers of your other hand. That application of pressure to a bleeding wound is the correct thing to do in all cases.

TO STOP BLEEDING

Press on the bleeding point with fingers or hands. As soon as possible apply a clean thick pad of folded handkerchief or towel. Use an inner surface of your handkerchiefs or towels. Keep up the pressure through this pad. Bandage the pad firmly in position over the wound. Be sure that the dressing is applied firmly enough to control the loss of blood. If there is still oozing of blood past or through the pad renew pressure over the whole dressing.

BLEEDING FROM ARM OR LEG

Press on the wound with fingers or hands. Apply a clean thick pad as soon as possible. Keep up pressure through the pad. Bandage the pad firmly over the wound. If this fails, pass a bandage, tie, handkerchief, elastic or fabric belt, or similar article, round the limb as close to the wound as possible, at a point between the wound and the trunk. Knot the fabric so that the limb is loosely encircled. Pass a stick through the slack loop and twist till the tightening of the band round the limb stops the blood loss, taking care not to pinch the skin. Hold tight till the First Aid Party arrives. If you have to do this, make a note of the time when you tighten the loop and give it to the patient or attach it to the limb. It is very important that the hospital surgeon should know this.

Left: First aid leaflet issued to the public

Right: ARP First Aid Party member Cyril Theaker in his St John's Ambulance uniform just before the outbreak of war

Above: Ambulance drivers – part of the ARP Casualty Service (Photograph courtesy of Nottingham Evening Post)

Above: Victoria Baths in Nottingham City - designated for use as a mortuary

injured people who were able to sit up. When the casualties had received first aid at the scene, they would then be transported to one of eleven first aid posts, each of which was staffed by two doctors and a team of nurses. Each post was equipped with a full range of medical requisites, including drugs, and they were strategically sited around the five city divisions. Posts were situated at St Catherine's Hall, The Children's Hospital, Ronald Street School, Queen's Drive Hall, Wells Road Hall, Noel Street Baths, Triumph Road Depot, Melbourne Road recreational ground, Basford Works and Ways Department, Vale Brook Lodge on Hucknall Road and the Bulwell Baptist Chapel.

The Casualty Service provided three mobile first aid units, which operated from St Catherine's Hall, Triumph Road Depot and the Bulwell Baptist Chapel. The units were adapted from single-deck corporation buses and were to be deployed as necessary in support of the other first aid posts. It was estimated that they would be functioning twenty minutes after arrival.

The 73 ambulances of the casualty service included three obsolete buses which could take up to 18 stretchers each. All the whole-time ambulance drivers were women and 56 of the 96 part-time drivers were also women.

Gas cleansing stations were a separate part of the ARP service but tended to be established at or near first aid posts. There were eight cleansing depots in the city and their role was one of decontaminating the streets and buildings in the event of a gas attack. The personnel needed for the stations had been recruited fairly easily amongst the corporation sanitation departments and the work and the equipment required was not tremendously different to what was expected of them in their day-to-day role. The key difference in the event of a gas attack was that they would have to work in either light or heavy gas suits and respirators depending upon the gas concentration.

The Department of Civilian Deaths was established to deal with deaths due to enemy action. Swimming baths in Nottingham were identified as ideal locations to set up temporary mortuaries. Those designated for use as mortuaries were Victoria, Northern, Noel Street, Portland and Radford Baths. The gruesome facts were that it was calculated the mortuaries could deal with up to 1,250 bodies in 48 hours and if that capacity were overwhelmed, a support scheme would be invoked where neighbouring authorities would be asked to help. Initially this would be within the region and then, if necessary, outside the region.

The Rescue Service was another vital element of the ARP Service and these squads had the task of extricating casualties from collapsed structures so that the first aid parties could render help. Nowadays we are used to seeing the words "Fire and Rescue Service" on the sides of our fire appliances and we accept it as normal practice that the fire service undertakes a wide range of rescue work. During the war years, however, there was the potential that a great many people would need to be rescued from partially collapsed buildings as a result of air attacks and it was anticipated that such rescue operations would in many cases be protracted. The fire brigades would have their hands full dealing with outbreaks of fire and while they would continue to rescue people trapped by fire or smoke and also those they could rescue from collapsed buildings during the course of their firefighting, they could not be expected to undertake the massive upsurge in rescue work. The Rescue Service was formed specifically to deal with rescuing people trapped as a result of enemy action, and many of those who joined this branch of the ARP Service were from building trades as they had some understanding of building construction and how a weakened structure might react as debris was moved.

The rescue service evolved so that there were light rescue squads and heavy rescue squads with additional equipment, which could be deployed appropriately depending upon the incident. In Nottingham there were six rescue depots which were controlled from the Rescue Service headquarters on North Church Street. There were 45 volunteer officers and 440 volunteer personnel as well as 200 whole-time men. The rescue squads usually consisted of ten men and were equipped with picks and shovels, crowbars, levers, ropes and jacks as well as propping and shoring equipment. This equipment was transported to the incident on the back of a lorry, often a builder's lorry, or in a trailer towed by a car with a powerful engine.

The job of extricating casualties was often slow and tiring. The dangers that these men had to face at times were immense. Working under piles of debris while a raid was still in progress was not for the faint-hearted. It is of considerable credit to these men and those who toiled alongside them that the stories of bodies being sealed up underneath buildings and air raid shelters are not true. There are no instances of facts bearing out the tales of this kind of thing happening. The rescue parties always worked hard until the last casualty or body had been recovered. We do them an injustice when we perpetuate the stories of entombing the dead where they lay rather than recovering them for a proper burial.

The Women's Voluntary Service, which is now known as the Women's Royal Voluntary Service, had a significant supporting role for those who were considered to be in the front line of civil defence. Their organiser for Nottingham City was Mrs Forman. At the outbreak of war in 1939, the WVS had 165,000 members, drawn from groups of people who were unable to join the armed forces or carry out essential war work. One of the first tasks undertaken by the WVS was assisting with the evacuation of one and a half million children from the large cities to the countryside, where they would be less at risk from bombing.

The WVS undertook work at emergency rest centres and provided meals for people displaced from their homes by air raids. Later on during the war, they often worked at incident inquiry points where relatives would seek information about missing relatives. Many of these women had to break bad news to people about their relatives and in some instances accompany them to the mortuary to offer support during the process of identifying those killed.

One of the things that they are most remembered for is driving mobile canteens to bombed cities so that, the morning after a raid, members of the public as well as ARP workers and firemen could get a hot drink and some food.

The WVS providing hot food from a kitchen set up in the street

2. The Auxiliary Fire Services

Above: Leyland Cub fire appliance DAU1 at Central Fire Station 1939 (Photograph Courtesy of Nottingham City Fire Brigade archives)

Above: Metz Turntable Ladder GTO 10 in the old fire station yard – The Guildhall c1938 (Photograph Courtesy of Nottingham City Fire Brigade archives)

Blue Watch at Central Fire Station 1939. Joe Springthorpe is 2nd from the right, front row (Photograph Courtesy of Nottingham City Fire Brigade archives)

The City of Nottingham Fire Brigade, the borough fire brigades and those of the urban district councils, although able to cope with the demands made upon them in peacetime, would be overwhelmed by the sheer numbers and size of the fires expected in wartime. The aggregate strength of whole-time firemen in England and Wales was only 6,600 and if the 13,800 part-time firemen were added to this tally, it still only gave a figure of just over 20,000. In 1935 an Air Raid Precautions circular recommended recruiting auxiliary firemen to support the regulars in the event of war. Some councils began to recruit for the Auxiliary Fire Service (AFS) in a half-hearted fashion. The Munich Crisis of 1938 prompted a few more to join the AFS, but it was not until 1939 that any real attempt was made to recruit men and women in the kind of numbers that would be needed if there was a war.

Men between the age of 25 and 50 were asked to volunteer for the AFS on the understanding that they would be expected to take up their duties as part-time firemen in the event of war. There would also be a number of these volunteers who would be selected by the Chief Fire Officer to perform whole-time duties and be paid accordingly as auxiliary firemen. A national syllabus was drawn up to cover sixty hours of training for the auxiliaries.

It is an interesting aside that the first sodium street lights in Nottingham were installed in the Guildhall yard to facilitate the training of auxiliary firemen at night after they had finished work at their regular occupations. Leenside Corporation Depot was soon equipped with sodium lights too as the training of auxiliaries commenced there.

Four of the regular firemen from the city brigade who became the AFS instructors were Fred Shipley for the Leenside Division, George Ragsdale for the Radford Division and Bill Page and Frank Straw for the City Division. The volunteers were certainly keen, but that on its own was not enough when it came to the type of work expected of these firemen. If they were not trained properly then they would be ineffective, and it was likely that at serious fires in wartime conditions they would not stay alive long enough to do much good.

Auxiliary Fire Service tunic badge, tunic button and cap badge

The instructors had to train them in the rudiments of fireman-ship and to bond them together as a team so that they could and would perform as a cohesive unit for long periods under adverse conditions. They had to try to impart a wealth of experience and knowledge, gained over many years, in just sixty hours. The fact that they turned out some excellent auxiliary firemen is a credit to these instructors.

Other people were needed in the AFS too if it was to be an effective arm of the Air Raid Precautions Service. Telephonists were needed for the control room and the watch rooms on fire stations as well as dispatch riders for taking urgent messages to and from the fireground. The control room jobs were mainly filled by women who volunteered, and some of them also became dispatch riders.

Auxiliary Fire Service dispatch riders at Carlton c1940 (Photograph courtesy of Nottingham City Fire Brigade archives)

The business of deciding how many auxiliary firemen would be needed was a matter for the Home Office. They had asked the country's fire brigades, of which there were over 1,000 before the war, to prepare and submit a fire scheme to provide for their area in the event of war. In conjunction with this, they then looked at towns and cities and worked out a street mileage. This was then "weighted" by an assessment of the fire risks these streets contained. A hypothetical town that had been provided for by nine whole-time and fifteen part-time firemen, crewing two fire pumps, might find itself needing 30 fire pumps and 300 auxiliary firemen. It was recognised that even with such massive increases in strength it would be impossible to deal with every eventuality. As a result of an attack by a single aircraft over a fairly closely populated area, 75 fires over a distance of three miles would result.

Just prior to the outbreak of war in September 1939, the strength of Nottingham's regular fire brigade stood at 82. Of this number, 68 were firemen, eight were sergeants, three were sub-inspectors, one was an inspector, one was a chief inspector and one was a superintendent. They had seven motor fire appliances, including an emergency tender and an 87-foot turntable ladder. All the appliances were crewed at one station on Shakespeare Street in the city. During the course of the year they had attended 468 fires and a further 149 calls which turned out to be false alarms. The city's fire loss had been kept down to £58,790 out of a value at risk of £1,067,275. The brigades in the county had not fared as well, as their fire loss was £110,000 out of a value at risk of £350,000.

The Auxiliary Fire Service soon recruited men and women up to a strength of 1,046 in Nottingham. They crewed 153 pumps throughout 66 AFS stations. In the main, the fire pumps provided by the Home Office were trailer pumps of various pumping capacities, from 250 gallons per minute to 500 gallons per minute, whereas some of the major pumping appliances used by the regulars could pump 1,000 gallons per minute. The trailer pumps were vital additions to the fire service and they were manufactured for a fraction of the cost of the fire appliances used by the regulars. They were simple in operation and robust, but the weak link was that they needed a vehicle to tow them; a vehicle that had a good-sized engine as these trailer pumps were no lightweights.

A Meadows AFS crew with their trailer pump in 1940 (Photograph courtesy of Harry Roe ex AFS)

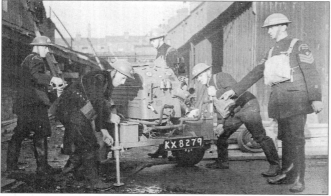

An Auxiliary Fire Service crew are put through their paces at Salisbury Street at Radford, by Sergeant Charlie Caunt of the Nottingham City Fire Brigade. 1939 (Photograph courtesy of Bert Caunt – ex Nottinghamshire Fire Service)

The scramble for the vehicles that were needed by all the civil defence services for various jobs meant that they all ended up with a motley assortment and the fire brigade, in common with the rescue service, found that some of their vehicles were underpowered for the weight of equipment they were expected to pull.

Elsewhere the recruitment of AFS personnel met with mixed success. Beeston, whose fire station was in Stoney Street, had recruited 278 peo-

Regular and Auxiliary fire service crews at Abbey Road Station, West Bridgford 1940. (Photograph courtesy of Nottinghamshire Fire & Rescue Service – West Bridgford)

Above: Bank Place – one of the standby locations for an AFS pump in the city

Above: AFS crew at the Cedars Hospital Fire Post. Ted Cawthorne is 1st on the left, front row (Photograph courtesy of Ted Cawthorne)

ple, whereas West Bridgford Fire Brigade, stationed in Abbey Road, had only managed to recruit 180. Basford had recruited 150 people, Arnold had managed 98, but Carlton had made a poor show with only 56. Bingham had three AFS stations under its control – Bingham town, Radcliffe on Trent and Tollerton – and they had recruited enough volunteers to crew the pumps stationed in them.

Nottingham's Central Fire Station continued to be crewed by the regular firemen, but now they had an AFS section attached to them with its own trailer pumps. Each of the other divisions in Nottingham had its own AFS station crewed by whole-time AFS personnel. A regular fireman who had been promoted, or a sergeant from the regulars, was transferred to each full-time AFS station to take charge. The full-time stations were situated at Commercial Road in Bulwell, Triumph Road in Radford, Alpine Street (which was known as Hyson Green) and the Eastcroft Depot off London Road, Leenside.

AFS substations were situated elsewhere too and these were crewed by part-time firemen on a nightly rota. These stations varied greatly in size and location and any creature comforts found in them were what the personnel had provided themselves or had managed to scrounge. The subsidiary AFS stations were known as either fire posts or "Action Stations". This name was given to them because they were intended to become fully operative only on the receipt of an air raid alert when all firemen, regulars, whole-time and part-time AFS were under instructions to report at once to their nearest fire station.

Fire posts were situated at the General, City and Cedars hospitals. Foreman's the printers on Hucknall Road also had a fire post, as did the drill hall on Derby Road, Ekowe Street in Hyson Green and St Peter's Gate in the city. The St Peter's Gate fire post was unusual in that the crew were stationed above a shop (where an estate agents now stands) and the trailer pump and car were parked in Bank Place directly opposite.

In addition to the trailer pumps that had been provided, the Home Office loaned Nottingham a 100-foot turntable ladder which in 1938 cost around £3,000. Two fire floats were organised for use on the River Trent and the canals as it was recognised that some industrial premises would benefit from having fires tackled from both the land and the river in the event of a major outbreak.

First aid vans were provided to deal with the expected casualties among the firemen so that the casualty service would not have to use its limited resources for this purpose, leaving them free to deal with civilian casualties.

The Home Office was having an expensive and difficult time trying to provide and pay for all the thousands of pieces of ancillary equipment required for firefighting. One measure that was taken to alleviate some of the problems of supplying uniforms was that the AFS firemen were issued with a boiler suit, steel helmet, rubber fireboots instead of leather, a webbing belt and axe, but no fire tunic or waterproof leggings until they had completed their basic training.

The supply of fire hose was a particularly difficult problem nationally. The manufacturers were unwilling to reveal their manufacturing costs to government departments who were making enquiries before placing substantial orders. It became apparent that price fixing was being organised among the manufacturers, who then pooled all the orders received and worked the situation to their advantage. These cartels were exposed in the national press and only then did the companies concerned give realistic prices for the manufacture of the hose. The scale of the problem can be better appreciated when it is realised that, even before the outbreak of war, orders for 3,400 miles of hose had been placed. It is a shameful indictment of these businessmen that when the country was preparing to defend itself against the most dire peril, their first thought was to make as much profit as possible at the country's expense while others freely gave their time and money to help with the defence.

The firemen, pumps and equipment were all essential but without adequate water supplies they would be unable to prevent fire from destroying industry, residential areas and the infrastructure necessary for civilised life. Fire hydrants were usually the quickest and most convenient way of obtaining water and there were 8,267 of them in the city. In addition there were 39 underground tanks at strategic points from which the fire brigade could draw water. The canals and the rivers were also convenient for certain districts, but in order to ensure that water would be immediately available in the industrial and business areas, emergency dams were constructed.

The total capacity of all the tanks came to 4,714,000 gallons. The fire brigade also had a supply of mobile dams which could hold 1,000 gallons. These mobile dams were used as collection points for water being pumped via a relay of pumps from open water supplies, such as the rivers Trent or Leen, to the fireground where it was needed.

Arrangements were made to obtain even more fire appliances and crews from other brigades if it became necessary. The reinforcement scheme worked in three stages.

Stage 1 meant that brigades could call on neighbouring fire services for assistance on a pre-arranged schedule, specifying which appliances they wanted to attend.

Stage 2 involved notifying the Assistant Regional Fire Officer that they needed more assistance. Further pumps would then be ordered to the scene of operations from specified brigades, up to a pre-arranged maximum.

Stage 3 required the Assistant Regional Fire Officer to notify the Regional Fire Officer that more assistance was required. If at all possible, reinforcing appliances would be ordered from within the region. If this was impractical, then the pumps would be obtained from other regions.

Above: Fire at Jacoby's Factory, Daybrook; 1939 (Photograph courtesy of Nottingham City Fire Brigade archives)

The end of an era; Nottingham Firemen Fred Shipley and Chris Raybould wear their brass helmets for the last time in 1938 (Photograph courtesy of Fred Shipley ex Nottingham City Fire Brigade)

It was a stipulation of the scheme that no brigade should be required to send more than one third of its total number of pumps outside its own area. This was so as not to leave areas deprived of fire cover in the event that they were also subjected to a raid.

Towards the end of 1938, it had been agreed that the AFS firemen and the Home Office pumps could be used in an emergency to save life or property in dealing with peacetime fires. It was a stipulation of this agreement that brigades were not to abuse the system by utilising AFS men and equipment to make up for deficiencies in the regular brigade.

In Nottingham the chance was taken to give the AFS men some experience of tackling real fires and they began to turn them out to incidents. However, as "insurance", the regulars from Central Fire Station were always sent too.

One such fire occurred at Jacoby's factory on Sherbrook Road in Daybrook, where £100,000 worth of damage was caused. Henry Strickson had been a part-time member of the AFS and had received his call-up papers as a whole-time AFS fireman. He viewed the scene at the Jacoby's fire from the bedroom window of his house as he got himself ready to report for his first day as a whole-time fireman. He felt despair as he thought of all the lengths of hose there would be to roll up that day and then to scrub clean back at the fire station. It was not the first time that Jacoby's had been gutted by fire: curiously it had also happened in 1914, just before the outbreak of the First World War.

On 30th August 1939 the government announced the rates of pay for AFS and civil defence workers. Men would receive £3.0s.0d per week and women would get £2.0s.0d. On the same day, almost as if it were a symbolic act, the firemen and policemen had their usual helmets withdrawn and were issued with steel ones.

The streets did not look quite the same without the reassuring sight of the "British Bobby" with his familiar helmet. For the firemen, it was the end of an era. Although their brass helmets had been replaced in 1938 when more men were recruited in order to reduce their working week, the replacement helmets were still magnificent. They were made of shiny black leather, liberally adorned with brass fitments. Now they had a dull grey service pattern "tin helmet". When the hostilities eventually ceased, they would return to the traditional shape of fireman's helmet, but never again would the helmets look dashing or spectacular. Instead they would be purely functional.

The country was now on the brink of war.

3. The Early Days of War

On Sunday 3rd September 1939, the Prime Minister, Neville Chamberlain informed the nation that the country was at war with Germany. This was the fulfilment of a warning issued on 1st September stating that unless Germany gave an undertaking that troops would be withdrawn from Poland, a state of war would exist. For many people there was a sense of the surreal about the situation, it seemed as though this was just another stage of the political posturing that had been conducted throughout Europe for the last few years. For others, the starkness of the situation was all too real. A woman living in Beeston explained the feelings she had on 3rd September 1939.

"I was expecting my first baby in November 1939 and I was apprehensive about the things that were happening. I had heard Mr Chamberlain's speech on the wireless and for the first time I didn't want my baby. I was afraid they would drop gas bombs on us. I know it must sound awful to say I didn't want my baby, but I just did not want to bring a baby into the world as it was then. I was so afraid of what may happen to it."

This very moving memory is one that would resonate with so many mothers-to-be and also those who had very young children at the time.

As the first day of war gave way to evening, the sirens in Nottingham wailed their warning. Throughout the city, air raid wardens took up their posts, and off-duty policemen and firemen reported to their stations. Grace Webster's recollections were typical of the apprehension that was felt that evening.

"We were living on Buckingham Road at Woodthorpe at the time and when the sirens sounded, we went down into the basement to shelter. The man who ran the chemist shop opposite us was an air raid warden and he went off to his ARP post when the sirens went and his wife came to shelter with us rather than be alone with her young baby. I remember thinking 'Oh no, not so soon.' We knew that they would bomb us at some time, but this was only a few hours after war had begun."

At the fire stations throughout the city, the firemen on picket duty, which was mounted 24 hours a day, stood at their posts rigged in fire kit with gas masks at the "alert position" strapped across their chests. The pickaxe handles that they had been issued with for protection in case of invasion by paratroopers did not seem much comfort now. They were under strict orders to remain at their posts even after the sirens had sounded and they were quite clear that they would be charged with disobedience to orders if they had gone into a shelter.

Jim Dunkerley was a police sergeant serving with the mechanised division of the city police at the time and he recalled that first air raid alert.

"I put on my uniform and made my way to Carrington Police Station as it was the nearest to my home. As I reached the top of Edwards Lane near Magnus Road, a chap came out to me and asked, 'What is going on?' I told him that there was an air raid alert.

This particular chap I had spoken to a week or so before and told him that he ought to dig a hole for the Anderson shelter that was lying idle in the garden. He said that he wouldn't bother as there would not be a war. Anyway, later on that evening when the all clear had sounded, I saw him again on my way home. He was in the garden with his spade digging for all he was worth!"

Air raid sirens were an integral part of the early warning system for the general public. Civil defence and armed forces, particularly the RAF, would be the first to be alerted of potential air attacks and the same system was in place the length and breadth of the United Kingdom.

Nottingham City had thirteen air raid sirens which had been installed and wired to the electrical supply by firemen who had previously been electricians by trade. The sirens were sited at strategic points to ensure that they could be heard everywhere. Nottingham Castle had a siren, as did the Adelphi cinema in Bulwell, the Peace Mills on Perry Road at Sherwood and the Player School at Bilborough. Each one had a four-mile radius and it was envisaged that they would be backed up by factory whistles and hooters and also police constables and air raid wardens blowing their whistles.

Initially the sirens were all actuated from a central point under the control of the police, but once war began in earnest it could be seen that it was a mistake to centralise the public warning system. If it became damaged in an air raid, then it would prove impossible to give adequate warning of any subsequent raids.

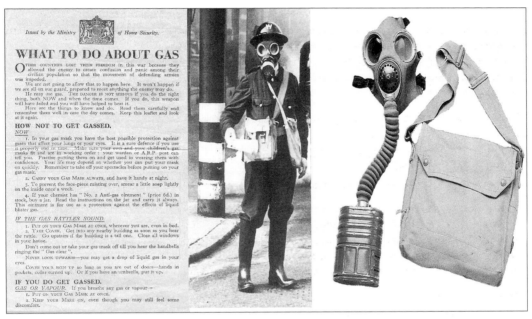

Above Left: Leaflet issued to the public giving advice about what to do if the enemy used caustic or nerve gas Centre: An ARP warden wearing a civilian type respirator during a gas training exercise in Nottingham (Photograph courtesy of Nottingham Evening Post). Above Right: Later in the war all ARP workers were issued with service type respirators of the same type used by the armed forces and the fire brigade as they gave better protection for longer

Above: Decontamination of a vehicle during a gas training exercise (Photograph courtesy of *Nottingham Evening Post*)

Above: Senior fire officers at an incident (Photograph courtesy of Nottingham City Fire Brigade archives)

Not very long after war broke out, it was found that there were problems with the air raid warning system and, for all the experience that the police had in dealing with matters affecting the public, it is fair to say that this was something so new and different that it was beyond their experience. It seemed that they were more intent on maintaining control of the populace than they were on giving sufficient early warning of air raids. Rumours began to circulate in Nottingham and elsewhere that air raid warnings would be withheld until an attack had actually commenced. Nottingham's Chief Constable, Captain Popkess, denounced this as nonsense and said that he would take action against any persons who spread such rumours against the national interest.

He was proved to be wrong later on in the war when people were killed and injured on several occasions by bombing in both the city and county before any warning was given. He remained remarkably silent on such occasions.

The most sensible arrangements would have been to put the air raid warning system under the control of the Air Raid Precautions Service for it was they who were in overall control in such situations and the police, much to their chagrin, were relegated to a secondary role. It is no wonder they were reluctant to sound the alarm, because once they had done so, the wardens and incident officers of the ARP Service reported for duty in large numbers and took up their duties with the full authority of local and national government behind them.

RAF controllers plotted enemy aircraft formations on maps and as they touched pre-determined circles drawn on those maps, part of the procedure was that warnings would be telephoned through to civil defence services and RAF sector stations. This was known as the Yellow Alert. When the plot from the enemy formations touched closer circles, this necessitated the Red Alert being issued, which was the trigger for the air raid sirens to sound in a given district. The government was concerned about the loss of war production resulting from workers taking shelter when no bombs actually fell in their district. It was often the case that the aircraft were flying over to attack somewhere else.

A scheme was introduced where vital industries sent selected personnel for training as ARP staff. When they were given warning, they would go to an observation post, usually on the roof of the factory, and would be vigilant for signs of an attack. The workforce would continue with production and only go down to the shelters if the factory's own ARP lookout sounded their local air raid alarm.

Another innovation was the introduction of the Purple Alert. This meant that the district was on the raiders' course, but was unlikely to be attacked. This decision must have been based upon the altitude that the raiders were flying at, which would give a clue as to whether they were likely to release their bombs imminently. The purple alert was relayed to key organisations such as the ARP service, the fire brigade and the police. Key personnel would then report to their posts for duty.

A study of the County ARP Control logbook shows that after the introduction of the purple alert, it became the exception rather than the rule for the red alert to be sounded. Putting this information together with the known facts of some of the air raids on Nottingham, it seems clear that there was a deliberate intention to only sound the air raid sirens if large formations of enemy aircraft approached, or if bombs actually fell in the district. The people of Nottingham were being very astute when they said that the sirens would not sound until bombs were actually falling.

The war on the home front entered a phase that became known as the "Phoney War". Hitler was busy dealing with Poland and it was not until 1940 that the majority of people at home began to be affected directly by the war.

The civil defence services and the fire services continued to be honed during this time and the pace of training within these organisations was increased. There was also a tightening-up of procedures that had been put into place in case of war and now needed to be rigorously enforced. Some amusing situations arose as these procedures were tested. Clifford McKenzie was an Auxiliary Fireman who was based in the

Above left: AFS crews at the fire station beside St Leodegarious Church, Alpine Street (Photograph courtesy of Clifford McKenzie ex AFS) Above right: ARP stretcher party during a county wide training exercise 4th May 1940 (Photograph courtesy of *Nottingham Evening Post*)

buildings at the side of St Leodegarius Church on Alpine Street, which was known as Hyson Green Fire Station. He recalled one such episode.

> *"One of our fire brigade officers climbed over the wall at the back of the yard which served as our fire station and he managed to get into one of the cars that were used for towing the trailer pumps. He did this without attracting the attention of the picket on duty and he scribbled a note and left it on the dashboard of the car before escaping back the way he had come. The following morning one of the firemen brought the note to the officer in charge of the station. It read:*
>
> *'If I had been a German spy or paratrooper, I could have driven off in this vehicle before you could have stopped me. You should be more vigilant.'*
>
> *The note was signed by the officer and he came in to see the men before they went off duty that morning. He asked the officer in charge if he had found the note and if, in future, he would take extra care.*
>
> *'Yes, sir,' he replied, 'I did find your note and all I have to say is that if a German spy or paratrooper managed to start that particular car, then he is a better man than any of us here. We have been complaining about not being able to start that car for months.'"*

The officer was not too pleased about this response and had the last say on the matter the next night when he had the men who were resting turned out of their beds on a "test turnout". He lined them up on Western Boulevard with their appliances and then required each of them in turn to show him their identity disc. They were all able to do so with the exception of one man who was not wearing his. He was reported for this along with his officer in charge and both men were subsequently put on a charge, the fireman for disobedience to a written order and his officer for neglect of duty (he should have checked that each man was wearing his identity disc). Both were fined for the breach of discipline and warned about their future conduct.

On Sunday 4th May 1940, 70,000 ARP workers took part in training exercises in seven different counties. In Nottinghamshire, 10,000 firemen and ARP staff dealt with 60 simulated incidents which ranged from small incendiary fires in dwellings to a realistic explosion and fire in a disused factory at Basford.

Incidents in the city were staged at Trent Bridge, Wilford Power Station overlooking the River Trent, Arkwright Street Railway Bridge and the Eastcroft Corporation Depot. The Greyfriars dance hall was also a designated incident, as were the Co-operative Hall, Springfield Hosiery in Radford, the Drill Hall on Derby Road, Hyson Green Police Station and the Nottingham Gas Works.

The scenario was that 80 high-explosive bombs, 12 gas bombs and 200 incendiaries had been dropped causing numerous casualties. The gas bombs had caused 23 injuries and the incendiaries had caused 112 more, but the high-explosive bombs had killed 323 people and injured 665 others. The exercise was watched

by Lord Trent, Commissioner of the North Midland (No. 3) Region for civil defence, Wing Commander Hodsall, the Inspector General for Civil Defence attached to the Home Office, and Major Ledbury, the Senior Regional Officer. The Nottinghamshire officials present included Lord Belper, Chief Air Raid Warden for the county, Captain Popkess, ARP Co-ordinating Officer, and Alderman Armitage, Chairman of the City Emergency Committee. The exercise was a great success and the official observers were impressed by the efficiency of the Nottinghamshire ARP and fire services.

The next time such scenes were witnessed in Nottinghamshire it would be for real.

Left Top: Firemen on Fletcher Gate near Weekday Cross providing a 'water curtain' to protect buildings during the exercise on 4th May 1940 (Photograph courtesy of Nottingham City Fire Brigade archives)

Bottom: The same view of Fletcher Gate from Weekday Cross in 2009. The car park on the right of the picture replaced a factory destroyed by enemy action in May 1941

Nottingham City AFS men take a break at the end of the May 1940 exercise. Fireman Charlie Bartles is in the centre of the group (Photograph courtesy of Charlie Bartles ex AFS)

4. The Raids Begin

"What General Weygand called the Battle of France, is over. I expect that the Battle of Britain is about to begin. Upon this battle depends the survival of Christian civilisation."

The words spoken by Winston Churchill on 18th June 1940, following the fall of France, were prophetic. What Churchill did not know was that the campaign about to be embarked upon would be unique in military history and would shape the way that the Luftwaffe would operate over Britain. In fact, it was to alter the entire course of the war. Sir Hugh Dowding was Air Chief Marshal of RAF Fighter Command and Air Vice Marshal Keith Park was the commander of 11 Group, which protected the south and south-east of the country. The industrial Midlands were protected by 12 Group under the command of Air Vice Marshal Leigh-Mallory, whose headquarters were at Watnall in Nottinghamshire. They knew that the ultimate test was now almost upon them.

The two nearest aerodromes to Nottingham were at Tollerton in the south and Hucknall to the north. Hucknall Aerodrome was part of Fighter Command at the outbreak of war and when the Polish unit based there moved out in June 1940, the number 1 Bomber Group Headquarters which had been evacuated from France was set up there. The Rolls-Royce experimental unit was also based at the aerodrome at this time and during the Battle of Britain Spitfires and Hurricanes were repaired at the works.

RAF Tollerton was brought into use as a scatter airfield for the Hampdens of 44 and 50 Squadrons from RAF Waddington. The aerodrome became a satellite station of RAF Newton later in the war.

On 2nd July 1940 Hitler formally directed his military commanders to proceed with planning to invade Britain. Attacks by the Luftwaffe on convoys of shipping in the English Channel increased in ferocity from 10th July and by the end of the month the channel had become untenable for convoys during daylight. Military targets and towns along the south coast had also been receiving attention from the Luftwaffe and it was this that prompted Leslie Nix to write to his family at Prospect Road in Carlton describing what it was like in Plymouth at that time. The letter was dated 23rd July 1940.

". . . unconsciously you are braced for the sound of the sirens. Every plane in the sky arouses excitement and all the time you are consciously, or unconsciously, on the alert. This, with all the hours of lost sleep is bound to have an effect on people. I hope for mother's sake that you are all spared this strain."

Unfortunately this was not to be. Nottingham was to have its share of raids with the Carlton and Sneinton areas being particularly badly affected. On 31st July, Hitler gave orders that the plans for Operation Sea Lion – the invasion of Britain – must be ready by 15th August. The destruction of the RAF was obviously vital to the success of any invasion of Britain. Hitler's planned invasion was over a 225-mile front, from Ramsgate to Weymouth. Hitler knew that to land his 13 divisions on English soil, he would have to control the English Channel, but first the Luftwaffe had to dispose of the RAF. Hitler instructed his command:

"The English air force must be so reduced morally and physically that it is unable to deliver any significant attack against an invasion across the channel."

The operation for driving the RAF from the sky was code-named "*Eagle*" and Eagle Day was set for 13th August. The Luftwaffe had 3,000 aircraft at their disposal, 1,600 of which were bombers, whereas the RAF only had 704 fighter aircraft in squadrons.

On 12th August, the Radio Direction Finding stations were attacked as a prelude to Eagle Day. One of them, at Ventnor on the Isle of Wight, was put out of action for eleven days. That night German aircraft roamed at will across the country and between midnight and 02:00 hours, ten high-explosive bombs and fifty incendiaries were dropped in Nottinghamshire. The aircraft followed the River Trent as far as Nottingham and then turned to the west. The raiders were probably searching for the Royal Ordnance Factory at Chilwell, but they were unsuccessful in their attempt to inflict damage on a vital part of the country's war economy.

Six high-explosive bombs plummeted down into Bramcote; one struck Balloon House and the other five cratered nearby fields. The aircraft then adopted a northerly course, skirting the edge of the city before dropping four more high-explosive bombs on the railway sidings at Annesley. The main London & North Eastern Railway (LNER) line was damaged along with some wagon sheds. Kirkby and Hucknall fire crews were kept busy for some time dealing with thirty fires in Annesley Plantation caused by incendiaries. On 15th August, seven major raids were launched involving all three German air fleets. The attacks on the Midlands and the north-east were launched by Luftflotte 5 from Norway. The formations were met before they reached the English east coast and were cut to ribbons by the Hurricanes and Spitfires of 12 Group from the Midlands. The German air staff had drawn an erroneous conclusion that fighters had been moved from 12 Group to make up for the heavy losses sustained by 11 Group in the south. They thought that the east coast had been left unprotected and that it was an easy way for them reach the industrial Midlands.

Following the heavy losses suffered by the Luftwaffe during these raids, no more daylight attacks were launched from across the North Sea. Between 8th and 18th August, the Luftwaffe lost 363 aircraft while the RAF lost 211. If the Germans were playing a game of attrition, they were losing.

The Luftwaffe then changed tactics by raiding airfields further inland. The plan was that more RAF fighters would engage them, which would mean they could be shot down in greater numbers and the Luftwaffe could keep to the timescales set for a mid-September invasion.

A fire officer saw one such attack on Croydon Aerodrome carried out unopposed by perfect formations of German aircraft. No air raid sirens had sounded to warn people to take cover. Fire crews from the AFS station adjacent to the airport attended rapidly as the bombs started to fall and were running out hose on the aerodrome to tackle the fires while the raiders were making their bombing runs.

On 19th August, the air raid sirens in Worksop, Retford and surrounding districts signalled another nocturnal visit by the Luftwaffe. At 00:45 hours an aircraft dropped incendiaries in an area one mile east of Worksop College while at the same time, eight high-explosive bombs fell 400 yards from the Budby crossroads on the Worksop to Ollerton Road and brought telephone wires down. The aircraft that had dropped the incendiaries maintained an easterly course and at 01:00 hours it dropped more incendiaries, this time in Clumber and around Appley Head Farm just off the A614. It continued eastwards and dropped incendiaries around Jockey House Farm, which was on the perimeter of RAF Gamston near Retford. By 01:20 the aircraft was dropping incendiaries at Gringley to the north of Retford and Gringley Brickworks received a high-explosive bomb.

Small-scale night attacks were still being carried out around coastal areas of Britain and, as can be seen from the bombing of north Nottinghamshire described above, the raiders began to range inland on more and more occasions. They were challenged by anti-aircraft guns, but of the 4,000 guns needed to defend Britain at a "*reasonable level*", only 2,000 were available.

Night fighters were feared by the Luftwaffe crews, but in reality the number of interceptions was small and actual kills were scarce. Nevertheless, a Heinkel He111 was shot down just off Skegness Pier, by a

Blenheim of 29 Squadron from RAF Digby. The Skegness lifeboat was launched but was unable to render service. Presumably the wreckage and crew had disappeared beneath the sea without a trace.

The majority of night raiders roamed unmolested and they were finding their targets too. This was not just a case of the bomber crews becoming more experienced at night navigation; there was an altogether more worrying explanation.

Doctor Reginald Jones, who was to become the scientific advisor to MI6 and assistant director of air intelligence, had detected German radio beams which he believed were being used by aircraft for navigation. At a meeting with the Prime Minister in June 1940, he had managed to convince him that the beams were not only leading enemy aircraft to their selected targets, but were also being used to release their bombs automatically. Jones was authorised to plan a way of jamming the beams and also to transmit other beams, similar enough to the originals, to lead the Luftwaffe pilots and navigators astray. Twenty officers and 200 men of No. 80 Wing (radio counter measures) RAF, began "Operation Headache". Doctor Jones provided information to 80 Wing, who were then able to transmit false signals. Unfortunately most coastal areas and London, because of the Thames Estuary, were still very easy to locate visually.

By the end of August there were 12 "Knickebein" transmitting stations operating and two of them, Kleve in Germany and Dieppe in France, were radiating beams on 27th August that intersected over Nottingham. Improvised jamming equipment was in use by 80 Wing on this occasion but despite the clever imitation being transmitted, the Germans realised that their beam was being interfered with in some way. One Luftwaffe pilot recalled how they realised that the British had detected the beam and therefore had advanced warning of the intended target.

"For all we knew the night fighters might be concentrating all the way along the beam to the target."

It was for this reason that many of the bomber crews kept out of the beam and only used it on the final run in to the target.

The Luftwaffe crews missed their target on this particular night as their aircraft droned past to the south of the city. From a pilot's eye view, seeing the River Trent pass below, a turn to the west would bring him over Chilwell; as with the raid on 12th August, they were probably searching for the Royal Ordnance Factory. The enemy aircraft were actually to the south of Chilwell but in a line parallel to it. The bombs went down onto New Sawley near Long Eaton, killing three people in Netherfield Road. The official account merely stated:

"Houses situated in a small town in the Midlands were demolished by Nazi air raiders."

When the alert sounded in Nottingham, people went to their shelters and ARP workers and firemen reported for duty. Five deaths occurred in the city as a result of this alert without a single bomb dropping within the city boundary.

Elizabeth Warner, of 41 Waterford Street, collapsed and died of a heart attack upon hearing the sirens. The same fate awaited William Holland of 99 Sneinton Boulevard. He was the stoker at Hollins Mills in Norton Street, Radford and he went into the air raid shelter when the warning sounded. A few minutes later he collapsed and died. George Ebohne was having his supper at 84 Park Lane when he heard the sirens; he immediately collapsed at the table and died of a heart attack.

One of the city's ARP shelter wardens, Herbert Hill, dashed out of his house at 76 Sneinton Dale in order to unlock the shelter for the people who were designated to use it. He was in such a hurry that he ran across the road and was struck by a bus, which caused fatal injuries. Saddest of all the accidental deaths was that of Laura Shires, who used the cellar at 67 Boundary Road in Beeston as an air raid shelter. Laura was pregnant at the time and as she hurried to get to a place of safety, she missed her footing on the steps and fell down them. She was admitted to hospital but died later of *"peritonitis consequent upon a septic abortion"*.

Aerial view of where bombs fell in Laxton

View of the Old School House at Laxton where Ruth Willis was killed

Shrapnel marks on the wall at the Old School House

Some of the Luftwaffe aircraft had been designated to attack industrial targets in Newark. Through not sticking rigidly to the navigation beams being transmitted, the bomber crews became lost and missed their target. The only thing they would have been sure of was whether they were off to one side of the target or the other. Whether they had overshot, or were still short of the target, would not be quite so clear. Obviously these crews would not want to spend any time over the supposed target area searching around before they dropped their bombs, as they believed that the RAF controllers would be able to vector night fighters straight to them. They did what most people would if they were in the same predicament; they jettisoned the bombs and immediately set a course for home.

Marjorie Sayer (née Bailey) produced a brief account of that night, in which she explained why the hamlet of Laxton was bombed.

"The first aid ladies [Laxton's ARP first aid party] had been to Southwell for a lecture and they returned by ambulance. It is thought that the bomber followed the ambulance light back to Laxton."

The blackout regulations only allowed vehicles to use headlights provided a cover was fitted which allowed a thin beam to illuminate the road. It is possible that one of the aircraft that had become lost over Southwell may have seen the narrow beam from the headlights of the ambulance and tracked them for a while before releasing its bombs as it saw buildings below. Marjorie's account continued:

"We lived at Top End Farm at the time and my father, Mark Bailey, had just turned the horse out into the field and he came back to the house to fetch me and mum out to look at all the searchlights. Whilst we were in the stock yard we heard a whistling noise and realised that bombs were dropping. We laid on the ground, tiles and bricks dropping all around us. It was a queer sensation not knowing whether we would be alive at the end."

It was 22:25 hours when the six high-explosive bombs fell in Laxton, along with two oil incendiary bombs and numerous one-kilogram incendiaries. Ruth Willis, a fifty-five-year-old who was a member of the village First Aid

Party, was by her front door at The Old School House in the village when the first bomb fell into her front garden. The shrapnel killed Ruth, blasted the front door off its hinges and peppered the front of the house, gouging chunks out of the brickwork. Two other people from the first aid party were just by the driveway of the property where the ambulance had parked and they were seriously injured by the blast. Damage was caused to the village school and outbuildings as well as breaking the windows of several houses.

The second bomb fell in the farmyard of Smithy Farm, next to what is now the Miller's House, killing the beasts in the farmyard as well as the family's dog. The third bomb fell on the buildings at the Bridle-croft, partially destroying it, and the fourth bomb fell into a grass field opposite Top Farm, also killing a farm beast. The shrapnel struck the side of the farmhouse, knocking lumps out of the brickwork and shat-tering the windows. Some of the shrapnel that penetrated the house sliced its way through the wooden bedroom doors and embedded itself into the wall opposite. Fortunately no one was injured.

The fifth bomb fell at Stoney Croft and caused one of the locals, on his way home from the pub, to dive for cover. He landed in the rhubarb patch, which was no real substitute for a shelter, but the shrapnel whizzed over the top of him. The following morning the proof of how close he had come to being killed or injured was evident from the marks on the wall of the building.

The sixth bomb fell just beyond Town End Farm and landed in an open field. This bomb was of larger calibre than the others and left a crater large enough to have put the farmhouse into.

Marjorie Sayer described the scene after the bombs had fallen.

"Mrs Dickenson had her hand injured by shrapnel whilst she was protecting her son's head. She was treated by the local first aid party. The others that were injured were treated and then taken to Newark Hospital. My husband, Ernest Sayer, was one of the firemen for Laxton and he dealt with Ruth Willis's body, which was very unpleasant. They could not find Ruth's dog, which was called Bunty, but several days later it was found hiding under the bed."

On the same night, fires were caused in Wellow Woods and also in Thoresby Park by incendiaries that had been scattered over a wide area. There was no doubt that everyone was in the front line now. You did not have to live near major industry in a large city to become a target. Enemy bomber crews jettisoning

Ruth Willis who was a member of the ARP first aid party at Laxton

The stables at Smithy Farm, Laxton. The area outlined in white shows where new brickwork has replaced the entire side of the building de-stroyed by a bomb

Above: Top Farm and Town End Farm in Laxton. A high explosive bomb fell in the field opposite Top Farm causing damage to the farmhouse. Inset: Shrapnel marks around the window at Top Farm

bombs were never fussy about where they fell and the bombs killed, maimed and destroyed just as if you and your hamlet had been the intended target all along.

Other aircraft that missed their target that night dropped incendiaries around the Hayton Lane and Chain Bridge area in Lound. During the early hours of the morning on 28th August, places as far apart as Normanton on Trent, Harworth, Blyth, Worksop and Bircotes all received incendiaries and some high-explosive bombs. To the south of the county, the raiders who hopelessly lost their way trying to find Chilwell dropped their bombs around East Leake, Gotham and Kingston on Soar.

The raiders returned again that night and dropped incendiaries and high-explosive bombs at Perlethorpe in the north of the county. Fires were started again in the woods at Thoresby Park and Wellow Woods. Budby received more high-explosive bombs and for such a rural part of the county, this was becoming a dangerous place to live in 1940.

Incendiaries were dropped around the junction of Eastgate and Kilton Road in Worksop, which were quickly put out, but a fire was started at the Carlton Road pit which required the attendance of the Auxiliary Fire Service to extinguish it. High-explosive bombs cut off communication between Nottinghamshire and Sheffield for around an hour before the telephone lines were restored.

Once again, the south of the county had its own small force of raiders, which dropped nine high-explosive bombs and two oil-bomb incendiaries over the area of Gotham, Kingston on Soar and Sutton Bonnington. The only "casualties" the Luftwaffe achieved for all their efforts were six sheep killed as a result of the oil-bomb incendiaries. Two nights later, the Luftwaffe visited Nottinghamshire again, dropping both high-explosive and incendiary bombs over a wide area. Aircraft from Luftflotte 2 in France followed the direction beam from Dieppe to Nottingham but, as before, they were reluctant to stick too closely to it. The aircraft began dropping high-explosive bombs on East Leake, Sutton Bonnington, Gotham and Ratcliffe on Soar but then the bomb aimers stopped briefly as open countryside and the River Trent passed beneath them. At the kind of speed they were travelling, it would have been another couple of minutes before they were over Chilwell and Bramcote.

Records of the County Air Raid Precautions Controller show that incendiaries were dropped in the Hains Road area of Chilwell at 22:36 hours and at 22:40 incendiaries dropped on Wollaton Golf Course. There was a pause in the raid at this point and no bombs are reported as having fallen again until 23:10, when

50 incendiaries were delivered over Costock and Rempstone. A high-explosive bomb was dropped between East Leake and Gotham and then, as before, the raiders flew on over Long Eaton towards Chilwell.

A high-explosive bomb fell on the 14th green of Beeston Fields golf course at 23:15, but failed to detonate, as did an oil-bomb incendiary which fell in the grounds of 77 Beeston Fields Drive. The oil container shattered and spread its flammable contents around, but the explosive agent intended to ignite the oil failed to detonate. Incendiaries scattered down around Trowell Forge and two high-explosive bombs fell just 150 yards away from the building. Then it was the turn of Kimberley, as high-explosive bombs fell at Norman Street, Parkham Road, Cliff Boulevard, two on Newdigate Lane and two on Holly Road. All the bombs failed to detonate. At 23:30 hours, an Anderson Shelter took a direct hit in the garden of 96 Bramcote Lane in Chilwell. Rebecca, May and Edna Barks all died instantly along with Gertrude Rushin. A house was set on fire by an incendiary bomb at Trowell and the raiders were then over Watnall, where they set Watnall Woods and Spring Woods, between Strelley and Kimberley, on fire with over 1,000 one-kilogram magnesium incendiaries. A high-explosive bomb crashed through the roof of 9 Allendene Avenue, killing Mary Lord and John Moult. Another seven houses in Common Lane at Watnall were also damaged as the deadly load spilled from the bombers.

A second group of bombers had approached Nottingham from airfields in Belgium. They had followed the radio beam radiating from Kleve in Germany, coming in over the Wash in Lincolnshire. As they approached from the east, searchlights began to sweep the sky searching for the raiders, and then anti-aircraft shells began to burst with a dull thud. All the way across Lincolnshire the flak burst around them, the defence being taken up by the Nottinghamshire guns as the aircraft approached.

Some of the bomber crews saw a built-up area beneath them and must have concluded that it was Newark. Wasting no time, they released their bombs onto the "secondary target" and headed for home. Back at their home base, they would be able to report that they had been unable to locate the primary target – Nottingham – and they had therefore bombed the secondary target – Newark. In reality, they had bombed Southwell. People in Sherwood heard aircraft approaching and as they listened, the reverberating sound filled the air. Two high-explosive bombs fell in Catfoot Lane at Lambley but these failed to detonate, as did the one that fell at Crimea Farm on Spring Lane at Lambley. At five minutes to midnight the first of the incendiaries fell on to the Mapperley and Sherwood area, around Woodthorpe Drive and Coronation Road. Most of the incendiaries were tackled safely before any serious damage was done to property, but Judges Bakery at the junction of Woodthorpe Drive and Mapperley Plains caught fire. Three fire appliances raced to the scene from Arnold, Mapperley and the city. They succeeded in extinguishing the blaze after some time, but the building was seriously damaged. The remains of six incendiary bombs were found in the bakery after the fire had been put out.

Around 100 incendiaries dropped in the area around Winchester Street in Sherwood, including the Mapperley Brickworks. An AFS crew began tackling the one-kilogram magnesium incendiaries with water spray and sand. The incendiaries burnt with a brilliant green/blue flame, throwing out showers of red hot sparks. A resident of Sherwood, Ernest Wilson, described how he dealt with one of the incendiaries.

"I was asleep in the front bedroom of the house and in the early hours I heard the droning of an aeroplane. As I lay listening to it, my attention was attracted by a whizzing sound. This noise became intensified and suddenly my bedroom was lit up. I sprang out of bed, drew aside the curtains and, looking out, saw an incendiary bomb well alight on the ground next to a wall. I slipped on my shirt and trousers and ran downstairs. Seizing my zinc alloy dolly tub, I went into the street and placed the tub over the bomb. Then I stood well back in case anything happened. The bomb burnt itself out inside the tub."

As the incendiaries began to drop just before midnight, one of the air raid wardens in the area telephoned a report through to the Nottingham Reporting Centre. As he did so, the unmistakable whistle

Above left: Bomb damage to 29 & 31 Fairbank Crescent, Sherwood (Photograph courtesy of Nottingham Evening Post) Above right: 29 & 31 Fairbank Crescent in 2009

of high-explosive bombs was heard. A 50-kilogram bomb fell on to houses at 29–31 Fairbank Crescent in Sherwood. The warden saw a "*huge flash and red glow*", followed by an explosion. There was a delay in the "*priority message*" being sent through to the reporting centre but at 00:10 hours the message was finally sent that a fire had been caused by a high-explosive bomb falling on to houses. What they did not realise at that stage was that there were 14 casualties at this one incident.

The Auxiliary Fire Service station at St Leodegarius Church on Western Boulevard was alerted and crews were dispatched to the incident. Other high-explosive bombs had fallen in the area, at numbers 11 and 13 Mapperley Street and also at number 1 Private Road and 480 Mansfield Road. The gas main in Mapperley Street had been fractured and was alight, requiring attention from the Auxiliary Fire Service.

Right top: Numbers 4 & 6 Fairbank Crescent where a bomb fell at the back of the houses killing 18 month old Kevin Betts in the air raid shelter of number 6. Right bottom: Anderson shelter in the garden of 4 Fairbank Crescent

The houses on Mansfield Road and Private Road were at the edge of an area that was only covered by three air raid wardens and they were already finding themselves hard pressed due to several simultaneous incidents. Incident Officer Leeds did some sterling work, not only in dealing with his own responsibilities but also in helping out the ARP wardens where possible. The rescue and demolition teams were delayed considerably in arriving at the incidents as a result of their lorry breaking down and a replacement having to be found. First aid parties, however, were on the scene quite quickly and no great harm came to anybody through the delay to the rescue party.

The Anderson Shelters had stood up well to the test, although four casualties occurred when a heavy piece of debris was blasted through the door of one shelter. A woman lying on one of the bunks in the shelter had a lucky escape when a piece of debris landed by the side of her head. After this, the authorities decided to advise the public to erect baffles approximately two feet away from the shelter door to prevent

Above top: Salvage work after an air raid in August 1940 (Photograph courtesy of Nottingham Evening Post)
Bottom: Numbers 1 & 3 Hood Street, Sherwood in 2009. Both were damaged in the August 1940 raid.

Above top: Anderson Shelter in the garden of 3 Hood Street after a raid (Photograph courtesy of *Nottingham Evening Post*). Bottom: View of the site of the Anderson Shelter in 2009

the blast from explosions throwing debris into the shelter.

Crantock House at 480 Mansfield Road was used as a club, and the incidents here and at 1 Private Road had caused no casualties. A police constable went to Crantock House and then reported to Carrington Police Station what he had found. The police were supposed to notify the ARP wardens, who were ultimately responsible for the incident, but they failed to do this and for some inexplicable reason they did not pass on the details of the incident to the Nottingham Reporting Centre either. Eventually, over an hour later, they telephoned the incident through to the police control room. Reading between the lines of official reports and documents, it appears that there was some resentment on the part of the police as a result of having to inform the ARP service of air raid incidents. The police had been used to operating in a completely autonomous fashion and did not respond well to this requirement of being accountable to the ARP Service when dealing with air raid incidents.

There were 25 casualties in Nottinghamshire that night: 18 injured and seven killed, including 18-month-old Kevin Betts of number 6 Fairbank Crescent, who died in Nottingham City Hospital. The Nottingham people had been given a small taste of what was to come and the city's ARP services had seen their first action. They had acquitted themselves well, as had the ARP services in the county.

On Sunday 1st September the sirens sounded again in Nottingham and, in an incident that was almost a repeat of that which had killed Herbert Hill four nights previously, William Dainty, a rescue team member was knocked down by a car in Lowater Street at Carlton. He died later in Nottingham General Hospital.

The Luftwaffe returned again on 2nd September and that made it eleven nights in a row that they had bombed the East Midlands. A high-explosive bomb fell at Thompson's Brickyard in Chilwell but failed to detonate and five high-explosive bombs caused damage to seven houses in Moor Lane at Bramcote.

Above: 480 Mansfield Road where a high explosive bomb fell in the grounds on 31st August 1940

Above Top: 11 – 13 Mapperley Street – bomb damage in August 1940 (Photograph courtesy of *Nottingham Evening Post*)

Bottom: 11 – 13 Mapperley Street in 2009

Incendiaries caused fires around Taylor's Farm at Bramcote and, across the River Trent, incendiaries fell around the railway in Wilford Lane at West Bridgford. Three houses were damaged by high-explosive bombs at Foxhill Road at Carlton and four other people were injured, making work for the first aid parties. The fire brigade were kept busy again dealing with fires from incendiaries, which fell over a wide area including Dale Avenue at Carlton, Scotgrave Farm at Gedling, Gedling Colliery tip, and a fire in a wheat field near the Calverton–Oxton crossroads.

On this same night, death visited Mapperley Hall Drive when a lorry carrying soldiers crashed into a tree on a bad bend during the blackout. Five of the soldiers were killed and thirteen others injured. On 4th September, a small-scale attack took place with high-explosive bombs falling on Attenborough and Ilkeston. This was the fifth raid on the county in the last eight nights.

Elsewhere in the country things had taken a turn for the worse. The fuel storage tanks at Thameshaven had been repeatedly attacked and firemen had extinguished the resulting fires only to see them started up again by another raid. It was one such attack on 24th August that had been particularly fateful.

London had been alerted by the sirens five times already that day and at 23:08 hours they sounded again. The enemy aircraft that made their way across a night sky studded with anti-aircraft fire were vainly searching for the Thameshaven fuel depot. The pilots knew that they should have been over the oil depot at 23:00 hours but as they turned their aircraft this way and that to avoid the anti-aircraft fire, they became concerned at not locating their target. The crews dared not return to their airfield with the bomb loads intact and so they decided to ditch their bombs and then set a course for home. Hitler had personally forbidden any attacks on London and, mindful of this order, they tried to establish their location. Satisfied that London lay to the south-east, they jettisoned their bombs.

St Giles in Cripplegate received a direct hit from the first stick of high-explosive bombs, and houses along the length of Fore Street in the City of London were peppered with incendiaries. Penetrating into roof spaces, the incendiaries quickly took hold and the first firemen on the scene were confronted with a rapidly developing fire situation. Several roofs were already well alight and thick black smoke poured skywards.

Fires had been started in the docks too. A fire in the West India Docks was threatening surrounding buildings and required the attendance of 100 pumping appliances and two fireboats. Another fire in the docks area needed 70 pumps and six fireboats to quell it, while the incident at Fore Street had 200 pumps attending it. Two other fires accounted for another 50 pumps and the resources at the disposal of the brigades were becoming stretched thin.

The toll of injuries among the London firemen was steep, particularly the inexperienced Auxiliary Fire Service crews. Civilians had been killed and injured by the bombs and destruction had been brought to London for the first time.

Churchill responded to this raid on London by demanding a retaliatory raid on Berlin. It was carried out the following night by 81 Whitley, Wellington and Hampden bombers. Only ten of them found the target and two Berliners were slightly injured during the raid.

The raids on the Thameshaven fuel depot continued and on the morning of 5th September a particularly heavy raid set five 2,000-ton oil tanks alight. A fire of that magnitude needed a sustained attack with foam and the local brigade had neither the massive amount of foam-making equipment nor the manpower to deliver such an attack. Although they struggled valiantly with the blaze there was no hope of extinguishing it without outside help.

The first of the reinforcements came in the form of 50 pumping appliances from the London Fire Brigade. There was no problem in locating the fire as a huge black pall of smoke hung in the sky, but this also meant that when the Luftwaffe returned they too would have no difficulty in locating Thameshaven, Shellhaven or Purfleet.

As darkness fell the fires were still out of control. A further seven oil tanks had steel plates starting to buckle due to radiated heat and it was only a matter of time before they ruptured and poured their contents into the inferno. An orange glow lit up the sky as the first of that night's raids got under way.

By daybreak the firefighting was beginning to have the edge and the fires were coming under control. The Luftwaffe continued to bomb the area throughout the day and, as the firemen could clearly be seen by the bomber crews, they began to strafe them with machine-gun fire. These tactics went on sporadically all day and although firemen had already been in the firing line indirectly, there was no doubt that the Luftwaffe was actually aiming at them now.

As the fires came under control, many of the London fire crews made up their firefighting equipment and headed back to their stations through the Essex suburbs. Crowds of people turned out to wave and cheer as the oil-soaked firemen returned. Firemen, the auxiliaries more so than the regulars, had come in for a good deal of abuse and contempt during the pre-war years and even during the "Phoney War" period of 1939 and early 1940. They had been derided as "Draft Dodgers", meaning that they were only in the fire service to avoid conscription into one of the three armed forces. People had changed their tune now though, and they were beginning to realise their worth and face up to the fact that a large number of firemen had seen more action than a great many men in the armed forces.

Infuriated by the RAF's attack on Berlin, Hitler gave orders for the Luftwaffe to be unleashed on London. Late in the afternoon of 7th September, 600 fighters escorted 300 bombers across the coast. Some attacked Thameshaven again, setting fire to previously undamaged oil tanks, but the main attack fell on London.

At 16:33 hours the air raid sirens gave the warning as the first wave of bombers approached. The bombs began to fall on East Ham, the Royal Docks, Silvertown, Canning Town and the Woolwich Arsenal. Minutes later, the Surrey Commercial Docks were hit with a devastating mixture of incendiary and high-explosive bombs. Terraced houses, shops, factories and warehouses were laid waste and others were threatened by the fires that were growing on a massive scale. The fire crews began the daunting task of extinguishing the fires, but even as they did so the second wave of the attack poured more high explosives and incendiaries down, starting more fires and smashing water mains that were the "ammunition" so desperately needed by the firemen.

Within thirty minutes of the start of the raid, West Ham Fire Brigade was requesting 500 pumps from the London Regional Fire Control to combat fires at the Royal Docks. With 200 pumps already committed to the Surrey Docks and another 500 at work between the London, St Katherine's and West India Docks, it was a request that would take some time to meet.

Bob Maslin was a full-time fireman with the Auxiliary Fire Service. He was later to serve in Nottingham, but at that time he was stationed at Wandsworth and he recalled the raid.

"We were sent to Silvertown and there were masses of people going the other way as we tried to get through. People were calling out to us, 'Good luck lads', as we drove along.

When we got to the docks a senior officer stopped us and said, 'Go down there and just pick a fire!' The wall of flames seemed to go on for ever. We drove on and then we saw a fireman in the middle of the street operating two Coventry Climax Pumps. There was a big flash and a bang and we saw him and the pumps blown right up into the air. We looked at each other and said, 'Blimey, is this what we're in for?'

We got to work on a sugar warehouse that was well alight and to our left there was another building well alight. From time to time aircraft machine-gunned us as they came over."

By 18:30 hours, when the all clear sounded, the raiders had ranged over the East End of London for more than one and a half hours and now the evening sky was lit up by the fires in the docklands. In the London Regional Fire Control, firefighting resources were thin on the ground. The Surrey Docks now had a fire zone of one square mile and altogether 19 conflagrations were logged. Conflagration was a term reserved to describe a fire officially out of control. Scores of fires needed between 10 and 30 pumps to deal with them, whilst other crews struggled alone to deal with over 1,000 smaller incidents. The request for more pumps came in from the various firegrounds, and fire brigades from further and further afield responded by mobilising some of their fire appliances. Number 3 Region, North Midlands, were asked to provide pumps and Nottingham sent crews from stations throughout the city divisions.

At 20:30 hours the air raid sirens sounded again and within a few minutes enemy aircraft were overhead. There was no need for them to locate the target using sophisticated navigation techniques: bomb aimers simply released their bombs at any point where they could see fires burning; they were sure to score hits. The firemen had to stand their ground as red hot shrapnel whizzed and clattered around them, the blast from nearby bombs pushing them as they struggled to control their powerful firefighting jets.

The German aircraft would continue the bombing for another eight and a half hours and by the morning 436 men, women and children would be dead and a further 1,600 injured.

As the waves of enemy aircraft swept inland towards London, the British authorities believed that this was the prelude to an invasion.

5. Invasion Alert

On 6th September 1940, the British authorities issued "Invasion Alert 2", which meant that attack was probable within three days. The decision to issue this alert had been based upon intelligence gathered about the German invasion preparations. Photographs taken by RAF Coastal Command showed that the number of invasion barges at Ostend had grown from 18 on 31st August, to 205 on 6th September.

A confidential report from the 1st Corps troop area to the Chief Constable of Nottinghamshire revealed that five enemy parachutes had been discovered at Buroughbridge near York and that two Germans had been captured, one wearing civilian clothes. The report went on to confirm that 25 enemy parachutists were at large in the area, with 11 others nearby at Sudbury in South Derbyshire and four more near the Nottinghamshire/Lincolnshire border. As waves of enemy aircraft attacked London on 7th September, the British believed that this was the precursor to an invasion and they issued "Invasion Alert 1", which meant that invasion was imminent and probable within 12 hours.

Issued by the Ministry of Information in co-operation with the War Office and the Ministry of Home Security

Beating the INVADER

A MESSAGE FROM THE PRIME MINISTER

IF invasion comes, everyone—young or old, men and women—will be eager to play their part worthily. By far the greater part of the country will not be immediately involved. Even along our coasts, the greater part will remain unaffected. But where the enemy lands, or tries to land, there will be most violent fighting. Not only will there be the battles when the enemy tries to come ashore, but afterwards there will fall upon his lodgments very heavy British counter-attacks, and all the time the lodgments will be under the heaviest attack by British bombers. The fewer civilians or non-combatants in these areas, the better—apart from essential workers who must remain. So if you are advised by the authorities to leave the place where you live, it is your duty to go elsewhere when you are told to leave. When the attack begins, it will be too late to go; and, unless you receive definite instructions to move, your duty then will be to stay where you are. You will have to get into the safest place you can find, and stay there until the battle is over. For all of you then the order and the duty will be : "STAND FIRM".

This also applies to people inland if any considerable number of parachutists or air-borne troops are landed in their neighbourhood. Above all, they must not cumber the roads. Like their fellow-countrymen on the coasts, they must "STAND FIRM". The Home Guard, supported by strong mobile columns wherever the enemy's numbers require it, will immediately come to grips with the invaders, and there is little doubt will soon destroy them.

Throughout the rest of the country where there is no fighting going on and no close cannon fire or rifle fire can be heard, everyone will govern his conduct by the second great order and duty, namely, "CARRY ON". It may easily be some weeks before the invader has been totally destroyed, that is to say, killed or captured to the last man who has landed on our shores. Meanwhile, all work must be continued to the utmost, and no time lost.

The following notes have been prepared to tell everyone in rather more detail what to do, and they should be carefully studied. Each man and woman should think out a clear plan of personal action in accordance with the general scheme.

Winston S. Churchill

STAND FIRM

1. What do I do if fighting breaks out in my neighbourhood?	as possible and only take cover when danger approaches If you are on your way to work, finish your journey if you can.
Keep indoors or in your shelter until the battle is over. If you can have a trench ready in your garden or field, so much the better. You may want to use it for protection if your house is damaged. But if you are at work, or if you have special orders, carry on as long	If you see an enemy tank, or a few enemy soldiers, do not assume that the enemy are in control of the area. What you have seen may be a party sent out in advance, or stragglers from the main body who can easily be rounded up.

Leaflet giving advice to the public about what to do in the event of an invasion

The large-scale air attack developed and continued long into the night and it seemed the authorities were right; if not tomorrow then certainly the next day, the Germans would come. That night the code word "*Cromwell*" went out to British home forces, bringing them to immediate readiness.

The fires in London's docklands gradually forced the defending firemen back and as the fires spread they were added to by each successive wave of bombers. As the firemen moved their jets of water on to another part of a building that was on fire, the part they had just extinguished would reignite. The fire crews had to fall back before this onslaught. The very means of continuing the battle were being destroyed by the fires and high-explosive bombs. Fire stations and sub control rooms were evacuated and became blazing shells in no time. Fire appliances that were urgently needed were cut off by the flames and when the water supply failed, crews had to abandon them in order to escape with their lives.

The firewomen at the sub control rooms found themselves setting up forward dressing stations to treat the stream of injured firemen being brought in with burns, cuts, broken bones and even scorched eyes. They had to turn their hands to tackling incendiary bombs that threatened their premises too. The whole situation was like a battlefield and it was clear that the battle was being lost.

Six fireboats were recalled from the Thameshaven blaze as they were needed desperately to fight massive riverside fires at Woolwich. At the Royal Arsenal, the fires within the area of the munitions factory set off the live rounds and the explosive nitroglycerine. As the officer in charge of one of the fireboats approached this area he was faced with a tunnel of fire. On both banks of the river the fires had formed into

Above Left: Soldiers of the 12th Battalion, Sherwood Foresters (Nottinghamshire and Derbyshire) Regiment, on anti invasion duty near Boston in Lincolnshire (Photograph courtesy *Nottingham Evening Post*) Right: Firemen being treated at a first aid post in London during the air raids of September 1940

a solid sheet of flame for over 1,000 yards. Ahead, the fires were stretching across the river and various river craft drifted past them ablaze while warehouses collapsed into the Thames.

Impossible as it had seemed the night before, by the morning of 8th September the firemen were beginning to win the battle. The conflagrations were under control and although it would be some time before they were extinguished, the danger to the capital was now contained. The civilian death toll stood at 430, the majority of whom had been killed by the blast from high-explosive bombs. Seven firemen had been killed during the night and many of those who had been injured were in a critical or serious condition. All things considered, the ARP and fire service had acquitted themselves well.

Bob Maslin was still firefighting at the dockside warehouse where his crew had been all night. They had been there for nearly 12 hours and they had not had anything to eat or drink for around 18 hours. They were tired out and were just staring at the fire and directing their jets of water as if they were in a trance. An officer suddenly rushed at them and pushed them violently to one side. They all fell into a mess of dirty water and molten sugar that had flowed out from the warehouse. A crane and jib weighing several tons fell from the top of the warehouse and crashed to the ground just a few feet from the men. Bob recalled the incident:

"There is no way we would have noticed it in time ourselves because we were so tired. Luckily the officer was further back from us and he saw it begin to lean before it fell. He shouted to warn us, but we did not hear him with all the noise around us.

I shall never forget one woman who came out of the basement of her house around 6.00 a.m. The whole street had been smashed up but she called across to us, 'All right, lads? Have you had a cup of tea?' We said that we hadn't and she scratched about in the ruins of her house and eventually found some tea and sugar then reappeared a little while later with tea and apologised for not having any milk. People were marvellous like that and in the early stages of the war, their spirit was unbreakable."

The Thameshaven, Shellhaven and Purfleet fires were still out of control on the morning of 8th September, the fire crews tackling these huge blazes sadly depleted by the recall to save London the night before. More pumps were desperately needed, and manpower to relieve the exhausted firemen. The reinforcements came from far afield and among them was a contingent from Nottingham.

As the fire crews arrived at the oil plant, they saw a scene from a nightmare. The concrete roads that led the way through the depot were smashed and cratered by the high-explosive bombs. Huge chunks of concrete lay strewn around and the ground was littered with all manner of debris from the explosions caused by the bombs. Some of the craters had an iron rod sticking out of them with a piece of rag tied to the top. These, the crews were later to learn, marked the sites of unexploded bombs.

The oil tanks blazed fiercely and continued to belch thick black smoke into the sky. Firemen who had been hard at work for several hours were coated in oil, barely recognisable as men. They staggered and slithered among the cratered ground, made slippery with oil, all the time trying to control their firefighting branches. The bund walls around the tanks were designed to hold any spills, but they were now full to overflowing. The tanks themselves glowed red and melted into the flames.

Frank Clay was a member of a Nottinghamshire Auxiliary Fire Service crew that made its way to Thameshaven. He had joined the AFS in 1937 and this would be the first taste of firefighting of any magnitude that he had experienced.

"We were firefighting at the Anglo-American oil docks using water jets to cool the tanks that were burning and those that were endangered by the radiated heat. At the part where we were, the fires stretched for miles and it seemed that we would never be able to put them out.

The aircraft came in low on their bombing runs and strafed us with their machine guns. It was very difficult to stand your ground and there were times when you felt like throwing the hose down and packing it all in. But you didn't, you stuck at it. I suppose it was because everybody else stuck at it; and they probably stayed because you did.

I can vividly remember one fireman who ran round an oil tank that had been pierced by shrapnel; he was desperately trying to plug the holes before the oil pouring out caught fire. We were surrounded by oil and also by water with oil floating on top of it. The fire had made it all hot and my biggest fear was of an incendiary dropping into the oil in which we were standing. If one had, then we would have been done for.

I remember seeing one fireman who had lost his hand; he was very calm. But there were others who were injured: some had their legs ripped off by shrapnel and they were in agony. The following day was very upsetting when we brought out some of the firemen who had been killed. They were cooked like chickens. I was a joiner and cabinet maker before the war and I had never had to deal with anything like that before.

We were firefighting for eight or nine hours without a break. But when the chance did come for a brief rest, crews used to go into a small concrete shelter. On one occasion there was five or six of us from Nottingham in there when a London fireman came bursting in. 'Am I bloody glad to get out of that,' he said. He was visibly shaking and we asked him where his mates were. He said, 'I have lost them'.

The idea of going to Thameshaven was so that we could relieve the crews that were already there, but that did not happen; we just got used up; there were so many fires they could not release anybody. We were there about eight days in the end and during that time they billeted us at a nunnery near Brentwood. I can't speak highly enough of those nuns. Our feet were in a terrible state because of the oil and hot water that we had been standing in. Our feet were very swollen and the skin was just hanging off in places and was very painful. The nuns bathed our feet and bandaged them. They were marvellous."

The night of 8th September brought another massive raid on London by 200 bombers of Luftflotte 3 from Norway. On 9th September cloudy weather restricted flying activity, but late in the afternoon 200 bombers with full escort made their way towards London. The unceasing attacks on RAF fighter bases had become accepted as the Luftwaffe's stock in trade and the daylight attack upon London on 7th September had been unexpected. To repeat it now, though, would be a different matter.

The RAF detected the raid and correctly supposed that London was the target. Subsequent plots of the enemy aircraft's route confirmed this and the RAF fighters had more time to get up to a reasonable height before intercepting the enemy because the raiders had further to travel. There was a second benefit to this too. The fighters of 12 Group, commanded from the headquarters at Watnall in Nottinghamshire, would also have sufficient time to get airborne and engage the enemy.

As the formations of aircraft droned towards London, the RAF intercepted and attacked fiercely, preventing about half the bombers from reaching their target. Douglas Bader's Duxford Wing of aircraft from 12 Group enjoyed notable success and a total of 28 German aircraft were shot down for the loss of 19 RAF fighters. In daylight it was starting to look as if the Luftwaffe would take a beating, but at night it was a different story. For over eight hours that night, German bombers passed across the London skyline, bringing death to 400 of its inhabitants and injury to 1,400 others. Massive fires had been caused again, and all this for negligible losses to the Luftwaffe.

The next day, 10th September, was cloudy and rain kept the Luftwaffe at bay in the daytime. At night, though, the raiders returned as usual and the following day they followed this up with three big raids on London. One young Nottingham soldier who was in London at that time was Gordon Needham. He had been called up for service in the Royal Army Medical Corps in January 1940 and along with others of 185 Field Ambulance had been moved from Stirling in Scotland to London in early September as part of the preparations for the expected German invasion. Their role in London was to assist with the casualties from the air raids.

"We were billeted in what had been a hotel and our army ambulances were parked in a schoolyard across the road. If we were needed to assist after a raid, a telephone call would come through and then they used to ring a big bell. We all had to grab our first aid satchels and dash for the ambulances.

The first couple of times we were called out everything had been taken care of by the Civil Defence first aid parties and ambulances. I remember we were called out on 11th September; I remember it particularly because I was 21 the following day. A heavy raid had occurred and when we arrived there were casualties everywhere. The dead lay amongst the dying and the whole scene was dreadful. We had all done our basic training but nothing prepared us for that. We did what we could for the injured and loaded them into our ambulances. One of the Civil Defence ambulances was a converted bread van.

As soon as we had our casualties we set off for the hospital. It never occurred to me how it was that our Service Corps drivers knew their way around, but I suppose they seconded Londoners to us for that reason.

Later on in the day we were called out again after other raids and on one occasion a couple of air raid wardens and a first aid party asked us to help out at a house that had been hit by a bomb. They told us that the family sheltered in the basement and asked if one of us would go down. I was the smallest so I volunteered.

They tied a rope around me and lowered me down the coal hole as it was the only way in. It was very dusty and dark down there but as I looked around I could make the family out; five of them in all. I checked each one of them for life, but they were all dead. There was barely a mark on them, but I saw quite a few like that during the Blitz: killed by the blast.

I had to drag them to the opening I had come down and tie the rope around them. The others pulled them up one by one and then finally I got out. I was absolutely filthy when I got out and I stood under the shower in my uniform to clean it when I got back."

At the end of August, Hitler had realised that a mid September invasion was not really practical to achieve and so he moved the date back to 21st September.

Nottingham Soldier Gordon Needham – Royal Army Medical Corps who dealt with casualties in London during the September 1940 air raids.(Medal group: 1939-45 Star. France-Germany Star. Defence Medal. War Medal)

Hitler gave the Luftwaffe commander, Field Marshal Göring, until 14th September to carry out his promise of destroying the RAF. The poor visibility on the 12th and 13th meant that large raids were out of the question, but London's nightly bombing went ahead, albeit on a reduced scale. Further postponements put the invasion back to 27th September. If the invasion did not go ahead then, the next date when the tides would be favourable would be 8th October, and that would be leaving it rather late unless Hitler was planning on fighting a winter campaign in England.

The Luftwaffe made one last all-out effort to destroy the RAF. Sunday 15th September began quietly;

it was a fine day with sunshine and cloud. Just before 11:00 hours the Radio Direction Finding equipment detected formations of aircraft over the Pas de Calais. The Observer Corps soon saw the approaching dots in the sky and as they grew closer, they were able to confirm they were enemy bomber formations.

The enemy bombers were attacked all the way to their target – London. The RAF planes harried them constantly and ferocious battles with the Luftwaffe fighters took place over the capital. The Luftwaffe turned for home having had mixed success with this massive raid. Two hours later they returned to find the Spitfires and Hurricanes waiting for them again.

Two smaller raids occurred during the day and that night 180 bombers continued the pounding of London. Göring had failed in his promise to destroy the RAF in four weeks and, despite the fact that he had sent 230 bombers and 700 fighters over in daylight raids, it was clear that he still did not command the skies over Britain. The Luftwaffe left its calling card in north Nottinghamshire again that night when three high-explosive bombs were dropped 300 yards to the north of Scaftworth Hall Grange and incendiaries were dropped around Scrooby.

The following night, Newark was paid another visit. The Luftwaffe announced its arrival by dropping incendiaries onto the village of Coddington and then a high-explosive bomb at North Road, Balderton. A high-explosive bomb also fell in Price's field at the end of Clay Lane in Newark, and two others that fell within 150 yards of the smallpox hospital failed to detonate. Only the caretaker had to be evacuated to safety as there were no patients in this wing of the hospital at the time. The unexploded bombs detonated 36 hours later without causing structural damage.

On 17th September, Hitler postponed Operation Sea Lion, the invasion of Britain, indefinitely. He gave orders for the concentrations of invasion barges to be split up so as to make them a less tempting target for the RAF bombers. Göring could not accept defeat and he continued to bomb London and also aircraft factories during the day whenever the weather permitted this. He mounted major raids on 18th, 27th and 30th September, but in truth his chance had gone.

Nottinghamshire was raided on the night of 18th September as incendiaries fell between Misterton Soss and Middle Broomston. A farmer's son managed to save a haystack from catching light by kicking the incendiaries away from it before they ignited. Retford was the target on the 19th when high-explosive bombs were dropped, but they failed to cause any significant damage. Other high-explosive bombs and incendiaries fell around Edingly, Farnsfield and Maplebeck. Air raid wardens at Kneeton extinguished incendiaries at Neale's Farm during a raid on the 20th and on the 26th it was the turn of Lound, Mattersey and Barnby Moor ARP workers to deal with a visit from the Luftwaffe. The night of 28th/29th September saw incendiaries dropped in a wide band across the county, including Sutton on Trent, Hockerton and Screveton in the east, with Blidworth receiving some further to the west and also damage at Peafield Lane and Leeming Lane in Mansfield.

Hitler formally cancelled Operation Sea Lion on 12th October and told his chiefs of staff that he would give them good warning if he intended to carry out an invasion in the spring of 1941. Towards the end of the month 36 bodies of German soldiers were washed up between Great Yarmouth on the east coast and Cornwall in the south-west. At the time it was assumed that these men had been part of the invasion armada that had set out for England around the 6th or 7th of September. They were in actual fact just unfortunate soldiers who had been killed during invasion exercises.

The invasion had been cancelled because the Luftwaffe had been denied the command of the skies; but at a terrible cost in human lives. During the period that was to become known as The Battle of Britain, RAF Fighter Command lost 438 aircrew, but the cost to the Luftwaffe was 3,089. Clearly the Luftwaffe could not continue to sustain such heavy casualties and yet, at night, when they roamed almost at will, their casualties were negligible. Night bombing was the way for the Luftwaffe to continue the air offensive against Britain. As the darkness fell earlier and earlier, the visits by night raiders became more frequent and the people of Britain learned what it was to be subjected to aerial bombardment night after night.

6. Night Raiders

Following the air raids on London in early September and the repeated bombing of the city at night, many Londoners had taken to sheltering in the tube stations deep beneath the city.

On 14th October, a high-explosive bomb struck Balham High Road and penetrated into the tube station beneath. The blast killed many of the 64 people who were sheltering there, but it is possible that some of those killed were drowned when water from the fractured mains gushed into the station. Bob Maslin was part of one of the fire crews that pumped the water out.

Balham High Road in London after a high explosive bomb had penetrated into a tube station and detonated

"There were a lot of other crews working on the same job and we were just one of many who were sent as reliefs several days after the incident. We had six Coventry Climax Pumps set up on a set of bogie wheels from a train. We had 107 lengths of hose laid out back up to street level. [This is about one and half miles of hose; as the hose would have been twinned to provide greater pumping capacity, the actual distance involved would have been around three quarters of a mile.] There was probably about eight feet of water to be pumped out of the station.

We had gone past this particular incident one morning on our way back to the station after firefighting and we noticed a bus had fallen into the crater, but we had no idea at the time that all those people had been killed. It was strange working down there and seeing a set of wheels belonging to a bus sticking down through the roof. We were working there about a fortnight altogether."

The recovery of the bodies was to go on for much longer than two weeks and it was not until Christmas that the last one was removed. The conditions that the fire crews and rescue parties worked in were grim to say the least and there was a high risk of contracting illness when recovering the bodies of those that had been underwater for two weeks and decomposing for ten weeks.

The Luftwaffe visited Nottinghamshire on Saturday 19th October and incendiaries were dropped on Bingham, at Radcliffe on Trent Golf Club and at Ingham Farm on Cropwell Road in Radcliffe on Trent. A house in Eton Road at West Bridgford typified the good fortune that the area had on that particular night. An incendiary glanced off the roof instead of penetrating it and it landed on a concrete path where it burned out harmlessly. A high-explosive bomb fell at Landmere Lane in West Bridgford, near to Wheatcroft's Rose Nursery. It fell into a field, leaving a crater, but caused no other damage. Incendiaries fell at Wysall and a high-explosive bomb fell about 500 yards to the north-west of the village near the Wysall to Bunny Road.

To the north of the county, incendiaries were dropped around Ordsall, Ranskill, Sutton cum Lound, Mattersey and Blyth. Two high-explosive bombs were dropped between Heck Dyke and West Stockwith, and exploded on the Nottinghamshire bank of the River Trent.

The raiders returned the following night and the aircraft were tracked across the southern part of the county. A landmine was dropped, which drifted down under its parachute and detonated in Orston at 22:05 hours. The explosion was terrific, rendering two houses in the village uninhabitable and damaging 60 others. Rose Haynes (née Carlisle) was ten years old at the time and she remembered events immediately following the explosion.

"I was staying at my grandmother's house at the time of this incident and I was asleep in one of the bedrooms. The whole house shook and I was thrown from my bed into another room. Part of the ceiling came down and other debris had landed on me. It was pitch dark and then I heard my granddad calling out my name. I answered him and then I heard him say: 'She is alive!' How I ended up in the other room I do not know, but I suppose I must have gone through the doorway. I was not badly hurt, but I was very shaken by what had happened."

Above left: Rose Haines (née Carlisle) stands in front of the replacement of the village hall at Orston, destroyed by a landmine on 20th October 1940. Rose was injured by the explosion. Above right: This house, opposite the village hall in Orston, was badly damaged by the blast from a landmine which fell in the village on 20th October 1940

The wooden building in the village which was used by the YMCA was seriously damaged and telephone lines and electricity cables were brought down. ARP wardens made their way to where the explosion had occurred and found a crater 40 feet in diameter and 18 feet deep. They reported the damage to the County ARP Control Centre in Nottingham and also informed them that one man and two women had been slightly injured.

Whilst ARP workers were dealing with the results of the landmine in Orston, another was dropped half a mile south of Hayton, near Retford. This detonated at 22:30 hours and fortunately the marshy ground into which it had fallen absorbed much of the blast. Hayton Castle Farm had its windows, doors and the roofs of buildings damaged and Wheatley Fields Farm and three cottages on the farmland were also damaged. When ARP wardens arrived, they found a crater 24

An aerial mine that failed to detonate and was subsequently defused and recovered by a bomb disposal squad of the Royal Navy (Photograph courtesy of Nottingham City Fire Brigade archives)

feet in diameter and 15 feet deep. Ten yards away from the crater a green parachute was found, which was the means by which the Luftwaffe delivered the 500kg (1,100lb) aerial mines.

Fifty incendiaries were dropped around Screveton and Flintham later during the night and at 00:20 hours a high-explosive bomb fell at Mr Cope's farm in Burton Joyce. The report of this bomb to the County ARP Control Centre was a little confused as wardens in Arnold had reported the sound of bombs falling in their district, but none were found. It is thought that the sound of the explosion at Burton Joyce led to reports of bombs falling in Arnold.

The raiders visited the county again on the night of 25th/26th October when Newark was the target. The contents of an army lorry were destroyed and a barn was also set on fire by incendiary bombs. Two houses, 65 and 85 Milton Street in Balderton, were also damaged in this raid.

On 29th October an unexploded bomb was discovered in Field Lane at Chilwell, which authorities believed had been there since the air raid on that district on the night of 30th/31st August. During the night of 30th October, Retford received incendiaries but no high-explosive bombs were reported as having fallen. The following night a raider over Attenborough dropped two high-explosive bombs that left craters 25 feet in diameter and 20 feet deep. Several houses were damaged and the windows of Attenborough Church were broken. Two high-explosive bombs also fell between Colston Bassett and Hickling in the south-east of the county.

Murky weather on 31st October probably prompted the daylight raid on the Chilwell Munitions Factory by a single aircraft. The raid was heralded by a high-explosive bomb falling in West Leake, about one mile west of the Gotham to East Leake Road. As the aircraft reached Nottingham, five heavy thuds were heard at about 14:40 hours, followed by machine-gun fire. Anti-aircraft guns began to fire but without any effect on the raider. Two high-explosive bombs and one 250kg oil-bomb incendiary fell near the Grove Inn on Chilwell Lane in Bramcote. A child who was seeking shelter at the Nether Street School in Beeston was slightly injured as a result of this raid. Another high-explosive bomb fell close to Wood Farm at Strelley. The Ministry of Information in Nottingham at first believed the explosions were fog signals being used on the nearby London Midland and Scottish railway! As the raider escaped to the north of the county, three more high-explosive bombs were dropped near to Ollerton Colliery.

On 3rd November 1940, a daring Luftwaffe pilot brought his aircraft very low as he approached Nottingham in broad daylight. In fact he was so low that the crew members could be seen clearly by people on the ground. The aircraft machine-gunned Trent Boulevard, Gertrude Road and George Road in West Bridgford. Three houses were hit by the bullets, but fortunately no one was injured. People described the raider suddenly appearing out of low cloud and machine-gunning before making off into the obscurity of the grey skies. He was flying far too low for anti-aircraft guns to locate him, let alone engage him. This sort of attack demonstrated clearly that the air defence network could be penetrated far inland with impunity.

In addition to the hazards caused by enemy action, the blackout caused casualties. One of Nottingham's firemen, Phillip Smith, was killed when the fire appliance he was travelling in was involved in a collision with a surface air raid shelter in Manning Street. Fireman Smith died of his injuries in hospital and an inquest was held into his death.

The Coroner heard evidence from Fireman Horace Danby and also from Herman Price, who had been driving the fire appliance at the time of the collision. They stated that three of the crew were travelling on the running board outside the vehicle. This was normal practice at the time. Fireman Price was under the impression that all the street shelters in Manning Street were on the left. He said that he did not see the shelter until he was right on top of it and although he braked and swerved, he collided with it. Fireman Smith was trapped between the vehicle and the brickwork and sustained fatal injuries.

The Coroner recorded a verdict of accidental death and said, *"It has been a matter for comment that the surface shelters were not visible on dark nights even to pedestrians."* Phillip Smith joined a list of firemen and ARP workers

Above left: Auxiliary Fireman Smith was killed when the vehicle used for towing the pump was involved in a collision with a street air raid shelter during the blackout (Photograph courtesy of Nottingham City Fire Brigade archives) Above right: The funeral cortege of Auxiliary Fireman Phillip Smith who was killed in Manning Street (photograph courtesy of Nottingham City Fire Brigade archives)

who had died on duty since the beginning of the war and it was a list that would continue to grow.

Nottingham continued to receive air raid alerts but nothing else fell within the city boundary until 12th November. Anti-aircraft guns set up a fearsome noise during the night when they fired off 107 rounds at an aircraft over the city. Two high-explosive bombs fell into the garden of Mrs Fowler, a 68-year-old widow who lived near Mapperley. Her house and a neighbour's were damaged but she escaped the ordeal without physical injury. Residents in 21 other houses had their windows broken and damage caused to roofs. At Huckerby Farm, Redhill, seven high-explosive bombs fell but there was no serious damage.

The incident that gave rise to the biggest problem occurred when three canisters measuring three feet long and nine inches in diameter were dropped in the Mapperley area. One of the canisters that fell into "Herring Field", ten yards from Killisick Lane in Arnold, was seen to have a parachute nearby. At first it was feared that this might be an unexploded aerial mine and 22 people were evacuated on the strength of this. Coppice Road, from its junction with Ravenswood Road to Mapperley Plains, was closed and the Admiralty was requested to send a bomb disposal team to inspect the canister. They did so the following day and declared it safe as it was an empty canister that had contained incendiary bombs. Mistakes like this were common as ARP wardens were unfamiliar with just how big an aerial mine was, or what an incendiary canister looked like. In fact the smallest of the aerial mines dropped by the Luftwaffe was 5 feet 6 inches long and weighed 500kg (1,100lb). The larger aerial mine was over 8 feet long and weighed 1,100kg (2,400lb).

The next day there was an anti-aircraft barrage in Nottingham again but this time it was in the middle of the afternoon. Thousands of people went out into the open to look at the lone enemy plane over the city. The aircraft was at an altitude of about 2,500 feet and although the sky was littered with puffs of smoke from the anti-aircraft shells, the aircraft was not hit. The concentrated anti-aircraft fire seemed to cause the pilot to change his direction and he turned from a northerly flight path onto an easterly course and headed in the direction of RAF Newton.

It appeared that the aircraft had been taking reconnaissance photographs of Nottingham and the chilling thought that crossed many people's minds was – "*How long before they come back and do to Nottingham what they have done to other cities?*"

On Thursday 14th November, the Nottingham people found out which city was next for special treatment from the Luftwaffe in a raid they code named Operation "*Moonlight Sonata*".

During that night, Nottingham's anti-aircraft guns fired shells at enemy bombers passing over the city, the intensity of the barrage being particularly noticeable at 23:25 hours and again at 02:00 and 04:00 hours.

On that night a new verb entered the English language: "*Coventrate*" – the systematic destruction of a city by bombing.

7. Moonlight Sonata

There has been much debate about the interception of radio messages to Luftwaffe units during the day on 14th November 1940 and whether the target of the raid was known in advance. It has been alleged that no warning was given to the people of Coventry on the direct instructions of Winston Churchill, so that the German High Command were not alerted to the fact that the Enigma Code had been deciphered.

Evidence points to Churchill being unaware of the target that night until the raid had actually commenced. In fact, Churchill returned to London on the basis of an intelligence report that led him to believe the target would be the capital city. On 11th November, the Air Ministry had decoded German signals in which the phrase "*Moonlight Sonata*" was used. Scientists concluded that the "*Moonlight*" part of the phrase meant that the raid would take place on a moonlit night; the period 15th to 20th November was a full moon. The code breakers had the names of three targets referred to in the "*Moonlight Sonata*" message:

The tower at Central Fire Station in Nottingham used for training. From the roof of the tower on the night of 14th November 1940, Alf Porkett could see the pulsing glow across the horizon as Coventry was systematically destroyed

Birmingham was code named "*Umbrella*", Wolverhampton was code named "*All one price*", but crucially, they did not connect the code name "*Corn*" to Coventry.

Evidence in Air Ministry files shows that the real meaning of the "*Moonlight Sonata*" message was misunderstood and it was believed that it referred to a raid that would be carried out against targets in the south of England, including London. The code names for Birmingham and Wolverhampton were thought to refer to raids that would take place on other nights and the British authorities did not know that Coventry was to be raided that night.

What does remain, however, are comments made by firemen from Nottingham who moved to "*standby locations*" during the late afternoon of 14th November before the raid had even started. In 1990, they expressed the opinion that "*somebody in authority knew that something was up*".

Whether this was true or not, the fact remains that some fire crews were moved and were not given any reason why. The explanation is probably no more than the fact that a heavy raid was expected and Midlands fire crews were moved further south in anticipation of forming relief columns. Senior Fire Officers probably suspected that they would be heading into London; we now know that it was to be Coventry.

Coventry was an obvious target for the Luftwaffe: it had a high percentage of factories contributing to the war effort. In the Air Defence Exercises of 1934, Coventry had been designated as one of the "key targets" assigned to the "enemy" bombers; London was the other. Although the industrial north–west was important to Britain in a war, it was thought that targets in the Midlands, along with those in the south and the east, were at most risk of attack. Coventry had already been bombed on 24 occasions by 12th November 1940 and this had led to large numbers of people leaving the city each night. Those who remained tended to go into their shelters early in the evening and stay there until daylight the next morning. A special constable who lived in St Paul's Road recalled that only twelve houses out of eighty had anyone living in them. He too had sent his family out of the city for safety.

On Thursday 14th November 1940, the air raid message "*Yellow*" was received at the ARP control room in Coventry at 19:07 hours, followed three minutes later by "*Red*". The wail of the sirens was still dying away as the first of the incendiary bombs began to fall. At first this raid appeared to be no different to any of the others that they had suffered, but within an hour the situation gave enough concern for the following report to be sent.

REPORT FROM ARP CONTROL CENTRE TO MIDLANDS REGIONAL H.Q.

Ref our report at 19:45 Coventry. A large number of IB's [incendiary bombs] *over a wide area. Fires reported at Rover Co., Courtahlds Ltd., Foleshill Road, Naval Ordnance Store, Stoney Stanton Road, O' Brien's works, Lloyds and Midland Bank High Street, Owen Owen's Store, Central Hotel, G.P.O. roof and warehouse at Foleshill Station. H.E.* [high-explosive] *bombs reported with people trapped.*

A report was also sent to the regional ARP HQ stating that a different type of incendiary bomb (IBEN: incendiary bomb exploding nose) was being dropped. This was the first time that such bombs had been used on the UK and the report was therefore forwarded to the war room at the Ministry of Home Security.

Around 20:00 hours, three incendiary bombs fell onto Coventry Cathedral. One of these was dealt with fairly quickly, but the other two burnt through the roof and one of them fell onto the wooden pews and started a small fire. The cathedral's fire-watchers put sand on this incendiary before scooping it up and throwing it out. The third incendiary proved more troublesome. It set fire to the wooden rafters and several buckets of water had to be pumped in with a stirrup pump before it was extinguished.

Just then another shower of incendiaries fell and the roof above the children's chapel caught fire. Smoke poured from the holes in the lead sheeting where the incendiaries had burned through, while inside the chapel a fire could be seen spreading rapidly across the ceiling. The fire party on this particular night consisted of Provost Howard, who was 56 years old, a 65-year-old stonemason and two men in their twenties. They tried to extinguish the fire, but found it beyond their physical strength. They ran out of water and sand to apply to the fire and it gained ground all the time until finally they conceded.

Coventry on the morning 15th November 1940 after the heaviest raid on a provincial city up to that point in the war. The landscape of the city changed overnight causing people to become disorientated in places that they had previously known well (Photograph courtesy of HMSO)

The fire brigade were called but it had been left too late and upon their arrival the roof was already well alight. Ladders were pitched and several lines of hose were hauled aloft and set to work on the flames. Burning material dropping down inside the cathedral had started fires among the pews and firemen tackling these were in danger of parts of the roof collapsing on to them. Molten lead began to drip down on to the crews inside the church and the water from the hoses of their colleagues on the roof was scalding hot as it cascaded on to them.

Before much impact was made on the fire, the water supply failed. The firemen got another supply from Priory Row but they quickly lost this when the main was shattered by a high-explosive bomb. At about 22:30 another water supply was relayed to the fireground and a firefighting jet was got to work. It had taken a significant amount of manpower to achieve this and a considerable quantity of hose and other equipment had been used simply to get water to the cathedral. Most of the cathedral was well alight now, but the firemen dragged their firefighting jet up the spiral staircase and through the sanctuary door in order to apply water to the fire in the Lady Chapel. The water pressure was low but they stuck at it until this supply failed too and then the firemen left the cathedral for the last time. This was a terrible blow to Provost Howard, who commented, "*We realised with consternation and horror that nothing more could be done.*" The cathedral became an inferno with just the outline of the main walls discernable amongst the flames.

The Midland Region ARP HQ was at Birmingham and when it was realised that the raid on Coventry was a major one, they asked for assistance from other regions. North Midland Region sent fire pumps and crews from Nottingham to help the hard-pressed Coventry firemen. One of the crews that went was from Triumph Road Fire Station (the forerunner of Dunkirk Fire Station). They met with disaster almost as soon as they arrived. They were firefighting when a high-explosive bomb fell right next to them. One of the crew, Fred Winstanley, described the moment as "*a big flash and then everything just disintegrated*". The crew were stunned by the blast and when they came to they found that Fireman Farndon was seriously injured. Fireman William Chadwick described the scene.

> *"Fireman Farndon was right next to me when the bomb fell and it was a terrible bang. You could have put a bus into the crater it left. Why the rest of us escaped serious injury I shall never know. We all got up after the explosion, but he couldn't, poor devil. I think he was unconscious and his leg was all smashed up with the bone sticking out. Our Patrol Officer, Sid Hucknall, decided that we would have to fetch an ambulance for him and so Sid and I made off in search of one. He found one first and I met him on the way back."*

Fireman Farndon was placed into the care of an ambulance crew and he was taken to Rugby Hospital. The crews then turned their attention back to the task of firefighting and inspected the damage caused by the bomb to their vehicle and pump.

Above: Part of the funeral cortege for Auxiliary Fireman Clifford Farndon killed during the air raid on Coventry on 14th November 1940 (Photograph courtesy of Nottingham City Fire Brigade archives)

By the KING'S Order the name of
William Chadwick,
Auxiliary Fireman.
Nottingham Aux Fire Service
was published in the London Gazette on
7 February. 1941.
as commended for brave conduct in
Civil Defence.
I am charged to record His Majesty's
high appreciation of the service rendered.

Prime Minister and First Lord
of the Treasury

Left: Auxiliary Fireman William Chadwick. One of four Nottingham Firemen who received a King's Commendation for their actions during the Coventry raid (Photograph courtesy of Nottingham City Fire Brigade archives)

The towing vehicle and equipment had been damaged by the explosion, but worst of all their trailer pump had been put out of action completely. Without this they could not provide pressure to the water to pump it on to any of the fires. At this stage, they could perhaps have been forgiven for deciding that there was nothing they could do to help, and in fact they would have been justified in finding a first aid post and getting their injuries seen to. Instead, they searched around until they found a trailer pump that had been abandoned by its crew. The reason quickly became obvious because, just like their own, the pump would not work. They set about remedying this situation and eventually got the engine to start. They found a water supply from a fire hydrant and recommenced the job they had been sent to do: put fires out.

All the time they had been working on the trailer pump, they had been aware of new fires starting up around them until it seemed that, whichever direction they looked, there was a building on fire. Later on during the night, while applying their firefighting jets to a row of houses which were on fire, they were warned that there was an unexploded bomb nearby. They had gone past the stage of caring what happened by now though, and rational thoughts were not at the forefront of their minds. This may have been partly due to the effects of the explosion, which no doubt had left them with concussion. The crew had become locked in to the desperate struggle to control the fires. They had entered a state of tunnel vision where nothing else mattered to them. They stuck at their task even though ARP wardens warned them of the risk of the bomb exploding.

Other Nottingham crews that had arrived in Coventry reported to the central fire station and from there they were dispatched to one of the many fires in the city. Frank Clay from Nottingham's Central Fire Station was in charge of a crew that was put to work on Coventry Cathedral. They got a water supply into their pump and tried to prevent the fire from spreading to nearby properties. Other crews were working close by and Frank found himself supervising three crews in the end. This is how he described the scene.

"The waves of aircraft kept coming over and dropping more bombs and it seemed at times as if they were aiming them personally at you. The radiated heat from the fires all around us was terrific. If you stayed still for too long without covering the skin on your face or hands, it became too painful and the heat scorched you. We were gasping for breath as the fires were using up the oxygen and any exertion made you feel as though you were suffocating. One of the crews I was in charge of was firefighting on the Dunlop warehouse near the cathedral and the smoke from that fire was absolutely choking.

I saw a little girl of about five or six in the street and she came up to me and took hold of my hand. Apparently she had been in a shelter and either it, or something close to it, had been blown up and so she had come out. I couldn't find out what had happened to her parents and so I kept her with me to try and look after her. She was crying at first, but she seemed to calm down once she was holding my hand and we went up and down the street from one crew to another, together. She was with me for quite a bit of the night, but when I saw a nurse, I took the girl to her so she could be taken away to safety. I sometimes wonder what happened to her and if she made it all right."

For Frank Clay's wife and two-year-old daughter at home in Nottingham, there was thankfully no knowledge that he was amidst the most devastating air raid to happen to a city so far during the war.

When interviewed in 1990, it was clear that Frank was deeply affected by the trauma that had been visited upon that little girl in Coventry. Even when describing the destruction and horror all around him, it was this more than anything else that brought the emotion to his voice. It was not difficult to understand that, as he held her hand through that terrible night, he wanted to protect her from what was happening. His thoughts must have wandered at times to his own daughter and the knowledge that one day soon she might be in the same situation. Frank felt a sadness that he did not know whether the little girl had survived or not. The bond that had been formed so briefly on that November night in 1940 was still there for Frank fifty years later.

The firemen at Nottingham's Central Fire Station knew that something serious was happening because of the number of crews that had been sent from the city divisions and also from the tremendous anti-air-craft barrage from the Nottingham and Derby guns. Alf Porkett was one of the firemen who went onto the roof of the drill tower in the station yard. From their vantage point seventy feet in the air, they could see what was happening to Coventry.

"The waves of aircraft passed over Nottingham and as you looked south you could see a glow all across the horizon. You couldn't hear anything at that distance but you could see the glow pulsing as the sticks of bombs went down into the fires."

Fire crews were still fighting the massive blaze at Owen Owen's store in Coventry. Their early attempts at putting out the fire inside the store had been delayed by the security grilles and the fire had gained a good hold. The fire spread above and around them, putting them in danger of being cut off, and they had to retreat until eventually they were forced to resort to fighting the fire from outside the building.

A parachute mine drifted silently down into the street and four firemen who saw it ran into a doorway to try to gain some cover. The officer in charge and his leading fireman were holding a jet and they did not have time to run. The terrific explosion blew them to the ground, but although they were dazed, they were not seriously injured. The other crew members had been buried under the rubble of what had been a shop. The officer and leading fireman managed to free one of the men, but sadly he died just a few minutes later.

Charlie Caunt was in charge of a Nottingham fire crew and they were firefighting on a factory in a narrow street with terraced houses opposite. The houses were ablaze and air raid wardens told the crew that a woman and two children who sheltered in the basement were trapped.

The heat was terrific and without the benefit of breathing apparatus it would be extremely difficult to get down to the basement. Charlie did not ask anyone else to undertake the task. He took a blanket from the appliance, soaked it with water and then draped it over himself. He crawled into the house and found his way down into the cellar by touch. He returned after a few minutes with a child, re-soaked the blanket and went down again. Charlie appeared again with the second child and without pause went down to the cellar a third time. When he reappeared dragging the almost unconscious woman, his colleagues went to his aid to bring her to safety. Charlie slumped on to the road, gasping for breath with steam coming from his fire tunic; they were safe. The family were taken to an ARP post and then on to a Rest Centre. The fire crew turned their attention back to the blazing factory.

A message had been sent at 00:45 hours from Midland Regional Control to London. It stated:

"Fire situation at Coventry extremely serious. City alight."

The central fire station which also contained the fire brigade's control room had been hit by a high-explosive bomb and no detailed records of fires were kept after this time. The mobilisation of firefighting resources was difficult and dispatch riders had to be sent from various incidents requesting more appliances and men. The water supplies had become woefully inadequate due to damaged water mains and the firemen were fighting a losing battle. Just like an army that has insufficient ammunition, they were forced back, and as they retreated the flames engulfed entire blocks of buildings.

The "*Raiders Passed*" signal reached Coventry at 06:16, but the all clear sirens did not sound as there was no electricity for them to operate. A mist of smoke and dust hung over the city, fires were burning out of control in all directions and buildings could be heard collapsing. People emerging from the air raid shelters were disorientated because familiar landmarks and entire streets had disappeared during the night. Even official messengers going to and from incidents in the city found themselves lost amongst the rubble and shattered buildings. The landscape had changed several times during the night and, in places where they had used a building as a marker, it was often no longer there and rubble blocked the street that they were intending to go down.

When daylight came there was a mass exodus by the civilian population out of the city. The flow of frightened and exhausted people carrying what few possessions they could was reminiscent of what the British public had watched earlier that year on the Pathé newsreels at cinemas as Dutch, Belgian and then French people had fled as the war advanced across their country. So this was what it was like to become a refugee. As the people flowed one way, relief fire crews and rescue squads edged their way through them going in the opposite direction.

The firemen and civil defence workers in Coventry were exhausted, but there was no time for them to rest. Coventry's Chief Fire Officer was still dirty and unshaven when he arrived for a meeting of the Emergency Committee that morning. He too was exhausted and fell asleep at the meeting.

George Wood had been firefighting all night with a crew from Mansfield Woodhouse.

"We were so weary the next morning and we would have given anything for a drink. We saw 'King's Messengers' going to and fro and they asked us if we wanted a cup of tea. Eventually we got a cup of tea each and a small piece of cake between five of us. We sat down on the steps of a theatre to drink the tea and then some people said to us, 'Don't sit there! There's some D.A.'s [delayed action bombs] in there.' Well, we were so tired we couldn't care less. So we just sat and drank the tea."

The Nottingham crew that had valiantly continued to work after being blown up the night before enquired after their injured colleague. They learned that he had died of his injuries during the night at St Cross Hospital in Rugby.

By 11:30 on that Friday morning, five major fires were still being tackled and countless other smaller fires were being dealt with. Not all the crews could be relieved the following morning, but 250 firemen from Coventry and other parts of the Midlands were eventually relieved by firemen from Manchester and Leeds. Four incidents were still in progress where people were trapped and Manchester rescue teams came to relieve at these incidents too. By Sunday only four fires were still smouldering and the casualty figures stood at 568 killed and 1,256 injured.

The Nottingham Air Raid Precautions HQ received another call for assistance on the Sunday night. This time it was to ask if they could supply breakfasts in Coventry on Monday morning at 08:00 hours. At the Eastcroft Depot kitchens on London Road, the Women's Voluntary Service set to work. Early the next morning, Mrs Weeks and four assistants from the WVS set out for Coventry. They supplied hot drinks and food from 08:00 hours on Monday 17th November until 15:00 hours on 18th November. The work of the WVS women was reported in the Nottingham *Guardian Journal*.

"A service some 5,000 Coventry people are never likely to forget was that rendered by volunteer staff of the mobile canteen sent from Nottingham Air Raid Precautions HQ.

One Sunday night a call was received at ARP HQ from the Regional ARP HQ to provide breakfasts in Coventry the next day. A whole sheep was procured along with large quantities of vegetables and work began at the kitchens of Eastcroft Depot on the production of a giant Irish stew.

The WVS volunteers had a problem with finding containers big enough to put the stew into once it was cooked. This was solved by providing brand new dustbins which were wrapped in blankets to keep the food warm. The ARP canteen set off at 5.00am with food for 500 people. By 8.00am it was serving stew or porridge and hot drinks from the side of a road in Coventry for all who asked for it.

Superintendent Pierce, Sub Controller of Air Raid Precautions for Nottingham spoke of the tremendous appreciation shown by the stricken people. He told the Nottingham Guardian Journal that a man in a bowler hat and carrying an umbrella asked for coffee and a sandwich at the canteen. These were supplied and he offered one pound in payment. He was told that the food and drink were free and that the canteen had been sent from Nottingham. He broke down and sobbed at that. The Coventry people were so grateful that others had so much thought for them that they could not express themselves.

Later in the day when the canteen was being cleaned up, a clergyman came by and asked what they were going to do with the scraps of food. He told them that he had lost his church and vicarage and was living in a cellar. He took some scraps of food away and was grateful for the kindness shown him.

More food was procured locally to keep the canteen going and the women of the WVS continued to help the Coventry people. The canteen from Nottingham was one of four sent from the North Midlands Region; the others were from Leicester, Northampton and Lindsey in Lincolnshire.

The canteen is normally stocked with food for 150 people and can call on one hundred loaves of bread day or night in order to provide food for ARP workers and firemen or civilians in an area affected by air raids."

The efforts of the women who took the mobile canteen to Coventry were worthy of the praise given them in the newspapers and the Nottingham fire crew who had one of their number killed also received praise, this time from Herbert Morrison, the Home Security Minister. He sent each of them a letter which said:

"Your devotion to duty was deserving of high praise. I have pleasure in informing you that His Majesty has been graciously pleased to give orders for the publication of your name as having received an expression of commendation of your services."

As a result of this King's Commendation, they were entitled to wear a Silver Oak Leaf on the ribbon of their Defence Medal.

The Earl of Dudley, Midland Regional ARP Officer, also sent the men a letter praising their work. The five recipients were:

Patrol Officer	Sid Hucknall	10 Cycle Road, Lenton.
Auxiliary Fireman	William Chadwick	8 Paignton Close, Aspley
Auxiliary Fireman	John Collins	61 Elstree Drive, Wollaton
Auxiliary Fireman	Bernard Hill	307 Denman Street, Radford
Auxiliary Fireman	Fred Winstanley	62 Noel Street, Forest Fields

While some of those involved in dealing with the raid on Coventry had their bravery and devotion to duty properly recognised, others were treated in a shabby fashion by the authorities. Auxiliary Fireman Flower from Nottingham was so badly injured in the raid that he had to be discharged from the service. From the date of his discharge on 5th January 1941, he did not receive a single penny from any source whatsoever for eleven weeks. When he finally did receive some money to keep himself and his family, it was only due to the fuss made that Nottingham's Emergency Committee gave him an allowance under the personal injury scheme until the Ministry of Pensions dealt with his case. Relying on the charity of his friends and family was a bitter pill to swallow when he had been permanently disabled protecting others from the worst that the Luftwaffe could throw at Britain.

On 16th November 1940, while some of the Nottinghamshire firemen and rescue teams were still at Coventry, Nottingham was bombed, but thankfully it was not a serious attack. Anti-aircraft fire began at 02:00 hours and two bombs fell near the Halfway House at Wollaton. One of the bombs fell into the canal and failed to explode, but the other fell into the market garden of Frank Earp and made a crater 30 feet in diameter and 10 feet deep. The windows of houses in Elstree Drive were blown in by the blast and for Fireman John Collins, who had just returned home from Coventry to recover from his injuries, it must have been a nasty shock.

Nottinghamshire firemen were called to another city again on 19th November. This time it was Birmingham. Pumps and crews from the city division were sent, along with the 100-foot turntable ladder.

Alf Porkett was on the turntable ladder that night and he remembers that the water supply situation was as grave as it had been in Coventry the week before. During the raid, one of the canals had a high-explosive bomb explode in it and this damaged the basin of the canal, causing a leak. The large number of pumps using the canal for firefighting water, combined with the leak, led to the canal being pumped dry.

Charlie Bartles was part of a crew from the Radford Division of Nottingham that was sent to Birmingham. They had been to Coventry the week before and were under no delusions about what to expect. Shortly after they arrived in Birmingham, there was a massive explosion as a chemical factory nearby was hit by a heavy-calibre bomb. A cocktail of chemicals poured into one of the canals that were being used for firefighting water.

Charlie's crew were sent to assist with the fire at the chemical factory and they had the

Newspaper article (8th February 1941) about the Commendation for the Nottingham Fire crew (Courtesy of *Nottingham Evening Post*)

task of getting their suction hose into the canal so that water could be pumped from there to the fire. The water had to be used even though it contained chemicals; there was simply no choice. Charlie remembers the firemen getting acid onto their skin and uniforms and on the pump and equipment.

The obvious danger from bombs when out in the open was not reduced to any great extent when crews went inside buildings to tackle fires. A high-explosive bomb fell close to where Charlie was firefighting and it sent shrapnel slicing through two doors before it slammed into a wall inches in front of his face.

When the fires were brought under control and they were relieved by other firemen from further afield, they were told to get some rest. They were billeted at Winson Green Prison. The prisoners had all been evacuated away to a place of safety. The conditions were far from ideal but the firemen were far too tired to worry about that. They drew their issue of two blankets and were thankful to able to take off their wet fire kit and sleep. They were too tired to eat or get themselves clean and they knew that there was every chance that the Luftwaffe would return again that night and they would have do it all over again.

The Luftwaffe had unleashed a Blitz on the cities of Britain of frightening magnitude; a Blitz that would continue through the dark months of 1940 and long into 1941.

8. The Blitz

The Luftwaffe continued its attacks on the provinces, but on 8th December 1940 it launched a major attack on London again for the first time in two months. The raid began at 18:12 hours and went on until 06:35 hours, during which time 413 aircraft found their way to the target area. They dropped 387 tonnes of high-explosive bombs during the raid and an unprecedented 114,700 incendiaries. The fire service had to deal with 1,700 fires and it was during this raid that the Houses of Parliament were set on fire as well as Westminster Abbey and the Royal Mint. Casualties were heavy in this raid, with 250 people killed and 630 seriously injured.

Auxiliary Fireman Bob Maslin was on duty at Wandsworth Fire Station that night and his crew were mobilised to Barnes Fire Station to "stand by" there. This procedure is known as a covering-up move and ensures that an area is not left without fire cover as the fire appliances that normally cover that area are committed to incidents.

> "As soon as we got to Barnes, the control room officer came out to us and said, 'You are to go straight back – your station has been hit.' We turned around and drove back as quickly as we could, but it was a fair distance. The ambulances had already taken the casualties away when we arrived and there was no hope for those still trapped inside.
>
> The whole place was just flattened. The control officer and our messenger boy were dead along with four of the firemen. We weren't there long before they said that they needed our pump and so we were sent to another job."

The twelve-hour bombing of London was one of the most devastating raids on the city and the fires caused by the raid stretched the fire brigade to the limit. Outside assistance was called in and the North Midland region responded along with others. Nottingham sent some of its fire crews to London and some of them were there for five days without a break. Charlie Bartles from the Triumph Road Station recalls:

> "We reported to a place at Luton before being moved in to the Clerkenwell district of London. You have never seen anything like it in your life. Whole streets were ablaze. Offices, warehouses, factories, shops, houses; it was like walking through an inferno.
>
> The firemen down there did a magnificent job, you know. Night after night they took it. We were tired out after just a few days; absolutely licked. You couldn't get any proper rest because you were firefighting all night and damping down and trying to sort your pump and equipment out during the day. We used to try and nap in the cab of the vehicle that we had travelled down in.
>
> Getting something to eat was a problem as well. The fire stations were reluctant to give us food as it meant they were depriving themselves of their rations. We used to scrounge what we could and rely on the goodwill of the public to give us some food. The voluntary services were very good to us and we could get something to eat and a cup of tea from them, but we were often too far away from them for that to be practical."

The Women's Voluntary Service and the Salvation Army frequently received praise for their "*Tea and a Wad*" (a cup of tea and a sandwich), which with a cigarette and a few words of encouragement meant so much to the weary firemen and civil defence workers.

The Luftwaffe turned their attention to Sheffield next, devastating it with a raid on 12th December 1940. German radio signals were intercepted and by 16:50 hours, the Air Commodore at RAF Fighter Command was able to confirm to all the RAF Fighter Groups and the Civil Defence Services that Sheffield was the target for that night. The code name "*Schmelzetiegel*", which meant Melting Crucible, was given to Sheffield by the Luftwaffe and the city was targeted because it was identified as a key location for the British steel industry. Luftflotte 2 and Luftflotte 3 sent 406 aircraft to attack Sheffield and 336 of the bomber crews claimed to have located and bombed the primary target. The attack began at 18:40 hours and continued until 03:00 the next morning, during which time 355 tonnes of high-explosive bombs were dropped as well as 16,452 incendiaries.

The most extensive damage was in the city centre, particularly amongst the commercial sector. Damage was also caused to dwellings and industry, which was mainly accounted for by fires started through incendiary bombs. Public utilities were very badly affected and the transport network in Sheffield, including trains, trams and other vehicles, had been brought to a standstill. By 06:15 hours, the fires in the city were under control but not yet extinguished and as the population began to emerge from their air raid shelters, they saw the effect on their city of just one night's bombing. It was predicted that the Luftwaffe would return and bomb the city again either that night or within a few days as this had become almost a standard tactic for them.

Nottinghamshire sent fire crews and rescue service personnel to Sheffield during the night to assist at the numerous incidents. The single biggest loss of life occurred when a high-explosive bomb fell at 23:45 hours on to the Marples Hotel at the corner of High Street and Fitzalan Square. The seven-storey building collapsed into the cellar, where 75 people were sheltering. The wreck of the building burned all night long and a rescue party sent to the premises was unable to carry out any rescues. At daylight, work began on reaching those trapped and by 14:00 hours the seven people who were the only survivors of this incident had been brought out safely. The search for the bodies and dismembered remains of the other 68 people took another twelve days. At the conclusion of this incident 64 bodies had been identified and the remains of those missing had been recovered.

The Luftwaffe returned to Sheffield on Sunday 15th December, attacking the city with 135 aircraft. The weather deteriorated after the aircraft had taken off on the raid and some were redirected to nearer targets. Visibility was poor and only 94 aircraft actually found Sheffield. The target area was again the north-eastern and central parts of the city and between 19:00 hours and 22:00 hours, 80 tonnes of high-explosive bombs and 21,600 incendiaries were dropped.

Industrial premises were more seriously damaged than they had been in the raid on 12th December and fires accounted for much of the damage. The fire service in Sheffield was once again bolstered by assistance from the North Midlands Region, including Nottinghamshire, and by 02:30 hours all the fires were being brought under control.

It is estimated that around 7,000 people had been rendered homeless by the two raids and 589 people had been killed, while a further 488 people had been seriously injured. The Luftwaffe was able to add another British city to the growing list of those devastated by raids.

Sheffield City Council sent an official thank you to Nottingham, praising the work of those who came to help them during the two raids. The lessons learned in Sheffield were taken seriously by Nottinghamshire and a report was compiled by senior ARP, Fire Service and Police officers who went to the city to observe at first hand the difficulties that arose from such attacks. The report made a number of recommendations and one that was of particular note was the necessity to provide relief crews for those who had been working all night during air raids. It commented on the exhaustion that came upon these people with daylight and the end of the raid. With the benefit of hindsight, it can be concluded that the ARP workers and firemen were kept going by adrenalin all night long, and as the level of danger receded they found that their minds and bodies slumped into the pit of exhaustion that awaits everyone who has worked under such terrific strain for hours. The net effect of this, however, was that these people could not overcome obstacles to progress that fresh crews were able to overcome. In some cases it was noted that rescue parties were demoralised by the

Above Top: Shops blazing in Sheffield city centre during the air raid on 15th December 1940 (Photograph courtesy of HMSO)

Above: Smoke swirls around burnt out buildings in Sheffield on the morning of 16th December 1940 (Photograph courtesy of HMSO)

slow progress at large incidents where masses of debris confronted them. Fresh crews arriving tackled the problem with energy and enthusiasm no longer available to their colleagues who had toiled all night.

Similarly, fire crews stupefied by tiredness and lack of food for energy poured water into the smouldering shells of burnt-out buildings, seemingly hypnotised and barely noticing obvious dangers around them from walls threatening to collapse. People living in north Nottinghamshire, particularly around Worksop, had seen the glow from the fires in Sheffield on the 12th and 15th December and could not help wondering when the Luftwaffe would turn on them. On 16th December, showers of incendiaries and flares fell around Nottingham at 20:40 hours, and the city seemed to be encircled. The people who witnessed this sight held their breath; was this it? Was it Nottingham's turn tonight?

Incendiaries fell in Thoresby Dale, Palmer Avenue, York Street, Whyburn Lane, Annesley Road and Wigwam Lane at Hucknall. A high-explosive bomb fell in the town causing a 9-foot diameter crater which was 6 feet deep. A large fire could be seen lighting up Hucknall from as far away as the city. This was in fact a house in Palmer Avenue, which the Auxiliary Fire Service extinguished. Incendiaries fell all around the railway station at Hucknall, but the raiders failed to locate the Rolls-Royce works and aerodrome. Incendiaries also fell at Annesley, Felley, Giltbrook, Kirkby and Bestwood Village. High-explosive bombs fell at Linby, Newstead and Woodhouse Eaves, where a gas main was set alight. A high-explosive bomb also fell at Papplewick and one at Kirkby, both of which failed to explode.

To the east of the county, incendiaries and high-explosive bombs were dropped over a wide area including Balderton, Southwell, East Bridgford, Thurgarton, Hazleford Ferry, Hoveringham and Calverton. The high-explosive bomb dropped in Balderton was close to the mental hospital in the town, but it failed to detonate, as did those that fell near to RAF Newton.

Fortunately the attack did not develop to any great degree due to poor visibility but nonetheless, the Luftwaffe was able to claim bomb damage and fires in Nottinghamshire, London, Birmingham and Manchester during the night.

The north-west was the next in line for special treatment by the Luftwaffe, as first Liverpool and then Manchester and Stockport were raided. Nottingham was required to send assistance again to help both fire crews and rescue teams. On Sunday 22nd December 1940, at around 17:15 hours, wireless transmissions by the Luftwaffe were intercepted and British Intelligence Officers at Bletchley Park interpreted the meaning of the messages. The target that night was going to be Manchester and they even knew some of the units that would take part in the raid.

The attack began on Manchester just after 19:30 and continued until 06:55 the next morning. Many of the 270 aircraft taking part in the raid were guided to the general area by the glow of fires still burning in Liverpool from the raids of the previous two nights. The aircraft dropped 272 tonnes of high-explosive bombs and 37,152 incendiaries on Manchester alone. The bombing was mainly on the west side of the city, the docks and industrial areas, with Trafford Park being particularly badly affected. The firemen had an insurmountable task to control over 400 fires that were consuming entire blocks of buildings. The water supply situation did not present the problems that it had elsewhere during heavy raids, but the sheer size of the job meant that most of the fires were still burning the next day.

Three Nottinghamshire firemen from Kirkby, Raymond Burrows, Joe Wright and Alan Day, were killed on 23rd December during the raid on Stockport and Manchester. Raymond was killed in Parket Street, Piccadilly and Joe was killed just a short distance away in Back George Street, Piccadilly. Alan Day was seriously injured and taken to the Roby Street Infirmary just a few hundred yards away. He died there of his injuries during the night.

Bert Dickson from Bulwell fire station had a lucky escape whilst fire fighting on the Metro-Vickers factory in Manchester. A one-kilogram (2.2lb) incendiary bomb hit him and glanced off his steel helmet. In other instances where someone was struck by an incendiary bomb, it often proved fatal or at the very least the person sustained serious injuries. Bert Dickson's helmet saved him, of that there is no doubt, but how he escaped a broken neck from the force of the impact was sheer chance.

Steel helmet of the same type worn by Auxiliary Fireman Bert Dickson when a 1kg incendiary bomb struck him on the head. The helmet was dented but saved Bert from death

The people of Nottingham had been kept in their shelters from 18:20 until 06:30 while the vast fleet of aircraft trooped across the night sky on its way to Manchester. They had heard the anti-aircraft guns pumping shells at the raiders, little knowing that their own firemen who were working alongside those in Manchester and Stockport were being slowly overwhelmed by the massive attack on the city.

During the night of 22nd/23rd December bombs had fallen in Nottinghamshire, in locations at Bingham, Gamston, Weston and Laxton. Twenty unexploded bombs had been reported to the Nottinghamshire ARP Control Centre to the south and east of the county. Ten high-explosive bombs plus two more that had failed to detonate were dropped around Kegworth, causing damage to the signal box of the London, Midland &

Scottish Railway Station (LMS) and around 40 yards of track. Incendiaries were dropped in Newthorpe, Kimberley and Giltbrook and at Alma Hill, Kirkby, by raiders making their way to Manchester who had become lost.

Bomb disposal squads dealt with three unexploded bombs in the county. One was at Lincoln Lodge Farm, one at Hickling in south Nottinghamshire and one at Cotham House Farm, which bordered on to RAF Balderton in Newark. Two more unexploded bombs were discovered in the county, one near Giltbrook chemical works and one at Kirkby in Ashfield. These bombs had been jettisoned by aircraft on their way to Manchester during the previous night. Manchester was attacked again that night and, as with the previous night's raid, the Air Commodore for RAF Fighter Command was able to warn that the target was Manchester. As darkness fell again, the Luftwaffe crews headed north-west; they could see the glow that was Manchester from as far away as London. No need to rely upon navigational beams now as they had done a few months before when raiding British cities. The bomber streams flowing from France and Belgium were in the ascendancy; it seemed that nothing could stop them now.

By 19:15 hours, the first of the 171 aircraft were over the target area and they bombed the city unopposed for five hours, during which time they unleashed 195 tonnes of high-explosive bombs and another 7,000 incendiaries. Some of the crews made use of the navigational beams for the final run on to the target, while others bombed visually and some just released their bomb load where they could see the glow of fires through the cloud that covered much of the target area. At 20:24 hours a message was received at

Above: Warehouses well alight in Manchester during the night of 23rd- 24th December 1940 (Photograph courtesy of HMSO)

Right: No escape! The wall of a burnt out building collapses in close proximity to fire crews who appear not to have reacted yet to the danger (Photograph courtesy of HMSO)

the Nottinghamshire County ARP control from the Regional ARP control requesting two rescue parties to report to Chapel en le Frith in Derbyshire at 07:00 the next morning. The rescue parties were to travel in convoy to Manchester with other rescue parties and ARP workers. They were to join their Fire Service colleagues who were already in the city rendering much-needed help. The rescue parties were sent from West Bridgford and one from the Western Division of Nottinghamshire.

During the raid, another of Nottinghamshire's firemen, Albert Cooke, was seriously injured and after being treated in hospital at Manchester, he was returned home. He subsequently died of his injuries. Christmas came and there was an unofficial truce. A communiqué received by the British Government via the German Embassy in Washington stated that there would be no air attacks on Britain provided that the RAF refrained from attacking Germany. The wives of firemen and rescue men often found themselves without their husbands for days at a time, not knowing where they had gone or for how long. Although their husbands were not serving with the armed forces, they nonetheless knew the men were in the front line of this particular battle. Each time their husbands reported for duty, they did not know if they would see them at the end of the shift or if they would be at the other end of the country.

Anne Cawthorn's husband, Ted, was a fireman at Bulwell and he went to Birmingham, Liverpool, Manchester and Stockport as well as firefighting in Nottingham. Anne recalled the comments she used to get from people at that time.

> "One of our neighbours always used to say, 'It's all right for you, your husband is at home.' Well, that used to make me mad because I hardly used to see him because of the long hours they had to work and he was also often away in another city firefighting. I had no idea where he was. I used to hear on the wireless about a big raid somewhere and wonder if Ted was there and if he was all right.
>
> When he did come home he was exhausted. He would be all scorched, with his eyebrows and eyelashes gone and cuts all over his hands and his feet swollen and blistered . . ."

Other firemen's wives recounted how their husbands came home with dirt engrained in their skin so that they looked as black as their fire tunics. It would take days of washing and scrubbing to get their skin clean again. George Woods was stationed at Mansfield Woodhouse and he recalls one particular occasion when they were mobilised to another city.

> "It was Sunday morning and we were preparing our dinner when we received a message to rendezvous at Chesterfield and that we were to set off at once. We did what we had been ordered to do; we didn't take any rations or anything, but I grabbed the Primus stove just in case we got chance to have a brew-up.
>
> We arrived at Chesterfield and we were hanging about with a lot of other crews for about four hours. Eventually they took us into a Sunday School and gave us all a mug of soup. It was getting dark by this time and we were told we were being sent to Manchester. [It was common practice to move large numbers of vehicles, such as fire columns, by night to avoid attacks by enemy aircraft.]
>
> We set off in column and eventually arrived in Manchester. The next thing, they said we were to go on to Liverpool. We drove all through the night, a terrible journey, but there was one incident that stands out.
>
> Our pump was one of the lead vehicles in the column and we were making slow progress. You couldn't drive too fast because you couldn't see the road in the blackout. Suddenly, fire appliances started racing past us. We thought, 'What's up? It must be something really urgent.' Some more shot past and then we realised that an enemy aircraft was dropping incendiaries and machine-gunning the vehicles at the back. Understandably they put their foot down and rushed to the front!
>
> We got to Liverpool on the Monday morning and we were very hungry. Apart from a mug of soup, we had not eaten for 24 hours. We were sent down to the docks, where we had to hang

around again, and then we were told that the Royal Navy were going to provide us with a hot breakfast on board one of the ships. We were starving for something to eat and so we all filed on board to get a meal. We were really grateful to the navy for that.

Once we were on board, someone noticed that the navy were loading our pumps on board the ship and lashing them down on deck. We asked what was happening and they just said that we had to go somewhere else but they wouldn't say where.

We embarked on the ship and once we were under way we were told we were going to Northern Ireland. That was a bit of a blow, I can tell you, but we were so tired that no one complained. Once in Northern Ireland, we were allowed to write a letter home to our wives and families, but we were not allowed to say where we were. We were told that if we did say where we were, the letter would be destroyed. What choice did we have? The letter was the only way of letting our families know we were all right, so we all obeyed and just said we had been sent away and would keep in touch by letter. [The fire brigade told the men's families that they had been "posted away", but refused to disclose where.]

Our billet in Northern Ireland was an old schoolroom and the conditions there were dreadful. We were given a mattress cover and some straw to stuff it with; this was to be our bed along with an issue of two blankets each. For food we were given a 7lb tin of Machonachy's stew between nine of us. That was all; no bread or anything else. We were there for three months protecting the docks and we became so rundown and malnourished that we got boils and skin sores. The day we left Mansfield Woodhouse we had just got the uniform that we stood up in. We did not receive any further issue of uniform for three months.

There were some bad air raids whilst we were there and I remember being at Harland and Wolff's where they were building cruisers for the Royal Navy. About one thousand tons of coke had caught fire from incendiary bombs and we were pumping water on to that. You can imagine the target that made from the air.

They used to drop magnetic mines to try and blow the shipping up and on one occasion they blew one of our firemen up. Bill Bough was in a small boat trying to keep our suction hose in the water when another boat set off a magnetic mine. A huge column of water shot up in the air and it lifted Bill's boat up with it. He smashed his ribs in on the side of the boat when it fell back into the water."

The year was drawing to a close and the British could only hope that next year things would improve. Surely this could not go on indefinitely? There had been 71 air raid alerts in Nottingham during 1940, the majority of them in the second half of the year. The strain of it all showed in the faces of the people. Official sources could issue whatever propaganda they liked, but it did not alter the fact that people were tired out and the population of cities like Coventry, Birmingham, Liverpool, Manchester and London were at the end of their tethers.

Nottingham's firemen, along with those from other parts of the country, were learning about blitz firefighting the hard way. The lessons learned, and the horrors endured by the firemen and rescue squads, would stiffen their resolve and stand them in good stead when their own cities became the target. For the time being all they could do was to deal with the effects of the air raids as night after night bombers brought destruction and death in the darkness.

9. Death in the Darkness

The New Year was ushered in by a cold night with a hard frost and the people of Nottinghamshire were spared from spending New Year's Eve in their shelters. The respite was short-lived, however, as just after 20:00 hours on New Year's Day, the air raid alert sounded and the now familiar sound of enemy aircraft could be heard overhead. It was a bitterly cold night again, but most people dutifully went to their shelters. Some decided to take their chances with the bombs rather than risk ill health through sleeping in a damp, cold Anderson Shelter.

The raiders continued on past Nottingham with further waves passing overhead intermittently; they were on their way to Cardiff. The all clear sounded for the Nottingham people in the early hours of the morning with no serious incidents happening in the county during the long hours of darkness. On 2nd January the alert sounded again at 21:50 hours and on 3rd January people's slumbers were disturbed by an alert at 00:15 hours.

Nottingham's neighbours at Grantham were bombed on 9th January and for a small town the casualties were heavy. The total casualty figure was 52 and of these 21 were fatalities. At 11:54 on the morning of 10th January, the North Midland Regional Control requested four rescue squads from Nottinghamshire to proceed to Grantham immediately. The Nottinghamshire ARP Control mobilised rescue parties from West Bridgford, Carlton, Mansfield and Sutton in Ashfield.

Another of Nottingham's neighbours, Derby, received attention from the Luftwaffe on 15th January. Aircraft were detected off the Dutch coast just before 18:30 hours and they made their way towards Flamborough Head on the east coast. The aircraft then set a course for the Midlands which brought them over Derby by 20:00 hours. Aircraft passed over the city in waves until 22:30, with further waves following at 23:20 and also between 02:00 and 04:00. A total of 49 aircraft dropped 59 tonnes of high-explosive bombs and 1,476 incendiaries.

The London, Midland & Scottish railway station was badly damaged by two high-explosive bombs and the Bliss factory, which was manufacturing munitions, was also damaged. Rolls-Royce escaped unscathed, probably due to low cloud and poor visibility making visual bombing difficult. Two high-explosive bombs fell in Offerton Avenue and caused fatalities there, while Derby Lane was straddled by three more high-explosive bombs. Houses in Rosehill Street, Litchurch Street and Canal Street were all damaged. Twenty people were killed and 48 injured during the raid.

The aircraft that failed to locate Derby dropped their bombs in Nottinghamshire. The raiders announced their arrival south of the city by dropping two high-explosive bombs at Moor Ends Farm at Ruddington. The craters were 75 feet in diameter and 10 feet deep. A high-explosive bomb was dropped near Fairham Brook between Keyworth and Widmerpool, two more at Willoughby Road, Whysall and another at Bradmore at around 22:00 hours, which failed to explode.

At 22:15 hours several high-explosive bombs fell at Carlton, causing damage to forty houses. One of the bombs fell in the garden at number 1 Hill View Road, badly damaging the house. Another bomb made a crater six feet in diameter in Hill View Road and six people had to be treated for shock. One fell at the corner of Florence Road and one at Pilkington Road, while eight others fell around Simkin Avenue and the nearby recreation ground. This was a serious incident, but it was in Sneinton that tragedy struck.

Three high-explosive bombs fell at about 22:30 hours, the first of which was a direct hit on Hutton Street, and another of particularly heavy calibre fell between Trent Lane and Kingsley Road. The third bomb fortunately failed to detonate. Mrs Thorpe was a resident in the area at the time and she described the event.

"When I first heard the bomb I made preparations to go to the shelter and covered up the baby in the crib. Then I switched out the light and I was flung against the door. When I recovered, slates and debris were showering down and my first thought was for the baby. I went to the crib and found it covered with glass. It was dark and I could not see if the baby was all right. I lifted him out and went to the shelter, expecting another bomb any minute."

At 31 Hutton Street, George Stafford was standing at the front door of his home while his wife Ada and nineteen-year-old daughter Joyce were sheltering under the stairs. When the aerial mine fell, the house disintegrated around them, killing Ada and George and burying Joyce under a mass of wreckage.

Bernard Chamberlain was a member of the scout messenger service at the time of the Hutton Street bombing and it so happened that on that particular night they were having a training meeting at St Christopher's Church Hall on Colwick Road. Bernard saw that the bombs had fallen on Hutton Street and Trent Lane and so he ran up Trent Road to report to the ARP post to which he was attached as a messenger. He quickly told them what had happened and gave the exact location. The air raid wardens at the post rang through to the Leenside Division Headquarters at Eastcroft and put Bernard on the line to pass on the information.

Bernard was instructed to go back to Hutton Street to await the arrival of the incident officer and to make himself available to relay any messages from the incident. The rescue squads were sent for along with ambulances, the fire brigade and the police.

The interim report sent by the Incident Officer to the Nottingham ARP Control stated:

". . . three high-explosive bombs have destroyed 16 houses and damaged 246 others. Two communal air raid shelters destroyed. A number of casualties, several people still trapped."

The bombs had rendered 180 people temporarily homeless, but worst of all, there was an unknown number of people missing under the wreckage of the houses.

Elsewhere in the county, the raiders dropped ten more high-explosive bombs at 23:30 hours. Three were dropped in East Bridgford near the Fosse Way and RAF Newton had two high-explosive bombs fall within its perimeter. Seven bombs fell at Car Colston, where phone lines were brought down, two barns were demolished and a bungalow was damaged by shrapnel and blast. At 03:15 hours the raiders dropped incendiaries at Weston, near the Great North Road, and four high-explosive bombs at Marnham, damaging phone lines. In Sneinton, the rescue operation was fully under way. Malcolm and Douglas Wood, who lived at 25 Trent Lane, had managed to climb out of the wreckage of their home on to the roof and they were brought down to safety by ladder. Once all those who could be rescued fairly quickly had been

Above: The replacements for the terraced houses destroyed in Trent Lane
Right: Close up of where the demolished houses ended in Trent Lane

taken to first aid posts, all the resources at the scene were directed towards locating and releasing those still trapped in the rubble.

It was clear that the extrication of all the casualties would be a long job, but rescuers managed to locate the three children of Leslie and Mabel Eggleston in what had been 37 Hutton Street. The children had been buried under the debris in the front room, where they had been put to bed for greater safety during the air raid alert; their parents, who had been in the kitchen, had escaped the blast unscathed. Bernard Chamberlain recalled the scene when they were found.

"I had not been there very long when Doctor O'Gorman arrived. I had never done artificial respiration before, but when they brought three kiddies out of a house who looked more or less dead, the doctor got me started on artificial respiration on them. He was doing artificial respiration himself and he handed me a little mirror so that I could keep checking for any signs of breathing [the type of artificial respiration applied was the Holger Nielsen method]. The children died; we didn't bring them round. They didn't appear to be marked; they had probably been killed by the blast."

Houses demolished by a aerial mine in Hutton Street on 15th January 1941 (Photograph courtesy of *Nottingham Evening Post*)

Searching the rubble for survivors at Hutton Street (Photograph courtesy of *Nottingham Evening Post*)

Hutton Street in 2009 showing its close proximity to the railway line; the likely target for the aerial mine

Gary Eggleston was the eldest child at three years, his brother was seventeen months old and his sister was just ten weeks. When the sirens had sounded, their parents had got them out of bed and brought them downstairs. Patricia was placed into her pram and the two boys put into a makeshift bed in an alcove in the front room, which Mabel and Leslie considered to be the safest part of the house. A rescue party eventually located Joyce Stafford in the rubble of what had been her home and she was dug out alive, but seriously injured. When she regained consciousness, she was in hospital, encased in plaster from her chest to her ankle. Her thigh bone was shattered and she had sustained internal injuries. She was to spend the next twelve months encased in plaster and was in a wheelchair for quite some time afterwards. At one stage, doctors thought that she would lose her sight due to the debris that had gone into her eyes.

In 1973 Joyce spoke of her ordeal to a *Nottingham Guardian Journal* reporter and mercifully, she could remember nothing about what happened after she went under the stairs to shelter with her mother.

"They told me afterwards that they found my father's body at the back of a chimney pot on the other side of the street. My mother, they told me, had an injury on her head."

The Staffords' other daughter, Ivy, and son-in-law George, escaped the fate of the rest of the family because they had gone home fifteen minutes earlier after visiting. Ivy recalled what happened.

"We'd just got home about 10.30 p.m. when the bomb fell nearby, shattering all the light bulbs and leaving us in the dark. We went down into the cellar which had been reinforced for use as an air raid shelter and linked to the cellars of the adjoining houses. We stayed there until the all clear went."

Volunteer Commander Hobson of the City Division of the ARP service was in charge of the incident for seven hours and even when relieved of that responsibility he remained on duty for sixteen hours. Rescue Team Leader Burton of the Leenside Division was in charge of the full-time rescue team that "did sterling work at the incident."

Burton worked under a mass of debris for two hours at great personal risk. He located a woman who was trapped and after a further hour managed to effect her release. He then heard sounds coming from inside the wreckage, which could only mean one thing: people were still alive, trapped amidst the tangle of timber, bricks and concrete. He tunnelled for a further two hours with the assistance of his team and was finally able to release a man from the wreckage. The final casualty figure for this incident was 15 killed and 11 injured, which included John (26) and Rebecca (22) Hopewell and their 17-month-old son, Terence, who died at number 33 Hutton Street. Their neighbour Albert Voce (40) died at number 35 and Brian Marshall died in number 29, along with Peter Marshall, another baby of 18 months. Gladys Green was extricated from the rubble of 27 Hutton Street but was dead when rescuers freed her. Samuel Pearson (67) was found in the rubble of 27 Trent Lane, but he was also dead. Evelyn Hughes, who lived at 16 Pelham Crescent in Beeston, was unlucky enough to be in the wrong place at the wrong time as she was killed at number 23 Trent Lane and Arthur Brewer (34), who lived at 9 Taylor Close in Sneinton, had the same bad luck and died at number 21.

The Lord Mayor, Alderman Halls, visited the scene to see for himself the rescue operation. As the work went on and casualties were brought out periodically, it was inevitable that for some of the ARP personnel there were periods of inactivity. Bernard Chamberlain tried to get involved with the removal of debris but the incident officer insisted that he should remain with him so that he knew where he was if he needed to send a message from the incident.

At 05:00 hours Bernard Chamberlain was finally released from the incident and he went to the Salvation Army canteen van parked outside St Christopher's Church. After a cup of tea, he made his way home to get himself cleaned up before setting off for his day's work building air raid shelters. Ivy Bettison (née Stafford) described the scene at Hutton Street on the morning of 16th January.

"It was getting daylight when we went to Hutton Street to see if everything was all right, but they wouldn't let us down the street. Where the houses had been, there was just a crater. I didn't know anything [about her family] until the afternoon. Later in the day they let us go down to see if there was anything we could salvage but there was nothing left."

The newspapers at the time had to compile their reports under the restrictions that were placed upon information that could be released to the public. There was no mention of the Nottingham casualties, but the raid on Derby was described thus:

"A number of high-explosive bombs were dropped in various parts of an East Midlands town last night and although considerable damage was done to residential property and a large number of families rendered homeless, the casualties are estimated at twenty, whilst a number of others were injured."

It is interesting to note that, in the newspaper speak of the day, the word "casualties" became a euphemism for dead. It seems that describing them as fatalities was unacceptable at that stage of the war. The reality of this newspaper report was typified in Sneinton, where people were still being dug out of the wreckage of the houses and families were grief-stricken at the loss of loved ones, while tears rolled down the cheeks of those who had survived, but their homes and precious possessions had been destroyed. On 16th January, the parliamentary secretary to the Minister of Home Security inspected the air raid damage and also the air raid shelters in the city.

Other matters relating to air raid precautions were introduced or amended in order to improve the city's defences. The ARP Controller stated that all swimming baths should be kept full of water for firefighting purposes, but if necessary, they should be drained at the request of the Director of Civilian Deaths as all the city's swimming baths were earmarked for use as temporary mortuaries. The purchase of 400 adult and 100 child size fibre board coffins had been a depressing enough matter, but the decision to purchase 500 more after the Hutton Street bombing showed that the authorities considered large numbers of deaths to be a reality.

A raid at 16:00 hours on the afternoon of 30th January by a Junkers Ju88 took people in the Newark area by surprise. The Newark Advertiser reported the incident under the following headline:

"Daylight Raid on North Midlands Town Two Fatal Casualties When Plane Swooped From Cloud

After 16 months at war, a North Midlands town suffered its first direct casualties through enemy action on Thursday afternoon when a single Nazi raider swooped through low-lying cloud and dropped several high-explosive bombs. The exact number is believed to have been 14, two of them considerably heavier calibre than the others. As a result Anthony Thompson, a 16-year-old boy was killed. Working close at hand at the time was Mr J.N. Saxby. Flying shrapnel inflicted on him wounds from which he later died in hospital."

According to the ARP controller's record of the incident, twelve bombs were dropped, ten of which landed in fields to the west of the River Devon and caused little damage. Two of the bombs caused damage to factories, shops and houses in the vicinity and injured two of the factory workers. The two men killed in the raid were Anthony Thompson of 2 Church Walk, who died of his injuries before reaching hospital, and 17-year-old Joseph Saxby, who lived at Farndon Ferry, and who died at Newark Hospital following the raid. Joseph's death was a particularly cruel blow for his parents as they had lost another of their sons, 20-year-old William, due to enemy action in May 1940. He was serving in the Royal Engineers and had been killed by a bomb while his unit were training. The couple were also to lose their eldest son, 22-year-old Charles, on 31st October 1941 while he was serving in Singapore with the Royal Leicestershire Regiment.

On Tuesday 4th February, forty aircraft attacked Derby in an attempt to damage the Rolls-Royce factory. The attack commenced at 19:45 hours and lasted just over two hours. The bombing was widely dispersed but no damage was inflicted on Rolls-Royce. At 19:49 hours, two high-explosive bombs fell into the gardens of 175 Wollaton Road and 28 Dennison Street in Beeston, dropped by aircraft that had become lost on the Derby raid. Neither bomb exploded, but they led to 40 people being evacuated to safety while roads around the area were closed. At 20:10 hours another lost aircraft scattered its load of incendiaries across Hollinwell golf course, to the west of the London & North Eastern Railway station at Bentinck, and also around Frander Ground Farm. In the south of the county, eight high-explosive bombs fell at the corner of Park Lane and the Rempstone Turnpike Road at Sutton Bonnington.

Just before midnight, an aircraft was picked up by a searchlight over Nottingham. It dived quickly, escaping the beam, and it then released a stick of three high-explosive bombs. A resident in Mapperley Park heard the bomber swooping down but thought that it sounded like a British fighter aircraft. This was wishful thinking, and it was generally the case that civilians could not distinguish between friendly and enemy aircraft by the sound of their engines.

"When the German plane came over, I thought it was a Spitfire. The noise I took for a Spitfire must have been the bomb whistling down, for as soon as the whistling stopped there was an explosion."

One of the high-explosive bombs fell in the garden of Victor and Ellen Thomas, who lived at 57 Mapperley Hall Drive with their 16-year-old son, Keith. They were sitting at the rear of their house at the time. *"We heard it coming and the explosion was very heavy."* Victor made his way through the debris and into the hallway. He kicked open his front door and led his wife and son out of the house to safety. No one was injured by this raid, but several properties, including nearby houses, St Jude's Church and the vicarage

Left: Bomb damage to 57 Mapperley Hall Drive. 4th February 1941 (Photograph courtesy of Zaf Iqbal)

Above left: 57 Mapperley Hall Drive in 2009. Middle: Side view of the damage to Mapperley Hall Drive (Photograph courtesy of Zaf Iqbal). Right: Comparative view in 2009

Left: Bomb damage to 92 Ribblesdale Road 14th March 1941 (Photograph courtesy of *Nottingham Evening Post*)

Below Left: 92 Ribblesdale Road where Hilda Allcock was killed (Photograph courtesy of *Nottingham Evening Post*) Right: 92 Ribblesdale Road in 2009

were all damaged. There was a huge crater in the garden of the Thomas family and the entire house had been moved about one and a half inches on its foundations, causing serious cracks in the structure. Masses of earth had been thrown into Mapperley Hall Drive. The next day, houses with shattered windows were displaying Union Jack flags in a show of defiance. When interviewed by a local journalist, Keith Thomas observed drily, "*So much for the sand I put into the loft to catch incendiary bombs.*"

On 6th February 1941, Hitler issued War Directive number 23, which set out the revised aims for operations against the British war economy. It acknowledged that it would not now be practical to invade Britain, but it stressed that every effort must be made to keep up the belief that this would occur later in the year. The night raids on the UK were to be intensified, along with minelaying off the British coast, to mask the declining strength in the west as a prelude to a spring invasion in the east. Luftwaffe crews had to fly double or triple sorties in one night to achieve this.

The week beginning Sunday 9th March had shown a definite increase in the number of air raid alerts in Nottingham. The bright moonlit nights during that week encouraged the bombers as it made navigating easier and also helped with visual bomb aiming. Anti-aircraft fire often accompanied these alerts, but no more bombs were dropped within the city boundary until Friday 14th March. Local opinion states that the target for this particular attack was the railway line and bridge in Daybrook Square. If this was the case, the aircraft missed the target completely and hit a residential area. Just before midnight, twelve bombs fell in a line across Bedale Road and Valley Road.

The first of the twelve bombs damaged a house in Bedale Road, one damaged a house in Ridsdale Road and the next hit number 92 Ribblesdale Road, partially destroying it and killing Hilda Allcock who lived there. Her husband, Joseph, had just gone out on fire-watch duties a few minutes earlier when the sirens had sounded, and because of this he was unhurt by the explosion. Two other fire-watchers and the street air raid warden threw themselves to the ground when they heard the bombs falling and they also managed to escape injury. A neighbour who was outside in his garden was lucky to escape unhurt as another bomb in the stick fell only twenty feet away from him. Mrs Riley and her daughter Joan, aged fourteen, were injured by this bomb, which blew the back of their house away. They were asleep, sheltering under a table in the downstairs front room at the time.

For Anne Cawthorn it was also a frightening time, with her husband on duty with the fire brigade at the nearby Cedars Hospital Fire Post. She had gone out to the Anderson shelter in the garden at Edward's Lane as soon as the sirens had sounded. She heard the bombs falling and got down on the ground inside the tiny shelter, covering her baby son with her own body. Her husband, Ted Cawthorn, was hurtling along Valley Road on a motorbike when the first bomb fell. He was under instructions to pick up the officer in charge of the fire post who was on his night off. Luckily for Ted, the stick of bombs leapfrogged the main road that he was travelling on.

Jill Dunkerley was married to a police sergeant and in her house on Danethorpe Vale she heard the bombs whistling down. She held her baby daughter tightly to her, bracing herself for the explosion. She heard the blast and was relieved that they had escaped harm. The discovery of a steel helmet on the edge of a crater in Ribblesdale Road caused a great deal of concern for the safety of an ARP warden, but it turned out that he had dropped it while running to his house to check that his wife was all right.

A water main had burst in Ribblesdale Road, which caused a problem for the fire crews from the Cedars and Hyson Green fire stations who arrived to deal with the numerous small fires. Scores of people had to be evacuated as there were two unexploded bombs near to Ribblesdale Road. One of the UXBs had gone through the footbridge over the brook and had buried itself into the ground. A fire crew from Hyson Green dammed the brook and pumped the bomb crater out so that a Royal Engineers bomb disposal squad could make the bomb safe.

Above Left: Bomb damage in Ennerdale Road 14th March 1941 (Photograph courtesy of *Nottingham Evening Post*)
Right: Comparative view of Ennerdale Road in 2009

10. Hit and Run Raids

Ransome & Marles

Photograph showing the close proximity of the railway and factory. This made it an easy target to find

Lt. Rudolph, pilot of the Heinkel HE111 that attacked Ransome & Marles factory on 7th March 1941

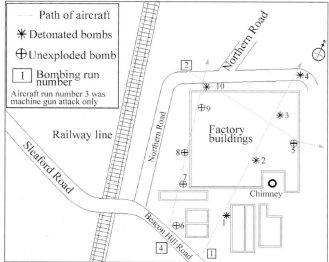

Diagram showing the direction of the bombing runs made on the factory

Low-level daylight raids were carried out by the Luftwaffe on single targets vital to the country's war effort. The Luftwaffe called them "*Pirate Attacks*" but in Britain they were called *"Hit and Run Raids"*.

The Ransome and Marles factory in Newark was selected as the target for one such raid on 7th March 1941. Newark had many factories producing war materials, such as Blagg and Johnson, which made parts for Bailey Bridges used by the British Army, Farrers, who were making tank turrets, and Worthington Simpson, who were assembling howitzers. The Ransome and Marles factory was selected because it manufactured ball bearings, which were essential to aircraft, tanks, lorries, searchlights and heavy guns.

Lieutenant Rudolph was at the controls of a Heinkel He111 as it approached Newark from the south. He had no trouble in locating the factory as he had followed the railway line all the way from Grantham. The weather was drizzly with low cloud and the aircraft swooped over the factory at an altitude of 1,000 feet. The raider was engaged by anti-aircraft fire from the factory as it started its first bombing run at 13:34 hours. The air raid sirens did not give their warning until 13:35 hours and the workers were still making their way to the air raid shelters when four high-explosive bombs were dropped on to the works. Two of the bombs landed on the factory, the third one fell on to the works underground air raid shelter next to Stanley Street, and the last one of the stick hit the road between the railway line and the factory.

Second Row—Messrs. Burrows, Facer, Hill
Front Row—Messrs. Savidge, Wood, Cook, Lathlane

Above: A fire crew at work after the factory had been bombed (Photograph courtesy of the Newark Advertiser)

Above: The Ransome & Marles Factory roof spotters. Their job was to sound the alarm to warn the workers inside the factory of an imminent attack (Photograph courtesy of NSK Europe Ltd.)

Right: Ransome & Marles ARP workers carrying out salvage inside the damaged factory (Photograph courtesy of the Newark Advertiser)

Three minutes later, the raider was making its second bombing run. It strafed the factory with machine-gun fire and dropped another high-explosive bomb, which failed to detonate. At 13:41 hours, the raider made its third run and machine-gunned the factory again before making off into the low cloud.

The damage to the works was serious and there were many casualties. A direct hit on the tool shop had destroyed it, along with the blacksmith's shop and a store opposite. The main machine shop had also suffered a direct hit and two internal air raid shelters there had collapsed. The other works shelter at the side of Stanley Street was fifteen feet underground. The third bomb had penetrated this and then detonated, completely destroying it. The fourth bomb, which had fallen in the roadway, had burst the water main and the sewer. The blast from this bomb overturned nearby railway trucks and damaged part of the factory.

Jack Griffin was a nineteen-year-old lad at the time and his recollection of the bombing was very clear.

"I went and fetched my tin helmet and gas mask and went to the shelter in the passageway. There was a large reinforced finishing table in the tool room and some took cover under that. A large 500lb bomb went through, taking the roof off. About 15 people were killed under that table.

The blast was imprinted in my eardrums. Then all I could hear was the rattle of machine guns as the aircraft strafed the workers."

Another worker in the factory described the scene inside the tool room.

"I was still at my milling machine when the air stood still and I felt like I had been moved by an unseen hand. My eardrums were buzzing and my mind was befuddled. I beheld the non-existence of the tool room as I had known it and collected myself in torn clothing but thankfully very much alive. Within minutes machine-gun fire was hitting what was left of the tool room and then a deadly silence took over."

As the raider passed over Newark, many people saw the low-flying aircraft and Greta Harrison, who was six years old at the time, recalled seeing the bomber from the living room window of her home.

"I vividly remember seeing the aeroplane coming over and seeing the pilot in the cockpit looking down at us. My father pushed me away from the window as they opened fire with machine guns, shattering our house windows."

Other witnesses described the aircraft as being so low that the crew could clearly be seen inside the cockpit. Allen Dickenson saw the bomber but did not realise it was German at first, until he saw the crosses on the wings. He stopped his bicycle and was rooted to the spot. As he looked up he saw the pilot looking down, waving a gloved hand at him. Ransome and Marles had their own ARP services set up in a similar way to those of the local authority and it was not long before they began to assess the situation and started rendering help. A confidential

RESCUE PARTIES

Third Row—Messrs. Robinson, Town, Sargison, Ducker
Second Row—Messrs. Sharpe, Neal, Jackson, Gravell, Beckett, Robinson, Hunt, Smith
Front Row—Messrs. Henton, Holland, Beckett, Johnson, Barlow, Cross, Tye

Ransome & Marles rescue parties (Photograph courtesy of NSK Europe Ltd.)

FIRST-AID

Fourth Row—Messrs. Postle, Bland, Bevis, Suter, Hopkinson, Corbitt, Capes, Newstead, Whitehead, Wilson
Third Row—Messrs. Walster, Derbyshire, Pask (F.), Pask (E.), Knyvett, Thompson, Cavey, Allen, Smith, Chambers, Lale
Second Row—Messrs. Hobson, Hunt, Grosse, Booth, Plummer, Lawrence, Miss R. Grant, Mrs. Beale, Miss E. Drewery, Messrs. Smith, Norledge, Parker, Walker, Capes
Front Row—Mr. Freshney, Mrs. Peck, Mr. Doncaster, Miss P. Jarman, Messrs. Bloodworth, Lockie, Mallory, Burden, Riley, Miss N. Watson, Mr. Johnson, Miss E. Hurt, Mr. Emmerson

Ransome & Marles First Aiders (Photograph courtesy of NSK Europe Ltd.)

FIRE BRIGADE

Fourth Row—Messrs. Sharpe, Davies, Henton, Rutter, Bentley, Harris, Garton, Sheppard, Seddon, Evans, Brittle
Third Row—Messrs. Doughty, Dethick, Hind, Rawson, Fletcher, Thorpe, Shaw, Wheatley, Wheeldon, Baggaley, Brader, Fletcher
Second Row—Messrs. Morris, Dalton, Edgar, Wheeldon, Roberts, Lawson, Fane, Grocock, Hawley, Bevell, Smith, Kettleborough, Hallam, Taylor
Front Row—Mr. Willis, Miss P. Tompkins, Mr. Salmon, Miss E. Hayes, Messrs. Lee, Thickett, Rogers, Hawley, Miss K. Knowles, Mr. Gilbert, Miss P. Knowles, Mr. Ellis, Miss L. Stephenson

Ransome & Marles Fire Brigade (Photograph courtesy of NSK Europe Ltd.)

report submitted by the works ARP subcontroller following the raid made it clear that Newark Borough Council ARP services were not expected to turn out to incidents unless a message was received at their control asking for assistance. It emphasised that the works ARP, fire service and medical service were intended to *"function as a complete unit"*.

The raid had knocked out the telephone system of the works, but despite adjacent premises still having their telephone system intact, the only message sent from the works was fifteen minutes after the raid. A motorcyclist pulled up outside the police station and shouted to a constable, *"Ransome's factory has been heavily bombed; send all the help you can!"*

The confidential report from the works subcontroller stated that an assistance message should include *"some indication as to the damage and number of casualties sustained"*. Clearly the message did not contain this information and it was just one of the elements of the works ARP scheme that did not function as planned.

At 13:50 hours, the Newark ARP control received a message from the London & North Eastern Railway Station, stating that they had an injured person. One minute later an ambulance and a first aid party was dispatched to the station. At almost the same instant, they were asked to send an ambulance and a first aid party to the factory, which they promptly did. At 13:56 hours, the sirens sounded out their steady note, signalling "All clear".

Two Newark rescue parties arrived at the factory at 14:05, but it was another 22 minutes before the works ARP subcontroller sent a proper message for assistance. Another ambulance was dispatched to the factory and three minutes later a further message got through to the ARP control, which requested another ambulance and first aid party. The situation at the factory was very confused at this stage as the works ARP subcontroller had not really taken effective charge of the situation. The company commander of the Newark Home Guard offered the assistance of his men and within five minutes they had closed the roads to the factory. The Officer Commanding, Royal Army Service Corps, arrived at the incident and offered assistance. He was asked to help with the removal of casualties, whereupon he produced two army ambulances, four cars and eight army lorries.

The road leading to the works entrance was 170 yards long and only 18 feet wide. Some of this width was blocked by debris and 500 men from the works were engaged in clearing this. The congestion and confusion was immense, with people trying to help vehicles to get through and another 1,500 people trying to make their way out of the works. Ransome and Marles' ARP Officer was wandering about from place to place and no one ever really knew where he was to be found. He was to come in for considerable criticism for this in subsequent reports into the incident. It was small wonder that, without adequate guidance or leadership, well-meaning soldiers began loading critically injured people into army lorries and driving them to hospital, while many of the ambulances transported the dead. Out of 82 people taken to hospital, only 14 arrived by ambulance. These statistics regarding the evacuation of casualties, provided through a Newark ARP report, are in direct contrast to what the works sub controller stated in his report:

"The majority of the dead were removed to the mortuary in army lorries, although several were taken in the police ambulance and in one or two cases in ARP ambulances."

No one gave any guidance as to where the casualties should be taken and consequently 76 were taken to Newark General Hospital, swamping the facilities available there, while only six were taken to the County Emergency Hospital. Both hospitals were an equal distance from the incident at Ransome and Marles.

At 14:24 hours the alert sounded again and even before the wail of the sirens had faded away a single aircraft was seen approaching at low level from the south. As before, anti-aircraft guns fired at the raider but could not deter it from making a bombing run on the factory. Five 250kg high-explosive bombs were dropped by this aircraft, but fortunately only one of these detonated. Many casualties were caused among the civil defence personnel and people from the factory who were making their way home when this bomb exploded. More damage was caused to the roadway and the "Old Stable" end of the factory.

Even after this second attack there was a delay in getting information to the Newark ARP Control centre. It was 18 minutes before a message was received which asked for *"further assistance"*. Two more ambulances were sent and then finally, at 14:58 hours, a message was sent to the Regional District Controller asking for another ambulance and first aid party to be sent to the factory. Both were dispatched from Collingham to the incident.

Above left: Some of the victims of the Ransome & Marles bombing. The graves are next to the military plot in Newark Cemetery

Above right: Memorial Plaque to the victims of the bombing inside the courtyard of the factory

Right: The grave of Gladys Cummings killed in Newark 7th March 1941 by the same aircraft that bombed Ransome & Marles

Rescue parties from other parts of the county began to arrive, the first being from West Bridgford, who arrived at 16:15 hours. Arnold and Sutton in Ashfield arrived five minutes later and then rescue parties from Carlton and Mansfield arrived at 16:30 hours. Mansfield Woodhouse was the final team to arrive at 17:15 hours. The rescue parties relieved their colleagues from Newark and continued with the grim task of extricating the casualties. It was not for want of effort on their part that no one was brought out alive after 16:30 hours. After all, it was by then over three hours since the incident had occurred.

Various officials began arriving at the site and inspected the work that was going on. Major Barefoot was accompanied by the Military Liaison Officer and Mr Banwell, the representative of the Senior Regional Controller. Banwell and the Military Liaison Officer were all for bringing in the military to take over the situation, but the leader of the rescue parties protested. In fact he went so far as to say that, if the military were brought in, he would withdraw the ARP rescue parties. At first glance, this seems very arrogant, but a closer look at the situation makes it look reasonable.

Over three hours had elapsed since the first raid and it was fair to say that the operation since then had the hallmark of inexperience. Any military help brought in would be equally inexperienced. For example, the ambulance and first aid party from Collingham had arrived, only to be sent away by soldiers as "*there were no more casualties to be dealt with*". At 16:10 hours, a message was received from the first aid post at Barnby Road School to the effect that first aiders there had so many casualties to deal with that the teachers were having to help.

The rescue parties' leader pointed out that to bring further large numbers of people on to the site would only further congest the works, to such a degree that it would become intolerable. Some of the county rescue parties at the scene were by now very experienced, having worked in the aftermath of heavy air raids on other cities. As recently as January some of them had been at Grantham extricating casualties there. As an experienced rescuer, he had every right to assert his position as there was nothing that inexperienced, ill-equipped if well-meaning amateurs could bring to the situation. He also had to consider what would happen if scores of inexperienced soldiers were unleashed upon the sites where his skilled rescuers were tunnelling through debris. The most likely effect would be to hamper the trained rescuers and in all probability cause additional, unnecessary danger to the ARP personnel. With hindsight, it does seem that the incident attracted all manner of people from the military who saw the incident as the opportunity to show themselves in a good light by utilising the troops under their command, albeit that they had no training or equipment for this kind of incident.

The workers from the factory who were beavering away at the rubble on the roadway were achieving little of any consequence, creditable though their actions were. In fact, had the military who were at the site shortly after the original bombing directed people home before the second aircraft had attacked the factory, there is no doubt that the casualty list would not have been so long. The most urgent work that needed addressing was the rescue of the casualties who were still trapped; the fire service had the fires under control and salvage work was in progress. At this point in the incident, it was not known that none of the casualties were still alive. It was pointed out to the Military Liaison Officer that only a relatively small number of people could be usefully put to work on the task of rescue and that these people needed to be part of a trained team. Arguing the various options with the officials was not helping the situation as the rescuers had only a few hours of daylight left. The rescue parties' leader obviously won the point and 60 ARP rescue workers began searching through the debris on the sites where people were still missing.

It is sad to say that this was not the end of the problems. There was some friction between the county rescue parties and the works rescue parties, but common sense should surely have made the works rescuers recognise the wealth of knowledge and experience that had come to their assistance. For the Ransome and Marles rescuers, this was their first incident of the war and unfortunately it was not uncommon for works parties to resent any outside help. They tended to forget that the people who were trapped and

View of the Stanley Street terraced houses which shows where part of the factory once stood

View of the factory car park near to Stanley Street. This was once part of the factory as the highlighted parts show – steel support columns cut off at ground level and other remains of steel columns still embedded in the wall Below Left: The cut off ends of steel support columns can be clearly made out in what is now the factory car park Below Right: One of the entrances to the underground shelter at the Stanley Street end of the factory now sealed up in the car park

injured had the right to the best help available, no matter where that help came from. The rescue parties ceased work at 22:00 hours that night, having turned over most of the debris. The casualty list was steep: forty people had been seriously injured and another forty had suffered injuries that were treated at hospital. The works first aid post had carried out some good work by treating between sixty and a hundred casualties. It was thought that thirty people had died as a result of the raid and, of the bodies lying in the mortuary, eight were still unidentified. The following morning at 08:30 hours, six rescue parties recommenced the search for missing people. The majority of the search was completed by 18:30 hours, but two crews, one from Arnold and one from Beeston, stayed until after 19:30 hours and two bodies were recovered from the blacksmith's shop. On Sunday 9th March, a full-time crew from West Bridgford, along with part-time crews from Beeston and Carlton, worked at the site. They recovered some human remains from the main factory, but no intact bodies. By this stage of the search it was soul-destroying work; no one had any illusions about finding people alive.

On Monday morning, four full-time crews recommenced work, which went on until after 18:00 hours. They were able to recover the bodies of another thirteen people as well as finding more dismembered body parts. Six people were still reported missing, but five of them could be accounted for by the number of unidentified bodies still remaining in the mortuary. A thorough search of the debris was made and it was finally accepted that the woman who remained missing would not be found. The rescue work was called off. The final death toll was 43, made up of 29 men and 14 women, including 19-year-old Esther Varney, who was never found. West Bridgford and Mansfield provided a crew each on Tuesday and Wednesday to assist with vital salvage work at the factory. The raid had caused £91,789 worth of damage to the factory, as well as causing disruption to vital war work.

The Confidential Report by the works ARP subcontroller is not dated but it appears to be a response to the report submitted by the Newark ARP services which was critical of some aspects of the incident. The "*congestion at the General Hospital*" was acknowledged as an error but the work carried out by the first aid parties was justifiably praised by all concerned. The works subcontroller's report also acknowledged the problem created by the sounding of the "Raiders Passed" signal at 13:54. "*An order was given for employees to leave the works. Unfortunately at 14:24 the 'Alert' was sounded again . . . There were still a large number of employees leaving the main entrance of the works and passing by the new road to Beacon Hill Road.*" Why were people still leaving the works 30 minutes after being instructed to leave? Possibly because they regarded the instruction in the same casual manner that they treated the instruction to take shelter.

Roy Lale was working at Ransome and Marles at the time of the bombing and his comments regarding taking shelter are very revealing.

> "*The usual practice during an air raid was to keep working. An imminent danger alert was relayed by the sounding of a gong over the tannoy. On the day of the bombing the alert was followed immediately by the gong, which had not happened before. We should have realised the urgency but we had evacuated so many times that we had become complacent and as usual took a leisurely walk to the shelters.*
>
> *I was as bad as the rest, taking my time strolling out of the workshop. As I got outside I heard machine-gun fire. I looked up and saw a German plane come into view. I saw the bombs released and with no time to run, dived to the back of a bike rack hoping for the best. A few seconds later the wall of the workshop came crashing down beside me.*"

One employee of the factory commented on the air raid warning procedure: "*We were always told that if the siren went we were to carry on working unless the danger was imminent and the bell went too.*" Even when the warning was given, some employees went to look at the guns engaging the bomber rather than going straight into the shelter. The works subcontroller's report states that the lateness of the warning was fortunate, as if it had been sounded sooner then more people would have been in the underground shelter, leading to greater loss of life. This cannot be used as a justification for the delay in sounding the alert. The shelter had been designated as a place of safety during a raid and if the shelter was not sufficiently deep, or as with most works and public shelters, too many people were allowed into one place, that is a different argument. The fact remains that people should have been given adequate warning.

In common with many large factories they had roof spotters who went to their designated posts upon receiving the "Purple Alert". It was their role to assess the need for workers to go into shelters, based upon whether the factory was about to be attacked. The need to continue production was impressed upon these spotters, to the point where bombs had to be virtually landing on the factory for them to sound the alert. There is no doubt that, whatever the reasons were on that day, the alert was given only one minute before the bombs hit the factory and not, as stated in the subcontroller's report, two to three minutes earlier. The slow response by employees to take shelter was a matter for the ARP Controller at the works to deal with and this issue should have been firmly corrected long before this fateful raid took place.

The report comments on the large number of people in Beacon Hill Road when the second German aircraft bombed the factory and states that it *"might have given the impression that there was a very large number of sightseers there who should have been prevented from approaching the works."* That certainly is the picture that is painted, and despite the subcontroller stating " *I consider that if too much force had been used to clear these roads of persons, who had undergone a very unnerving experience, panic might have been caused"*, it was not a decision he should have been making; it was a matter for the police and the military. There was no need for panic to be caused by moving people along and directing them to go home, as figures suggest that there could have been no more than 1,500 people at most in the area, and given that it is possible to clear a football stadium and the immediate area of up to 70,000 people in half the time available between the two alerts in Newark, it should have been possible to achieve an orderly clearance.

A factor that may have had a bearing on the reluctance of people to leave was the presence of two WVS canteens that arrived at the site. Ostensibly these were for the refreshment of the ARP workers and fire crews at the site, but in fact they provided tea to anyone who requested it, thus unwittingly encouraging people to stay in the area. The justification for this in the report was given as that people were suffering from "shock". This is a fallacious argument as anyone suffering from shock should have been taken to one of the first aid posts or to hospital. However, the use of the term "shock" has been used in this report in the loosest sense, possibly in an attempt to divert criticism. The report had already stated that people had been through an unnerving experience and that is what they were suffering from – not "shock". The best thing for them was to be sent home and to have a cup of tea there, away from the incident, so that the ARP workers could get on with what needed to be done.

The Luftwaffe crew who carried out the raid, Lieutenant Rudolph, Lieutenant Metzmacher, Unterofficer Groper and Unterofficer Hahn, were praised as heroes for pressing home their attack. An official German communiqué said:

> *"A daring low level attack took place on an armaments factory in Newark causing heavy damage in the workshops."*

It is perhaps hard to accept, but the Luftwaffe crews were only doing the same as our own RAF crews who carried out similar low-level raids. The German crews believed they were doing what was right, just as our own boys did. The *Newark Advertiser* for 12th March carried the headline:

> *"RAID ON BUILDINGS IN NORTH MIDLAND TOWN: SOME DEATHS*
>
> *Hard work by rescue parties and others"*

What else could they have said under the reporting restrictions?

11. Lone Raiders

Lone aircraft often roamed about at night, dropping incendiaries here and there and two or three high-explosive bombs in one location and then some more elsewhere in an effort to cause as much disruption as possible. Sam Swain lived in Beeston all his life and was in the Home Guard. When on duty at night, he often saw low-flying lone raiders. One night Sam was on fire-watching duties up the tower of Beeston Parish Church when a raider passed so low overhead that he clearly saw the bomb bay doors open. He also recalled seeing a crippled German bomber when on duty with the Home Guard at the Acacia Walk Telephone Exchange.

> *"One night when the sirens went and the ack-ack guns were firing, we saw an aircraft coming very low straight up Acacia Walk. It had obviously been damaged. The man in charge of us was Sergeant Straw, an 'old sweat' from the First World War. He called out: 'Aircraft approaching! Five rounds rapid fire!' There was about ten of us and we all fired off our five rounds. As the aircraft passed over the top of us, the rear gunner lowered his guns right down and let fly at us. The bullets blasted lumps out of the road and the holes were big enough to put a bucket in.*
>
> *The next morning, the sergeant logged the incident: 'Aircraft overhead, believed to be hostile.' I said to him, 'I wouldn't want to be with you, Sergeant Straw, if you knew the bugger was hostile'."*

There was a sharp raid on the Bramcote, Beeston and Chilwell area at 02:25 hours on 8th April 1941. This was yet another occasion when the sirens had not sounded and the first people knew of the raid was when the bombs were falling. Hundreds of incendiaries were dropped, as well as a number of high-explosive bombs. The majority of the damage in Beeston was in an area bounded by the railway lines at the bottom of Mona Street, Station Road and Beeston High Road. A high-explosive bomb fell on 24 Mona Street. Sarah Cox and her daughter Edna were both seriously injured and Sarah died later the same day of her injuries at Nottingham General Hospital. The Queens pub on the corner of Mona Street and Queen's Drive had a 250kg high-explosive bomb fall next to it. It caused a massive crater which took up the whole width of the road, but at first glance appeared to have left the pub undamaged. A closer inspection after the raid revealed that the entire building had been moved about 12 inches on its foundations. It was shored up

The Queen's public house on the corner of Mona Street which was badly damaged by a high-explosive bomb in April 1941 and had to be shored up to prevent it collapsing

for a long time afterwards to prevent it from collapsing.

The fire brigade in Beeston found itself dealing with 25 houses on fire, while many other small fires were dealt with by ARP wardens or householders themselves with stirrup pumps. Monica Carrott (née Emery) was only seven years old at the time of this air raid and she was fast asleep in bed with her sister. Two incendiary bombs hit their house: one crashed through her parents' bedroom window at the back of the house and the other plunged through the roof and ceiling of the front bedroom.

"The bomb at the back of the house landed between my mum and dad in bed and just caught my mum's shoulder. Their mattress and bedclothes caught fire. In the front bedroom, my sister Alma and I awoke to find our beds and the curtains on fire. There were flames over by the bedroom door too and our dad was on the landing by this time and he called out to us to get out of the bedroom. My sister's hair and the bottom of her nightie were on fire by then and we just ran through the flames to get out.

Neighbours were queuing up in the hallway and on the stairs to throw buckets of water on to the fire. The bedding and mattress were all thrown out of the window. Someone took my mum [Frances Emery] up to the first aid post but she didn't go to hospital. Later on her arm swelled up and turned black through the poison caused by the powder in the incendiary bomb getting into her burns. Her arm wasn't right for about a year, but she never received any medical treatment. What pain she must have gone through."

Two other people, Constance Spen- also injured during this air raid. A bomb fell into the yard of Beeston Boiler Works and, although it failed to explode, people nearby had to be evacuated. Another UXB landed in Schofield's wet fish shop on Station Road which led to the road being closed off. The next day, the tail fins of the bomb could still be seen poking up from behind the counter. Windsor Street and Regent Street were littered with incendiary bombs but fortunately many fell into the roadway and gardens, where they burnt themselves out without setting light to property. Two houses with the sides blown away had beds and other furniture hanging precariously out of them.

While the air raid on Beeston was in progress, other raiders were in the north-east of the county, where they dropped three high-explosive bombs and 60 incendiaries onto RAF Ossington. Three nights later, on Good Friday, the raiders were back again. A heavy anti-aircraft barrage started at around 02:00 hours as enemy aircraft turned over the city from the River

Top: Bomb damage 24 Mona Street in Beeston where Sarah Cox was killed on 8th April 1941 (Photograph courtesy of Nottingham Evening Post) Bottom: 24 Mona Street in 2009

46 Charlbury Road (right) where Maude Tomlinson was killed on Good Friday, 11th April 1941

Trent. They made a bombing run in a line from Castle Boulevard, over Triumph Road and towards Radford Bridge Road and Beechdale. Jim Dunkerley was the sergeant in charge of the police mechanised division at Triumph Road. He remembered how the raid started.

"We heard this droning overhead and so we went outside to see if we could see the aircraft. One of the lads said, 'It's all right, mate, it's one of ours.' The next thing, we heard a swishing sound coming down and then the scream of the bombs falling. They must have aimed for the gasometer as it used to stand out a mile even in the blackout, but the bombs missed it. Some bombs in the stick fell short of their target and others passed over the gasometer and our police station and the fire station and they hit a house on Charlbury Road."

The high-explosive bomb on Charlbury Road scored a direct hit on number 46, where Maude Tomlinson was sleeping downstairs. She was killed, but her husband, who was upstairs in the house, survived, although he was injured. He was just making his way down the stairs when the bomb struck and the staircase enclosure protected him from the blast. A large number of houses were damaged and fourteen of them were rendered uninhabitable. Two more high-explosive bombs fell on to the housing estate on Beechdale Road and Felstead Road, but no serious damage was caused. An Anderson shelter took a direct hit, but thankfully it was unoccupied. On Charlbury Road there were fifteen people slightly injured; one of them was Inspector Frank Bennett of the Nottingham City Fire Brigade. The Bennetts lived opposite number 46 and they were lucky to escape serious injury, as were neighbours either side of the house.

The Vickerstaffes lived next door to number 38, and they were afraid for their baby daughter when they found the cot covered with plaster and glass, but the baby was unhurt. Hetty Walker, who lived on the opposite side of the road to the bombed house, recalled what happened when her house was seriously damaged by the blast.

"I was in bed with the baby in the downstairs front room when I heard a plane swoop low and then there was a deafening crash. The whole house rocked. My first thought was for the baby and instinctively I flung a pillow over it and so saved it from injury. The glass of the windows was smashed to fragments and I was covered in plaster from the ceiling. Fortunately the head of the bed was towards the window and this stopped the direct effect of the flying glass.

We had a piano in front of the window and although the doors were blown off in the house, the piano gave us some protection from the blast."

Hetty Walker received a cut to her forehead but was otherwise none the worse for her ordeal and her five-year-old daughter, asleep in the back bedroom, was unharmed. The raiders passed on over Aspley,

Cinderhill and Bulwell, where they dropped large numbers of incendiaries and more high-explosive bombs. The Co-op store at Aspley had its windows blown in by the blast and fire-watchers were quick off the mark in dealing with many of the incendiaries. Florence Calladine of Babbington Cottages was injured by a high-explosive bomb while trying to deal with an incendiary. The bomb was on open ground and could have been left to burn itself out, but Florence was typical of many people who believed it was their duty to tackle incendiaries, regardless of the risk. In Bulwell, some buildings were set alight, including a church, but fire crews extinguished the fires before they caused much damage.

The raid had been similar in format to the Beeston raid three nights before and, once again, just as at Beeston, the raid was under way long before the sirens gave the warning. The alert was not given on this particular night until 02:20 hours, according to official records. The population was mightily fed up with being sent to their shelters night after night when the aircraft passed high overhead without dropping any bombs, but when their town was bombed, they received no warning. People were often asleep in their beds when this happened, which left them at their most vulnerable.

The proof, if proof were needed, that the sirens were not being sounded until bombs were actually falling in a district, is contained in a message from the Nottingham City ARP Control to the North Midlands Regional Control. The message was sent at 04:30, reporting the raid and stating the number of casualties and damage caused.

"NOTTINGHAM CITY INTERIM SITUATION REPORT.

02:16 4 H.E. and incendiary bombs fell in Radford Division and Bulwell Division STOP. All fires now put out STOP. 1 dead, 7 seriously injured, 10 slightly injured, several minor injuries STOP. 3 houses demolished, 5 seriously damaged, 50 slightly damaged STOP."

Here then were the unequivocal facts to show that the Nottinghamshire populace had been right all along when they said that the sirens would not be sounded until bombs were actually falling. And despite the threats by the Chief Constable that he would take action against anyone spreading this opinion, he could not dispute that the bombs had been falling for more than four minutes before the alert was sounded. His silence was notable. Nottingham came under red alert again on 16th, 17th and 20th April, but no bombs were dropped. Newark was bombed on 21st April, when a lone aircraft dropped high-explosive bombs around the London Road area. The original reports written in pencil on scraps of paper from the ARP post have survived and recorded the situation as follows:

"Supplementary message No. 1
Section 39 Elm Avenue – Falstone
Six people trapped under debris at 'Mondello'. Casualties from broken glass from Falstone Ave, London Rd and Elm Ave accounted for and names taken.
Time 20:40
Message ends.
JLW 20:50

Supplementary message No. 2
Section 39 Elm Avenue – Falstone Avenue
Six casualties have been removed to hospital. 27 casualties from broken glass sent to fixed [first] aid post. All casualties have now been removed. Police and wardens standing by.
Message ends.
JLW 20:53"

The two messages are annotated in orange crayon, which shows that the casualty figures had been noted and passed on and also the times of the messages. The apparent discrepancy in the times on the first message are explained by the time it was sent and the time when the ARP control in Newark logged it. The names of the casualties have disappeared from the records with the passage of time. Nottinghamshire was visited again on the night of 30th April and 1st May. RAF Newton was bombed with high explosives and also oil incendiary bombs and one man was injured at the aerodrome. Liverpool had been the major target for the Luftwaffe on 26th April and with hindsight it seems likely that this was a trial run for what was to follow. From 1st May, Liverpool was bombed every night for a week, with a particularly heavy raid on 3rd May. On that night a 7,600-ton ammunition ship, the *Makaland*, received a direct hit. The resulting explosion wrecked the south Huskisson Dock.

The series of raids became the most prolonged of any that had been carried out against provincial towns and cities. Road and rail links were severed, docks were blocked by sunken ships and 75 per cent of the shipping berths were out of action. The situation for the nation was very serious, but for the people of Liverpool, and particularly those in and around Bootle, it was more than they could bear. The Minister of Home Security said at a civil defence meeting on 7th May:

> *"The people cannot stand this intensive bombing indefinitely and sooner or later the morale of other towns will go, even as Plymouth's has already gone."*

The casualty list was high: 1,900 dead and 1,450 seriously injured. Entire areas of Liverpool had been laid waste, 66,000 houses had been destroyed, and the docks and commercial areas were smashed beyond recovery. For the firemen who had been sent as part of the regional reinforcements scheme, it was yet another round of battling against hopeless odds. The fires were always too numerous and the firefighting resources were always too thinly spread to be able to halt the advancing flames. But, just as they had done for London, Coventry, Birmingham, Sheffield, Manchester and other cities, they stuck to their task. Nottingham fireman Charlie Bartles was a veteran of blitz firefighting by this time and he remembers the Liverpool raids.

> *"The fire situation was hopeless, just massive blazes all around. But it was the civilians I felt sorry for. I stuck my head into a communal air raid shelter on one occasion and I saw rows of people slumped against the walls, and leaning on one another. They looked like zombies. They didn't seem to have any life left in them at all. Not one of them spoke. By god, I did feel sorry for them.*
>
> *The raids just seemed to go on and on and we were becoming exhausted by it all because we got virtually no sleep in the daytime and we were firefighting all night surrounded by great danger. It just wore us down. One night when the sirens sounded again, some of the men I was working with just vomited; their nerves were shot to pieces after a week of being under aerial bombardment.*
>
> *I remember one morning, one of the dockers come up to us as he was going to work. He could see that the place where he normally worked was just a heap of rubble with fires burning all around it. He gave us his sandwiches that he had brought with him for his dinner. We were starving and when we opened them we couldn't believe our eyes; they were <u>EGG</u> sandwiches and he had given them to us!"*

On the night of 7th and 8th May, a raid on Liverpool went ahead and again serious fires broke out. Bryant and May's at Bootle, Brunswick Cold Storage, Atholl Street Gas Works and Walton Prison were all serious blazes. Manchester took a pounding again too. The Manchester Oil Refinery was seriously damaged by fire, and Eccles, the fuel tank manufacturers, and the Ingersoll Rand works were both gutted by fire. Nottingham's firemen were in action alongside their Liverpool and Manchester colleagues again, little knowing that tomorrow night they would be desperately needed in their own city.

12. Bomber's Moon

Thursday 8th May was a fine, warm day and it was so welcome after the seemingly endless dark nights of winter during which the country had endured the Blitz. As the Nottingham people listened to the BBC morning news bulletins they learned that Liverpool had been raided again, but the BBC did not reveal that the situation was extremely serious for the city.

People outside Liverpool had no idea how close the people were to breaking. The raid they had endured during that Wednesday night and Thursday morning had been of massive proportions. They had been on the receiving end of 232 tonnes of high-explosive bombs and over 29,000 incendiaries. Part of the bomber force had been diverted to Hull as weather conditions deteriorated over Liverpool. The 110 tonnes of high-explosive bombs and over 9,500 incendiaries that the other city received had spared Liverpool from even greater destruction.

The people of Nottingham were tired out because they had been under air raid warning from ten minutes to midnight until 05:00 that morning. For the seventh consecutive night they had sheltered in basements, under stairs and in cold, damp Anderson shelters in gardens. They had heard the bombers making their way to the north-west knowing where the likely target was and at the same time thanking their lucky stars that it was not them.

One of the raiders, a Heinkel of Kampfgeschwader 53, the Condor Legion, was on its way to Liverpool when it was shot down by a night fighter over Nottinghamshire. Sergeant Johnson was at the controls of a Boulton Paul Defiant from 255 Squadron of RAF Kirton in Lindsey. He closed in on the unsuspecting Heinkel and then his gunner, Sergeant Aitchison, gave it a burst from his twin machine guns. The Heinkel caught fire and crashed into a sand and gravel quarry at Scrooby near Retford. Its crew – Feldwebel (Corporal) Gunter Merten (pilot). Gefreiter (Sergeant) Erhardt Schönberger (wireless operator), Feldwebel H. Müller (flight engineer) and Gefreiter O. Wilfingseder (gunner) – all parachuted out of the aircraft safely.

Tail fin of a high explosive bomb from a Heinkel He 111 shot down near Scrooby on the night of 7th – 8th May 1941 (Photograph courtesy of William Taylor)

ARP personnel knew that the Heinkel had crashed and the police and local military headquarters were informed. A search for the German airmen began and three of them were eventually found walking along the trunk road at Scaftworth. They were immediately taken into custody by a police special constable, assisted by a number of fire-watchers who had accompanied him in the search. The three airmen offered no resistance, even though at least one of them was armed with a handgun. The captured airmen were taken to the army camp at Retford for initial interrogation.

Later on during the night a fourth member of the crew was captured at Everton Carr, by a gamekeeper. The fifth member of the crew, Hauptmann (Squadron Leader) E. Kölmel, was found by a bridge over the River Idle. His parachute was unopened and it is thought that as he jumped from the aircraft he may have been struck by the tailplane and killed outright.

The newspapers were restricted in what they could report about such events and confined themselves to the following comments at the bottom of a column.

"NIGHT RAIDER DOWN. An enemy raider crashed in flames in the North Midlands early yesterday morning. Four members of the crew who had baled out were taken prisoner."

Charlie Shelton finished reading the report of the enemy aircraft being destroyed and then put his newspaper down and began eating his tea. Charlie lived in Roseberry Avenue at the back of the Nottingham Forest football ground in West Bridgford. Each morning at 02:00 he went to the Co-op Bakery and Co-op Dairy on Meadow Lane and then drove his lorry load of milk and bread to Skegness. He usually arrived back in Nottingham about 13:00. Today was no exception and he had slept during the afternoon, awakening in time for his tea.

The Nottingham populace was making its way home, unaware that tonight the target for the enemy aircraft would be their city. At airfields in France, Belgium and Holland, the Luftwaffe was making its final preparations before embarking on the night's mission. It began to get dark just before 22:00 hours and half an hour later the first of the raiders were already crossing the south coast and heading for the Midlands. Subsequent waves of bombers came from the Dieppe area and took a north-easterly course over the Strait of Dover before joining streams of aircraft from Belgium and Holland. They continued up the east coast and then turned inland over East Anglia towards the Midlands.

A total of 210 aircraft were dispatched with three key targets in mind: Nottingham, Hull and Barrow-in-Furness. Nottingham had been assigned 107 aircraft with the target area being the south-east of the city. The Luftwaffe had highly trained units that carried out the same function as the RAF Pathfinder Squadrons. The German bomber groups, Kampfgeschwader 100 and Kampfgeschwader 26, located targets with the aid of navigation beams and on-board navigation equipment. Marking the target for the main bomber force following behind was often achieved with flares, or by ringing it with a vapour trail if visibility was good.

The air raids usually commenced with large numbers of incendiaries to start plenty of fires and then the high-explosive bombs were poured in once the civil defence personnel and the firemen were at work. Later waves of aircraft would continue with more incendiaries, which would burn without being noticed as the high-explosive bombs would have driven all the civilians into their shelters. More high-explosive bombs would then go in to keep them in the shelters while the fires spread and destroyed the city. The firemen would be pounded by the bombs being aimed where the fires burned brightest, with the intention that they would give up and seek shelter from the explosions.

At 23:26 hours, the yellow alert was telephoned through to the city and county ARP controls, followed four minutes later by the purple alert. They began at once relaying the purple warning to the police and fire brigade controls as well as alerting their own staff within the ARP organisation. At 23:37 hours a Heinkel of Kampfgeschwader 26 approached the city from the south-east. It was flying at a height of around 4,000 feet and it began to mark out a rectangular box in the sky by means of a vapour trail. The box extended from Tollerton to just past Trent Bridge and then ran downriver to Colwick, enclosing the south-east part of the city.

Air Raid Warden Salter was at his post in West Bridgford and he watched the aircraft marking out the box in the sky and then he noticed flares burning down the Trent Valley. These were the guide markers for the Luftwaffe bombers to follow along the river to Nottingham. As he looked eastwards he could see a faint glow on the horizon. Unknown to him, bombs were already falling on and around RAF Newton and the glow he could see was from the fires at the aerodrome. He went up to the roof of Trent Bridge flats to try to see what was on fire and from this vantage point he was able to conclude that it was the aerodrome.

Further to the south, twelve high-explosive bombs had already fallen between Barnstone and Granby, along with 500 incendiaries. A house had been set on fire and the police house at Barnstone and a farm building had been damaged by the blast. Bombs continued to fall well to the south of the city and 16 more high-explosive bombs fell around Langar, Granby and Whatton. More incendiaries were dropped and Whatton Manor had its windows damaged by the blast from one of the high-explosive bombs. The south Nottinghamshire villages found themselves cut off from their reporting centre in Nottingham as the telephone wires were brought down by explosions. Half a mile from the village of Elton, there was a series of loud explosions as bombs fell around the Nottingham to Grantham road, causing a large crater that restricted it to one-way traffic only. Five of the bombs failed to detonate but nonetheless still created a problem of their own.

The sound of aircraft began to fill the air as searchlights burst into life one after another and began sweeping the night sky looking for the raiders. A flare dropped very close by and Warden Salter watched as it descended slowly to earth. In any other circumstances it would have been quite a pretty sight, but his attention was brought sharply back as the first wave of bombers passed directly overhead. The night was clear and brilliantly lit by a full moon. They would have no difficulty in finding the target tonight; it was a bomber's moon.

Across the river in the city, the rising and falling note of the air raid sirens began to fill the air, mingling with the unmistakable engine note of German bombers. Fireman Chris Raybould was manning the fire-watching post on top of Central Fire Station. It was usual practice to send a man up there as soon as the purple alert was received and, at the same time, all the fire appliances were driven out of the station to standby points. The idea was that if the station received a direct hit, the firefighting capability in the city would not be totally destroyed. The sound of high-explosive bombs could now be heard coming from the direction of the Leenside Division to the south of the city and then there was the clatter of incendiary bombs as they fell onto the city rooftops.

Chris could hear the aircraft overheard when the whistle of a falling bomb warned him to dive for cover. The next moment the Masonic Hall on Goldsmith Street was struck by a heavy-calibre bomb. Mr Sandell was the caretaker of the Masonic Hall and he was on fire-watch duty there with a companion.

"I was on the roof, which is about forty feet high, when we heard the screech of a falling bomb. We ducked down just as the building received a direct hit. The next thing I realised was that I was on the ground floor."

Mr Sandell suffered concussion, but his wife and child, who were in the building at the time, as well as the other fire-watcher, were all uninjured.

The force of the blast could be felt at the fire station and Reg Miller, who was at his standby point on the corner of Burton Street, decided that it would be wise to take cover. It was out of the question for him to leave his post, but there was nothing to say that he had to stand in the open and run the risk of being hit by shrapnel. He did the common-sense thing and lay down underneath the turntable ladder that he was crewing.

Above: The position on the roof of Central Fire Station where the spotter's post was situated. Fireman Chris Raybould watched the raid on Nottingham develop from here

Above: The rebuilt Masonic Hall which was hit by a high explosive bomb on 8th May 1941

The control operators in the basement of the fire station were already taking calls to fires and although such a close detonation caused them to look up for a moment, they had no time to dwell on it. The bells rang out at Central Fire Station, sending the firemen running to their machines. It would be eighteen hours before most of them got back to the station again. Chris Raybould went helter-skelter down the main staircase of the station, grabbed his turnout message and then went through the revolving door on to Burton Street. He told Reg Miller that they were to go to Snook's Factory on Hounds Gate as it had been struck by a bomb.

A call had also been received to C & A Modes on Lister Gate and the second turntable ladder was mobilised to the premises. As it raced through the streets a bomb exploded, sending a piece of shrapnel whizzing across the open cab of the appliance, which slashed open the fire tunic of Sergeant Arthur Wright without seriously injuring him. He looked down at the gaping hole across the chest of his tunic and knew that he had escaped death by an inch or two. By some quirk of fate, the shrapnel passed out of the cab without hitting the driver and five other chunks of shrapnel slammed into the metalwork of the turntable ladder without hitting either of the men.

As the calls mounted up, the control room mobilised pumps from the city AFS stations. On the edge of the Lace Market, an AFS pump crew was at work tackling incendiary bombs that encircled St Peter's Church on Wheeler Gate. They had heard the whistle of the high-explosive bomb that had fallen into Snook's Factory on Hounds Gate followed by the explosion. It had caused

Snook's Factory on Hound's Gate which was hit by a high explosive bomb which set it on fire

massive damage to the factory and started a fire. The crew were torn between going to deal with that or sticking to the job in hand. Their decision was made for them when another pump and the 87-foot turntable ladder arrived within a few minutes.

Chris Raybould and Reg Miller arrived at Snook's Factory and could see that the turntable ladder would not be needed at this particular job. They were told to go to the Severn's building, a medieval timber-framed structure,

St Peter's Church which was surrounded by incendiary bombs at the start of Nottingham's heaviest air raid. An Auxiliary Fire Service crew from Bank Place put them out

which at that time stood on the corner of Middle Pavement and Weekday Cross. The fire at the Severn's building turned out to be just an incendiary in the back yard and it was soon dealt with by a line of hose from a fire hydrant.

The fire-watchers at Smith's factory on Short Hill were being put to the test by this time. Irene Sharp recalled what happened.

Left: The site of the Severn's building in 2009 Right: The original half timbered Severn's building that stood on the site

"Once the raid started we could hear bombs falling a little distance away and then we saw that the factory roof was on fire. Trudie and Frank [the other fire-watchers] and myself went up to the third floor to get the stirrup pumps and buckets and then went up to the sixth floor, which was the top of the building. It was no use; we hadn't had much training and no practice. The fire was spreading and new ones were starting up so we went down into the street.

Fires were starting up all around and the firemen were there running hose out. I tried to get back into the factory to save my typewriter but the firemen stopped me and said that the whole place was starting to go up. We watched them for a while and then they got us down into the basement of the Shire Hall where we stayed the night."

As soon as they had put out the incendiary at the Severn's, Chris Raybould and Reg Miller were sent to another job. This time it was the Shire Hall on High Pavement. This building housed the ARP Control for the county and pumps were already in attendance trying to tackle the fire on the roof. The turntable ladder could not get through from Middle Pavement because of the number of hose lines already criss-crossing the street and so they had to go the long way around via Hockley.

The St Peter's Church AFS crew had already dealt with all the incendiaries around the church when an ARP warden came up to them and asked them if they would deal with a fire that had broken out on the roof of a bank at the junction of Bottle Lane and Fletcher Gate.

The crew had pitched their wheeled escape ladder to the roof of the bank and had the fire under control when there was an explosion no more than fifty yards away; the Allied Paper Company had been

The bank at the corner of Bottle Lane and Fletcher Gate which had incendiaries on its roof tackled by an AFS crew

hit. Dense smoke billowed upwards and through it could be seen dirty orange flames. They moved their appliance and equipment down the road and got firefighting jets to work inside the building.

Off-duty firemen and part-time firemen throughout the city had tumbled out of their beds when the air raid sirens went and were racing to their nearest fire stations. The air raid was gathering momentum now and there was a constant drone of aircraft overhead.

Fred Shipley bundled his wife, Coris, and young family under the stairs of their house and then sped off on his motorbike for Central Fire Station. As he reached the end of Parkdale Road at the junction with

The site of the Allied Paper Company Factory in 2009 – now a car park

St Christopher's Church on Colwick Road which was completely burnt out by 250kg oil bomb

Oakdale Road, he was blown off his motorbike and on to the pavement by the blast from a high-explosive bomb. Fred was to discover later that a childhood pal, Charlie Brown, who was a speedway rider and a volunteer ARP warden, was killed by this bomb. Fred remounted his motorbike and carried on down Sneinton Dale.

As he approached the railway bridge by Edale Road he was flagged down by someone who warned him that there was a bomb crater across the width of the road. Fred turned off on to Sneinton Boulevard but found his path blocked again by a bomb crater. He drove down Trent Road, where St Christopher's Church was already ablaze from the oil bomb incendiary that had fallen on to it. Fred was aware of the bombs that were falling on the city and also of the fires that were beginning to show themselves as a glow inside the buildings as he raced past. He opened the throttle wide as he screeched round on to Manvers Street and the next instant he crashed into something and was thrown from his motorbike again. Picking himself up, he found that he had collided with a length of railway line that had been blasted from the goods yard. The front forks of his motorbike were buckled but he was able to hobble into the station on it.

George Hodson also had some difficulty making his way into Central Fire Station on his bicycle. As he cycled down Sneinton Dale he could see a bomber ahead and the shriek of bombs as they fell made him feel that each one was about to hit him. As he reached the bottom of Carlton Hill, he went headlong into a bomb crater that stretched across the road in front of Cooper and Roe's Factory. He managed to scramble out and continued on his way to the fire station. Alf Porkett had to leave his family in the care of a neighbour and then cycle as quickly as he could from his Wollaton home to Triumph Road Fire Station. The anti-aircraft guns were firing and shrapnel was clattering into the street, searchlights were sweeping across the sky and the dark shape of the bombers could be seen in the beams, or as they passed across the moon. At the station Alf remembers a cluster of incendiaries that had fallen into the canal next to the buildings. They burnt fiercely at the bottom of the canal and it occurred to him that this did not bode well for their chances with jets of water.

Fireman Charlie Bartles could not respond to the sirens immediately as his neighbour's house had been set alight by an incendiary. He dashed up the stairs to the bedroom of the old man who lived there. He picked him up off the bed and carried him to safety. The smoke was acrid and choking and the poor old man was barely breathing when Charlie laid him down in the front garden. He did what he could and, once satisfied that the man was not going to asphyxiate, he went back into the house to tackle the fire. He threw the bedding that was alight out of the window as the blankets and horsehair stuffed mattress were responsible for most of the smoke. He then tackled the rest of the fire with a stirrup pump.

Once he was sure his neighbour was safe, he then fulfilled his obligation to "turn in" at his nearest fire station. Leading Fireman Marshall had been preoccupied too. His own house was alight and although he was able to extinguish the fire, he ended up in hospital with burns.

The incendiary bombs that had fallen across Sneinton and Carlton had started many fires in domestic properties. Bernard Chamberlain, who was a messenger with the ARP service, went out on fire watch with his brother George, his father George senior and his cousin, Bill Laxton.

"I had been up to the ARP post at the top of Kentwood Road and everything was all right so I went back down to the family. Just then incendiaries started dropping and we went under cover. Only a few dropped and then I noticed that Mr and Mrs Tyers' house opposite had a fire in the front bedroom.

I ran across the road and went into the house, calling to them down the cellar that the house was on fire, but they wouldn't come out. There was the old boy down there with his wife and son and daughter. We went upstairs and put the incendiary out with sand.

Not many minutes after that, incendiaries started dropping from the Sneinton Dale end of the road and we all dived into the entry between the houses. First Bill, followed by George, me and then Dad. An incendiary came down and clipped the stone lintel over the entry just as we went in. It took a lump out of the lintel and then hit Dad on the arm and broke his elbow. It glanced off his arm and struck my hand. When I looked it had gashed my hand open and left one of my fingers hanging by the skin.

We went up to the first aid post to get it seen to and on the way we had to dive for cover when a high-explosive bomb fell nearby. Eventually we were taken to hospital."

The explosion that had caused Bernard and his father to dive for cover as they were going to the first aid post had been caused by a stick of bombs falling across Kentwood Road, Westwood Road, Lyndhurst Road, Baden Powell Road, Port Arthur Road and Lichfield Road. A shop was wrecked on the corner of Port Arthur Road and the gas main in the street was blazing fiercely. Thirty-five-year-old William Bush lay dead and his thirty-

The site of the shop on the corner of Port Arthur Road and Sneinton Boulevard which was wrecked by a 50kg high explosive bomb and which also killed two men

three-year-old companion, Robert Barber, was critically injured. Barber was to die later at the General Hospital.

In Baden Powell Road, four men were out in the street when the bomb fell at the junction with Sneinton Boulevard. Charles Gooding was the ARP warden for that area and Cyril Theaker was a member of the first aid party as well as a fire-watcher. Not long after the raid had begun, they had been joined outside by Cyril Parkes and a nineteen-year-old soldier, Joseph Murquis, who was on embarkation leave.

When the bomb fell they had no chance to run for cover and the blast killed Gooding, Murquis and Theaker. Cyril Parkes was badly injured and later developed gangrene in his leg. He suffered from ill health for over forty years as a result of his injuries and underwent a series of operations, even into the 1960s, to remove pieces of shrapnel from his leg and arm. Arthur Theaker was only five years old at the time of the air raid but remembers his dad calling through the coal grate down into the cellar where he

Number 36 Baden Powell Road now stands where two terraced houses were destroyed by a bomb. Inset: Some of the shrapnel marks on the wall of the house opposite. There are extensive marks on the wall from roof to floor level

Arthur Theaker and David Parkes in Baden Powell Road where Arthur's father was killed along with Charles Gooding and Joseph Murquis. David Parkes father Cyril was seriously injured when a bomb destroyed two houses at the top of the road. The men killed were standing approximately where the telegraph pole is, Cyril Parkes was on the opposite side of the road. Inset: The coal grate into the cellar where Arthur and his mother were sheltering. Arthur's father called down to them through this grate just minutes before he was killed

Cyril Theaker - one of the men killed in Baden Powell Road (Photograph courtesy of Arthur Theaker) Right: Cyril Parkes seriously injured by a bomb that killed three of his friends

and his mother were sheltering. Satisfied that they were all right, Cyril went back to his colleagues up the road. It was shortly after this that the bomb fell that killed them.

The firemen who were racing to the various fires, or who were making all haste to the nearest station, had no idea if their loved ones would be safe, or whether they would come back to find their own house burnt to the ground while they had been saving the property of others. Harry Roe had to leave his disabled wife behind and turn in at the fire station, but he would have felt sick to the stomach if he had known that incendiary and high-explosive bombs were falling all around his home in Lyndhurst Road.

Even as Fred Shipley was risking life and limb just to get to the fire station, so his family were in jeopardy as a bomb fell at the back of Hollydale Road where they lived. Tall poplar trees were uprooted by the blast and thrown against the back of the house. Reports were coming in to the County ARP Control room from Beeston by this time, stating that high-explosive bombs were falling in the vicinity of the River Trent. The aircraft dropping these bombs were certainly outside the designated target area and it is likely that their navigational error had occurred due to the similarity of three distinctive bends in the River Trent. The actual turning point for the aircraft making their way along the Trent was the "Hook of the Trent" at West Bridgford where the river bends between two built-up areas. The spread of bombs outside the designated target area for the raid suggests that some pilots and navigators were unsure of their exact location and turned over other bends in the River Trent so that the flight path took them over parts of West Bridgford, Beeston, Chilwell or Stapleford.

At 00:45 a high-explosive bomb fell in

Bessel Lane in Stapleford and two more damaged the Government Stores at Chilwell Depot. High-explosive bombs fell into Meadow Lane at Chilwell, seriously damaging a house and injuring Henry Gill, a fire-watcher. He died later during the night at Nottingham General Hospital. One of the bombs failed to explode, which created a different kind of problem as wardens now needed to evacuate people from their homes and shelters close to the bomb. Three minutes later high-explosive bombs fell a quarter of a mile from the Toton Lane and Brookhill Street junction in Stapleford and damaged several houses there.

At 01:07 Beech Avenue in Beeston was rocked when a high-explosive bomb fell on to a house and also destroyed a surface air raid shelter, but fortunately no one was in it at the time. The occupants of the house that had been struck were in another surface shelter which was undamaged by the blast. This incident demonstrates the randomness of surviving unscathed or becoming a casualty. The same aircraft dropped high-explosive bombs on to Ashfield Avenue, where gas and water mains were damaged, and also on to 27 and 29 Maple Avenue where both houses were virtually destroyed. The next street along the course of the bomber was Layton Crescent and a high-explosive bomb struck numbers 17 and 19, demolishing both houses.

High-explosive bombs from another aircraft crashed down on to 61 King Street in Beeston and six people were trapped in the wreckage. Bombs from this aircraft also fell into Regent Street and Queen's Road in Beeston. A rescue party was dispatched at once to King Street and they were soon involved in the painstaking task of extricating people from the wreckage of their home as they had been following the raid on Beeston in April. As with the previous raid it was the areas near to the railway line and the river that attracted most of the bombs. Over in West Bridgford, Air Raid Warden Salter was still patrolling his sector, accompanied by his wife. They were making their way towards Musters Road where they lived, from Warden Post number 9 when the first high-explosive bombs fell in this part of the suburb.

Number 61 King Street in Beeston which was struck by a high explosive bomb on 9th May 1941

The enemy bombers that had followed the river as far as the "Hook of the Trent" began releasing their bomb loads over West Bridgford at 01:00. Three high-explosive bombs exploded in fields by Pinder's Pond near Adbolton Grove, killing two beasts. Bombs fell on to numbers 80 to 90 and 113 to 115 Trent Boulevard, destroying eight houses, killing two people and causing multiple casualties, many of whom were trapped. The water mains and gas mains in Trent Boulevard were damaged by the explosions and all around was a scene of chaos. High-explosive bombs also fell across Julian Road, Gertrude Road, Mona Road, Pierrepont Road and Ropsley Crescent. The roads were cratered, all the mains supplies were damaged and more people were injured and trapped in the wreckage of their homes. Large numbers of incendiaries fell around Ropsley Crescent and a high-explosive bomb that fell into the canal failed to explode, as did three more high-explosive bombs that buried themselves into the Boot's playing fields at Lady Bay. In addition to dealing with several incidents within a small area, the air raid wardens now had to evacuate sixteen houses because of the unexploded bombs.

As the aircraft passed over Ella Road and Radcliffe Road more high-explosive bombs went down on to the houses, along with showers of incendiaries. On Fox Road and Hound Road, four houses were partially demolished. In a short space of time the flicker of fires could be seen lighting up bedrooms of other houses as the incendiaries did their work. Air Raid Warden Salter takes up the story.

"We heard the bombs exploding nearer and nearer and then there was the whistle of bombs falling and we immediately fell flat on the ground. After the explosion we went to investigate in the direction of Musters Road, which is where we thought they had dropped."

Left: Fox Road in West Bridgford showing the style of the original houses and the replacements for those destroyed in May 1941

Realising that the ARP post on Musters Road had almost certainly been hit, he made his way there to give what assistance he could and at the same time sent his wife back to number 9 Post to telephone a report through asking for a rescue squad and an ambulance. Bill Shaw lived at number 4 Bridge Grove, just off Musters Road, and he remembered well the moment when the stick of bombs struck.

Right: The junction of Musters Road and Rushworth Avenue showing the building that replaced the shop on the corner

"My dad had noticed the vapour trail square up in the sky earlier on and we listened as large numbers of bombers passed overhead. As the raid developed he commented, 'We are going to catch it tonight.' The next thing, we heard the noise of bombs falling, they whistled as they came down, and the next instant there was a tremendous explosion with bricks and glass crashing down. The windows of our house were sucked out and part of the roof had gone. We decided that we ought to go to the brick air raid shelter opposite Bridge Grove on Musters Road as we would probably be much safer there."

As they ran to the shelter, they saw that the block of shops on Musters Road, both sides of the Bridge Grove junction, had been hit. Cliff Price's chemists shop was blazing fiercely and rubble was strewn all across the road. Warden Salter arrived a few minutes later.

"When I arrived there was a thick black pall of smoke in the road and it was difficult to see the extent of the damage, but it was apparent that some buildings had been demolished."

What Warden Salter could not see at that time was that further up Musters Road, the Co-op store at the junction of Rushworth Avenue and the house on the corner of Millicent Road had both been struck by bombs.

"I was greatly concerned for the safety of my family and I was relieved to see them emerge from our house unscathed. I took them to the safety of the shelter and then began helping people to get out of the rubble. People were still calling out at this time and it was realised that a man was trapped at number 12 Musters Road."

An "Express Report" had been telephoned through from Warden Post 9 asking for a rescue squad, but they did not realise that fires had also broken out and so no request for the fire brigade was made. Two wardens from ARP Post number 1 made their way along Loughborough Road towards the incident when they saw smoke. They turned down Rushworth Avenue and when they reached the junction with Musters Road they could at once see the scale of the incident. The Divisional Warden made his way quickly towards the rubble at Bridge Grove, where he could see flames shooting up, while Warden Brown ran to the social club on Loughborough Road from where he could telephone the fire brigade When the Divisional Warden arrived

Number 12 Musters Road (left) where a man was trapped in the wreckage of his home

on the scene, Warden Salter informed him that two ARP wardens, the Irene and Gladys Hall, were both unaccounted for and thought to be trapped in the rubble. The Divisional Warden telephoned through again for a rescue party and an ambulance at 01:10 hours.

"The fire engines were quickly on the spot and although they were prevented from approaching very close due to rubble in the roadway, the firemen ran hose out and quickly got the blaze under control.

The ambulances were next on the scene and I showed them to where the casualties were. We were doing what we could to release those trapped, but desperately needed a rescue squad. I telephoned through again and was relieved when they arrived at about 01:30 hours.

I left Warden Salter helping the rescue party and made my way to ARP Post number nine where I was able to direct other wardens to assist in the sector. We started receiving reports of fires at the Plaza cinema, the county cricket ground and The Boat House, all over by the River Trent. I telephoned through to the fire brigade, who arrived quickly and brought the fires under control, saving what could have been a serious situation had it spread to the large timber yard and garage nearby."

Even as the firemen were fighting to contain the outbreaks of fire, more incendiaries were falling on to other properties and fires were springing up in the shops on Radcliffe Road. Soon the rescuers and firemen at the site of the bombing on Musters Road could see the glow from the properties that were burning on Radcliffe Road, but there was nothing they could do as they were fully committed. They could only rely on other fire appliances arriving as soon as possible to contain the fires. A massive detonation was heard from the direction of Radcliffe Road as an enemy aircraft dropped a high-explosive bomb where fires could be seen burning below.

At around 01:30 a stick of high-explosive bombs fell on Melton Road at the junction with Henry Road, as well as on Loughborough Road, Victoria Road and the junction of Wilford Lane. Five houses had been destroyed on Loughborough Road and over a dozen people were missing.

Air raid wardens from the Wilford Lane sector were on the scene quickly amid scores of incendiaries that were falling. They had to ignore these and leave them to burn as they focused their initial efforts on helping those who were trapped. They quickly located a casualty at number 24 Loughborough Road and rescued the injured girl, Sheila Relph, from the rubble, using a deckchair as an improvised stretcher until the first aid party arrived. Warden Brown located three people at number 23 Loughborough Road and was able to assist them out. He took them to the warden's post for safety. It was clear by this time that no further rescues would be achieved until the heavy rescue squad arrived. They were on the scene about thirty minutes after the bombs had fallen and began work at once on number 24. The rescue operations

Above: The rear of number 34 Loughborough Road where a high explosive bomb partially destroyed the house and trapped a man in the wreckage of the kitchen

Middle: The Church Hall in West Bridgford used as a first aid post. Above: The cottages next to the church hall which were set on fire by an incendiary bomb

were extremely difficult as the rescuers were tunnelling under masses of loose debris. Their labours were rewarded when they located two people, but the rescuers' hopes came to nothing: Dorris Relph and Edith Briggs were pronounced dead when they were recovered from the wreckage.

A rescue party from Ruddington had been summoned to help in the extrication of eleven people missing in what had been numbers 32 and 34 Loughborough Road. As they were making their way to the incident, they found themselves amid 200 incendiaries that fell around Landmere Lane at Ruddington and they saw a bright flash followed by the sound of an explosion from a bomb that had fallen near to Wheatcroft's. The rescue party arrived unscathed and began work on the partially demolished house. During the night, Mr Blyth was rescued from the kitchen of number 34 and, sadly, he was the last person to be brought out alive.

Casualties from the various incidents were taken to the Church Hall on Stratford Road, which was designated as a first aid post. The cottages opposite were on fire as a result of incendiaries but a quick-thinking warden summoned the fire brigade, who tackled the blaze with urgency. The last thing anyone needed that night was a fire near a first aid post or rest centre. Fires attracted high-explosive bombs and a hit on one of these places would cause catastrophic loss of life.

At Shelford village, nine miles from Nottingham, three air raid wardens had watched the enemy raiders heading for the city for over an hour. The drone of the engines had now grown to a constant roar and through this noise they could hear the church bells ringing in a strange way. It was absolutely forbidden to ring church bells under any circumstances except to warn of an actual enemy invasion.

"The church verger came rushing along and asked what the bells were ringing for. We told him we had no idea but that we would go up the church tower and find out.

We went up the tower and from there we could see the light over the fields from the fires in Nottingham. We realised that the bells were vibrating and making a ringing sound because of the noise of the aircraft; it absolutely filled the air."

Across the fields in the direction of Nottingham an orange and red glow could be seen on the skyline. Just as they had done in other cities, the firemen in Nottingham were now fighting a battle with the flames.

13. The Battle of the Flames

"There is a battle being fought that is just as important for the outcome of the war as any battle of tanks in the Middle East or of ships in the Atlantic. It is the battle against fire and high explosives

I want people to sit up and take notice of the Battle of the Flames as they do the ebb and flow of military conflicts."

Herbert Morrison
Minister of Home Security
24th April 1941

An aerial view of the Old Market Square in 1939 showing where some of the high explosive bombs fell in the city centre

Up at the General Hospital in Nottingham, the fire crew stationed there had watched the raid begin and then develop into a major attack. During the early part of the raid they had seen a stick of bombs go down across the city centre and then, shortly after, others exploded very close by. The Old Moot Hall on Friar Lane was destroyed, Lloyds Bank on Beastmarket Hill was damaged and the road was cratered on Angel Row in front of the Odeon cinema. The bombs that had struck Snook's on Hounds Gate, A. & B. Gibson's food store on Upper Parliament Street and the Masonic Hall on Goldsmith Street had all been in the same stick of bombs dropped from one of the aircraft as it flew low over the city centre. A little further away on Victoria Street, Victoria Stores was struck by a high-explosive bomb and a crater was made in the road. The bomb which struck the Allied Paper Factory on Fletcher Gate had been dropped by the same aircraft.

Left: Site of the Moot Hall, on the corner of Friar Lane: inset plaque on the wall recording the destruction of the building by enemy action: Below the bomb damage in May 1941 (Photograph courtesy of Nottingham Evening Post)

Left: Angel Row in the city centre with the spot where a high explosive bomb fell in front of the Odeon Cinema marked

Above Left: Trivett's Factory well alight on the night of 8th / 9th May 1941. (Photograph courtesy of Nottingham City Fire Brigade archives) Right: The site in 2009

The fire crew at the General Hospital were stationed there principally to provide cover for it. If incendiaries started fires at the hospital the outcome would be disastrous unless they were extinguished quickly. Unfortunately the fire brigade could no longer afford the luxury of a pump and fire crew waiting to put fires out that may not happen. They were receiving so many calls for assistance that many fires were burning unchecked and were destroying manufacturing capacity vital to the war effort. The decision was taken to mobilise the crew to Trivett's factory on Short Hill, where reinforcements were needed, but Sergeant Caunt, the officer in charge of the crew, ordered auxiliary fireman Bob Rose to stay behind. Bob could barely contain his frustration as he watched the city burning and the crew turned out without him.

Sergeant Caunt had ordered Bob to remain behind at the hospital so that he could immediately deal with any incendiaries that fell on it. He wanted an experienced person to be there so that if a fire began to get out of control he would know when it was time to send for assistance. Charlie Caunt knew only too well what had happened to hospitals in other cities during air raids and the frantic struggle to rescue the patients before they were literally burned to death as the building caught light. Bob Rose knew the decision was the correct one, but it was still hard for him to bear.

Thomas Patrick was the caretaker at the Public Assistance Office at number 50 Shakespeare Street. Although he was not on duty on this particular night, he had joined four members of staff who were on fire-watching duty at the premises. When the bomb fell on the Masonic Hall quite early on in the raid, he had arranged for his family to take shelter in the basement of the Public Assistance building. The raid had been in progress for about an hour when he and one of the fire-watchers went to open the front doors. Thomas had decided that he would do this to allow ARP workers to take shelter inside if they wished. It was typical of him to think of other people. As they opened the doors, a 250kg bomb struck the University College Library at the junction of Shakespeare Street and South Sherwood Street; the library was demolished.

Debris and shrapnel peppered the side wall of the Central Fire Station opposite the library as well as the Esplanade Hotel. The blast caused a partial collapse of the Public Assistance building and Thomas Patrick was trapped underneath the debris. His colleague, Samual Boaler, was killed instantly when he was hurled several yards up the street. Patricia Patrick, Thomas's daughter, was aged 15 at the time and she remembered what happened next.

Left: The Public Assistance Office, number 50 Shakespeare Street, in 2009, was badly damaged by a bomb which killed the caretaker, Thomas Patrick Right: Doorway of 50 Shakespeare Street after the raid (Photograph courtesy of *Nottingham Evening Post*)

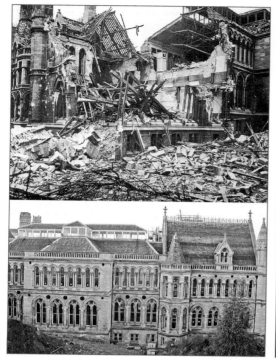

Above left: The building that was the University College Library. It was rebuilt to match the part of the building still standing after a heavy calibre bomb caused its partial destruction.

Above right: The Fire Brigade control room in the basement of Central Fire Station (Photograph courtesy of Nottingham City Fire Brigade archives) When a bomb hit the University College Library the entire fire station shook on its foundations and the control operators thought it would collapse on top of them. Below right: The basement in 2009

Left: The extensive air raid shelter complex beneath the central police and fire station. People were taken into shelter there after bombs had partially demolished buildings on Shakespeare Street. Right: The deeper level of shelters accessed by spiral stairs that can be seen in the centre of the left hand picture

"Mother and me were able to make our own way out of the cellar and the ARP workers helped us from the building. We were taken across the road to the fire station where we were sent down into the deep shelters beneath the station."

The blast from the bomb that had destroyed the library had rocked the fire station on its foundations. Ida Wilson was a Fire Control Room Officer on duty that night and she recollected the moment when the bomb struck.

"The control room was in the basement of the station and was on the side facing the library. It was very frightening as the whole building shook and we did not know what had happened. We weren't sure if the station had been hit or another building. I think we half expected everything to suddenly collapse on to us."

The calls for assistance steadily mounted and the pressure on the resources at the disposal of the control staff grew. The only picture of what was happening was the one that they were able to form in their minds based upon the incident reports that they were plotting on the maps. It was obvious to them that this was the biggest raid on Nottingham so far and it was also obvious that things would get worse before they got better. The fires in and around the Lace Market were spreading rapidly and the water mains had been fractured. Fire crews had to start the lengthy process of setting up water relays from underground water tanks and the emergency water supplies that had been strategically sited for just this eventuality. Other cities had been swept by fire as crews struggled to get adequate water supplies to the fireground quickly enough to do some good. Now the same battle was being waged in Nottingham; men and water against high-explosive and fire bombs: The Battle of the Flames.

Clifford McKenzie was a full-time Auxiliary Fire Service fireman and he was one of those tackling the Allied Paper Factory blaze. The dense smoke from the cigar manufacturers in the same building had finally driven the crew out into the street. Their eyes were streaming and they were coughing and retching, almost unable to breathe. As Clifford and another fireman stumbled about amid the rubble and blinding smoke they were thrown to the ground by the jet reaction from the hose they were holding; then the water supply failed. Clifford picked himself up; his colleague was winded but seemed as if he would be OK, and so Clifford ran towards their pump to find out why the water supply had failed. The hose supplying it was flat, no water was coming in and so Clifford ran in the direction of Pelham Street to try to get another supply for their pump. He met another fireman from a pump crew working down Hockley who was on the same mission as himself. Both men knew each other as they had worked at Boots Printing Works before the war. As they toiled to try to get a water supply for their respective pumps the enemy aircraft were destroying their old place of work.

Boots Island Street works had been hit as well as the printing works and a pump crew on their way to the fires at the railway goods yard were straddled by high-explosive bombs. The Triumph Road crew had just passed Boots Printing Works when it was hit. They continued on, knowing that that other crews would be sent to it and that they were required at the goods yard. As they rounded the corner on to London Road, the rest of the stick of bombs went down across the road, hitting the Great Northern Pub and Boots Island Street works again. Roy Wolfe was a member of the fire crew.

"When the blast from one of the bombs hit us it seemed to suck the breath out of your body. The pressure wave was so strong that it all but stopped the towing vehicle. Smoke filled the road and we couldn't see a thing; gradually it began to clear and we saw this huge crater. It was almost directly underneath the railway bridge.

When we realised that we could not get past the crater in the road we decided to go back the way we had come. It was virtually impossible to reverse with the trailer pump hitched, so we unhitched it and manhandled it into a position so that we could move off again. We knew that we were badly needed at the incident we had been sent to and we just had to find a way of getting through."

Samuel Mitchell was an ARP warden responsible for air raid precautions at the Boots Island Street site and he recounted his experience of what happened during the raid.

"We had received messages that the Boots shop on Wheeler Gate had been damaged by a bomb and also that Boots in Beeston had been struck by a bomb at the main gates.

Then, bombs fell on our site and also on the local gasworks [Eastcroft gasworks]. All around was ablaze and tireless firemen fought with unflagging desperation to save the buildings. We did not know if we could get pumps from the city brigade. It was certain that they were as hard pressed as we were."

Above: The view along the canal looking towards what was the site of Boot's Island Street works. Buildings were well alight all around this area on the night of 8th / 9th May 1941 and fire crews had numerous trailer pumps set into the canal to provide firefighting water

Above left: Damage to the Boot's works by Nottingham Canal (Photograph courtesy of Nottingham Evening Post)

Left: the same view in 2009

The city did respond with pumps and their men joined the Boots AFS crews, desperately trying to save a vital piece of the nation's industry. In Station Street, three men and a lad of sixteen who had been fire-watching at the print works were trapped in the wreckage and there seemed to be little hope for them as the fire burned out of control.

Fire crews were already at full stretch at the railway goods yard and a retained crew from Carlton were at this incident along with city AFS men. Two gasometers received direct hits at the nearby Eastcroft works and provided a spectacular sight as the gas burned off like giant fireworks. A third gas holder was damaged by shrapnel and the escaping gas ignited with a huge whoosh. It blazed furiously, providing a beacon to the enemy bombers stalking across the Nottingham sky. The fireman who was operating a trailer pump which was set into the canal nearby did not like the idea of such a bright and obvious fire being close to him as he felt sure that it would attract some high-explosive bombs before the night was out.

Around 100 incendiaries had fallen on to the gasworks about half an hour before and Percy Hague, a gasworks employee, had gone on to the top of one of the gasometers and kicked three incendiaries off that were burning on the crown. Hague later helped gasworks superintendent Eric Morrison to isolate the plant by closing down valves. Both men's clothing began to smoulder while they were doing this, but they were not badly injured. For his actions during the raid, Hague was awarded the George Medal. Morrison later received an OBE for his part in limiting the damage to the gasworks.

Part of the citation for Percy Hague was as follows:

Above: The Eastcroft gas works off London Road which were badly damaged in the air raid of May 1941. Percy Hague was awarded the George Medal for his bravery in tackling incendiaries at the works; George Morrison was awarded an OBE

"His coolness was without doubt an inspiration to other men and whilst other factories were completely gutted by fire, the gasworks was only put out of action for five weeks due to his courage and leadership in tackling the incendiary bombs and rendering assistance to the superintendent."

On Newark Street, firemen Joe Springthorpe and Fred Shipley were tackling a fire at I. & R. Morley's along with about five other crews. They had managed to get a water supply relayed from the canal via the railway arches but it was a hopeless task. The building was already seriously damaged and the crews were working under the constant threat of the gable end collapsing onto them. Earlier during the raid, Joe Springthorpe's crew had tackled a series of incendiaries on roofs all around London Road, Poplar Street and Lower Parliament Street. They had done a tremendous job of stopping some of the fires from getting a good hold, but could do nothing to stop the 66,000 square feet of cold storage space at the Boots food store being made useless by a high-explosive bomb.

Fireman George Hodson was working with a crew under the directions of Jack Garside and they too had to face the danger of collapsing buildings. They had crossed over the railway sidings and climbed up the embankment to gain access to the rear of a five-storey warehouse in Station Street.

"We went up the external fire escape that gave access to the internal wooden staircase. We were dragging our line of hose up this staircase so that we could tackle the fire on the top floor and the roof. Jack Garside was a very experienced fireman and he suddenly warned us to withdraw as the building was about to collapse. We had just got away when the whole roof caved in. There is no doubt that he saved us."

Just around the corner from the I. & R. Morley's blaze in Newark Street, Edgar Sharp's crew were struggling to contain a fire in Wheldon's factory on Manvers Street.

"We had been turned out originally to the railway sidings, but an AFS officer flagged us down just before we got there. He told us to get a jet to work on Wheldon's factory and that a crew from Beech Avenue [Forest Fields] were setting their pump into the canal to supply us with water. Well, it was just hopeless. We were the only crew firefighting there for most of the night and there was very little we could do on our own. We kept the jet moving to stop other buildings catching light and tried to hold the fire back, but the building was well alight at the other end. Whilst we were doing this, bombs were still falling and one dropped about a hundred yards away from us. We felt the blast from it pushing against us."

Above: A factory well alight in Nottingham during the air raid of 8th / 9th May 1941 (Photograph courtesy of Nottingham City Fire Brigade archives)

Above: The remains of a factory on the corner of Manvers Street and Pennyfoot Street which now looks out of place with empty space to its left and a modern building to its right

Not far down the road from us a pub had been damaged by blast. After we had been firefighting for some time, I went down there to see if I could manage to find anyone who would let us have some cigarettes. I found a family sitting around the fireplace in the back room with all the doors blown off and glass and plaster everywhere. The landlord just looked at me and asked, 'What do you want?' I asked him if they were all alright and could he let us have some cigarettes. He told me just to go and help myself. I went and got a packet from the bar and the family just stayed in the back room staring into space."

The Lace Market situation was deteriorating now and although fire control were mobilising additional pumps as soon as they had crews to man them, there simply were not enough firemen or pumps to go round. Firemen Stan Mitchell's experience was typical of the situation.

"Simon and May's factory on Weekday Cross was on fire from an incendiary bomb but there was no pump or crew available to deal with it. I got some hose and a branch from an appliance and managed to get a hoseline shut down just long enough for me to put a dividing breaching in. Then I started tackling the fire."

From where he was positioned, Stan could see some of the firefighting efforts on buildings further up on High Pavement. The noise was tremendous, as the roar of the fires and the constant reverberating of the

Above: Simon & Mays building on Weekday Cross (centre of picture) where Stan Mitchell tackled a fire alone and prevented it spreading to adjacent property

Above Right: A view along Broadway showing the close proximity of the buildings which allowed fires to spread quickly across the roofs. A conflagration developed in the Lace Market on the night of 8th / 9th May 1941

Right: A building well alight due to enemy action (Photograph courtesy of Nottingham City Fire Brigade archives)

enemy bombers mingled with the engine noise from the fire pumps. Occasionally the sound of firemen shouting instructions or warnings to one another reached his ears, but he had no real idea of how well or how badly things were going for them. He leaned into the jet reaction from the powerful hose he was holding and tried to tuck his head down a little to prevent the water which was streaming down his helmet from running into his eyes. Another fireman dashed past him with a rolled-up length of hose under his arm. He was on a mission that no doubt involved him in replacing a burst length of hose and restoring a precious water supply for a crew somewhere. He disappeared from view into the thick smoke that was filling the street from the Allied Paper factory fire.

"After a while I had the fire under control enough for me to be able to get inside the building. Once inside I was soon able to finish the job off, but it was very awkward manhandling a charged length of hose on your own. I could not get the water shut down and I was soaked to the skin with cold water as I made my way up the staircase. There was broken glass and debris all over the staircase and I thought that if I once lost my footing, the jet reaction would throw me down the stairs and at the very least the hose with its metal branch would give me a battering. [In reality, the power from the jet reaction combined with the metal branch and coupling could have killed Stan if they had hit his head.] It took me about an hour all together to put the fire out and then I managed to get someone to shut my hose line down and I went up towards the Shire Hall. It was obvious that they needed all the help they could get and so I pitched in."

Alf Porkett was part of Sergeant Muir's crew who were hard at work on the roof of a factory on Stoney Street and they were having some success in holding a fire in check that was threatening to link up with one from another building.

"We could see fires all around from up there. Trivett's factory stood out in silhouette against the glow with its roof on fire. Bombs were still falling but the fire and collapsing buildings seemed to be the most imminent danger. You couldn't spend your time worrying whether the next bomb was going to hit you.

The next time I looked across towards Trivett's, the fire had spread to the top floor and I watched each floor catch light until it was just a blazing shell, but there was nothing we could do; we were fully committed with our fire.

When fires started up in other buildings close by, it was sometimes possible to redirect your firefighting jet for a short time to put it out or at least hold it in check until someone else got another jet on to it. But then you would have to go back to the original job. The buildings on both sides of the street were on fire and the heat was scorching. We just had to stick at it. We knew that if we didn't put the fires out they would come back the following night and would find us from the glow. It was a fight for survival; we were in no doubt about that."

The Shire Hall normally had its own civilian full-time fire party of eight whose job it was to man two concrete fire posts on top of the building. This fire party would have been in touch with the County ARP Control Room in the basement. When the raid started two of the party, Bill Johnson and Tim Mears, were sitting on the steps of their office in Kayes Walk. As the incendiaries had started fires in buildings close by, the two men went for their buckets and stirrup pumps and axes. Bill Johnson recounts the events of that night.

"We went to the top floor of the Taxation Office. One of the offices of the Medical Officer was on fire and we just threw the full buckets of water into the room to no avail. Now, of course, we had no buckets. Tim managed to find coal buckets which we had to fill with hot water as the mains supply had failed and after a while we got the fire out. An incendiary had gone through the roof and had penetrated a steel filing cabinet but there was no key. We managed to chop it open with an axe to get at the bomb.

Left: St Mary's on High Pavement. The fire on the roof that threatened the destruction of the church was extinguished by the persistence of Chris Raybould and Reg Miller

Below left: St John's Church it was entirely gutted by fire on 8th / 9th May 1941 which caused despair for Bishop Talbot when he saw it in flames as St Mary's in the Lace Market also began to burn

Below right: St John's in 2009

We went outside and saw that the Education Offices at the rear of the Shire Hall were well alight. Men from the city brigade were trying to axe their way through the main doors of the Shire Hall. I unlocked and then went round and opened the doors from the inside."

The city firemen had been surprised to find the Shire Hall and the adjacent police station locked and apparently abandoned. Chris Raybould was expertly wielding the axe when Bill Johnson arrived with the keys. Only now could the fire crews gain the access required and start to attack the fire from where they wanted to: inside the building. Bishop Talbot approached Bill Johnson and Tim Mears and said: "*Will someone help me save my church?*" [St Mary's on High Pavement]. They took Bishop Talbot to where he could see across Leenside and showed him the fires. They pointed out St John's Church, which was a sheet of flames. In order to satisfy him they went up to the roof of the church and tried to put out the incendiary bomb but had no success. Dr Blandy, the churchwarden, and Roger Donald had already tried to put the fire out with a stirrup pump.

"The bomb had burned through the lead and was inside the roof and we could not get at it. Although smoke was coming out under our feet we could not get at the seat of the fire."

So far, this particular fire was an almost exact rerun of the destruction of Coventry Cathedral that had happened six months earlier. While St Mary's is not a cathedral, it is certainly the largest and best-known church in Nottingham city. Dr Blandy ran up to Reg Miller and Chris Raybould and pleaded with them to save the church. Chris drove the turntable ladder down to the church but had to go the long way around. He could not get past the fire appliances and firemen that were in High Pavement fighting other fires. Lines of hose snaked everywhere. When he arrived at the church he found that siting the turntable ladder would be difficult. The fire was on the St Mary's Gate end of the church, but mainly on the Kayes Walk side. In other words, it was inaccessible to the fire appliance. He sited the turntable ladder in the best position he could and then extended the ladder with Reg Miller at the top of it. Carefully he lowered the ladder in towards the building and Reg began to tackle the fire with the hose reel from the head of the ladder. It was no use: the fire was too deep-seated, and even the hose reel jet would not do the job. Chris brought the ladder down.

Reg was relieved to be down at ground level again as he had felt particularly vulnerable nearly 90 feet in the air with bombs still falling. The two firemen decided that they would have to tackle the fire from inside with a main jet. The only problem was finding some hose and a branch that was not already in use.

They cast around and eventually found a few lengths of hose and a branch. Now all they had to do was find a pump near enough to reach the fire with the hose they had available and with some spare pumping capacity to supply their jet with water. They managed to persuade a pump operator supplying some jets up Stoney Street that he could manage their jet as well. They ran their hose out to the church.

Once inside, they got to work and soon began to improve the situation. Provided the water supply could be maintained and no other fires were started in the church, they were in with a good chance. All around the church, fire ripped through factories and warehouses. A high-explosive bomb screamed down and detonated inside the Lace Market Theatre on St Mary's Gate. Chris and Reg, firefighting inside the church, felt the ground shake from the explosion. They did not know what had been hit, but they knew that the bomb had been very close to them. Meanwhile Bill Johnson had joined some people who were trying to save a few bits and pieces from the Public Assistance Office in Commerce Square.

"The director of Public Assistance was there and he was telling us what to save. He said, 'Could you get the safe out? It is rather important.' So we started rolling it over and over towards the top of the stairs. He said, 'Don't roll it down the stairs; it will spoil the carpet.' As the building was on fire we just let it roll down into the street."

The fires in the Lace Market were on the verge of joining up and becoming one massive inferno. High Pavement, Stoney Street, Pilcher Gate, Broadway, Warser Gate and Fletcher Gate all had major fires. St Mary's Gate and Halifax Place had by this time been declared conflagrations, which was a term used for fires officially out of control. The Poplar district, London Road, Canal Street, Manvers

The site of the theatre on St Mary's Gate in the Lace Market which was destroyed by a direct hit on 9th May 1941

Street, Newark Street and Pennyfoot Street were also all seriously affected. Just as in other cities the odds were becoming overwhelming. It was a battle of firemen, pumps and water against the fires raging across rooftops and linking up to form solid walls of flames. It was becoming increasingly clear that, just as had happened elsewhere, the balance was starting to swing against the firemen. They were being forced back; having to give ground to the enemy, often because they had nothing to fight with when the water supplies failed. Determination on its own was not enough and worse was yet to come.

14. Death in the Moonlight

Elsie Singleton looked towards Nottingham from Ruddington and could see the massive fires that seemed to be flaring up in every direction. She was employed by the Co-op Bakery on Meadow Lane, where her colleagues were still working as the factory ARP wardens had not deemed it necessary for them to go into the shelters yet. By pure chance, Elsie had made arrangements to stay with a friend at Ruddington on this particular night.

As the aircraft droned endlessly towards the city she could hear the muffled crump of the bombs and the thump-thump of the anti-aircraft shells as they exploded. Her thoughts turned to her family in Lenton and she wondered what was happening where they lived; were they all right? The women in the fire control room beneath Central Fire Station were working non-stop, taking calls for assistance and passing messages to and receiving messages from the police and ARP control rooms. Many of the telephone lines had failed by this time and fire crews who needed additional help at the various fires could no longer rely on this means of communication. Group Fire Control Officer Ida Wilson recalled the scene.

Group Fire Control Officer Ida Wilson who was on duty in the control room in the basement of Central Fire Station during the blitz on Nottingham

"After a while firemen started bringing in messages by hand from the fireground as well as dispatch riders arriving. Some of them were bleeding and needed first aid. I remember them being dirty and smoky; some of them looked as if they had been having a bad time of it.

The control girls were very good; there were no outward signs of panic, they just got on with the job in hand, although I think we were all frightened as to whether we would come out of it alive, especially when we saw the state of our firemen coming in from outside."

Roy Sanderson was one of the brigade's dispatch riders and he was blown up by a high-explosive bomb in London Road as he was on his way from Leenside Divisional HQ to the Fire Control at Shakespeare Street with an urgent assistance message.

"High-explosive bombs were raining down all around when I heard a piercing whistle. A black object fell into the gutter about fifteen yards from my motorcycle and exploded with a blinding flash. My steel helmet flew right over an adjacent building."

Roy was partially buried by debris when he regained his senses, but he managed to free himself and his motorbike only to find that it was unusable. His head was still swimming from the explosion and he found that his vision was blurred and the air raid going on all around him seemed muffled. In fact he had burst his eardrums and had sustained concussion, but he made his way back to Leenside and obtained another motorbike. He set off on his journey for the second time and somehow managed to arrive at Central Fire Station, where he delivered the message. Roy was another one of those civil defence workers whose devotion to duty that night was beyond question. He had an urgent assistance message to deliver and a fire crew desperately needed help. To fail to deliver that message to the control room was unthinkable to him; no matter how bad things got.

He looked in a fearful state when he got to the control room and was relieved of his duties on the spot. Control staff gave him first aid and then an ambulance took him to the General Hospital where he was admitted with burns and lacerations to his eyes, mouth, face, wrists, legs, back and chest in addition to his ear injuries and concussion. He was to be detained in hospital for a considerable time while he underwent skin grafts to his face. The Regional ARP Control had now given the order for the decoy fires at Cropwell Butler to be lit. These decoy sites were known by the code name "Starfish" and they were intended to cause the enemy aircraft to drop bombs on the decoy site instead of the actual target.

The site at Cropwell Butler was on the same navigational line as Nottingham and Derby and it is approximately the same distance from Nottingham that Nottingham is from Derby. Number 80 Wing of the RAF had detected the Luftwaffe's navigational beams earlier on during the evening and had succeeded in jamming the Derby one. Why the Nottingham beam could not be jammed as well is unclear. It does, however, pose the question of whether Nottingham was to be sacrificed in order to save Derby and Rolls-Royce. It was now hoped that the fires that could be clearly seen in Nottingham would be thought of as Derby and that those on the starfish site in Cropwell Butler would be thought of as Nottingham. This meant that Derby stood a chance of escaping the raid, but whichever way you look at it, Nottingham was going to get a pounding; either in its own right, or in lieu of Derby.

The attack on Nottingham began to be drawn off to the decoys a little while after the fires were lit, but unfortunately the fires at the Starfish site went out and attempts to contact another site at Barton in Fabis, six miles south-west of Nottingham, were unsuccessful. The next wave of bombers was now approaching the city, some as low as 1,500 feet, and their deadly load of high-explosive bombs fell over the Meadow Lane area and part of West Bridgford. Roseberry Avenue, off Pavilion Road, took a hard blow. Four houses were hit and many others damaged. Charlie Shelton, who lived at number 27, had dashed out to put sand on an incendiary at the bottom of their garden not long after the raid had begun. Hilton's woodyard was there and he reasoned that if it caught light Roseberry Avenue would certainly attract some high-explosive bombs. This was the same woodyard that firemen had managed to prevent from catching light when they halted the spread of fires along Radcliffe Road. As he was going back into his house a 50kg bomb exploded in his garden and left a crater.

The raid continued and Charlie stood on his doorstep and watched the bombers streaming towards the city. His wife, Doris, and the daughter of the Smiths at number 23 were due to take their turn at fire-watching duties that night. Constance Smith went to her front door just as high-explosive bombs hit numbers 23, 25 and 29 Roseberry Avenue.

The explosion was tremendous. It flattened number 29, which was unoccupied at the time, and it ripped apart numbers 23 and 25. Constance Smith was killed in the most appalling manner, she was literally blown to pieces and her mother was critically injured. Kate and Jessie Robinson lived at number 25 with their elderly mother Ida and one of them, Jessie, died when falling masonry broke her neck.

Left: Roseberry Avenue at the back of Nottingham Forest Football Ground where two women were killed and houses were destroyed by a bomb

Right: The tail fin from one of the incendiary bombs that fell into the garden of Charlie Shelton at 27 Roseberry Avenue

Left: Lady Bay Bridge over the River Trent, in 1941 this bridge carried rail traffic and was within the target area for the Luftwaffe's attack. Right: Meadow Grove which was close to Lady Bay Bridge. In 1941 this was a street of houses where Ray Brown sheltered from the bombs in the basement of their house. Nothing remains to show the devastation that was wrought upon the houses and shops here

Charlie Shelton was knocked over by the blast and the windows of his house were sucked out as his greenhouse and a nine-foot-high garden wall disintegrated. Charlie took his wife, two children and father–in–law into the brick-built gents' toilets in Nottingham Forest's football ground. This backed right up to their garden and the wooden fence had now gone so they had no problems getting in. The communal air raid shelter designated for their use had been buried under a pile of debris. Other people were huddled in the toilets too, including the neighbours from number 21, whose house was threatening to collapse. The football ground was littered with incendiaries embedded in the pitch, as was the county cricket ground. Notts County football ground received five high-explosive bombs which silenced the Bofors anti-aircraft gun sited there. One of the bombs damaged the dressing rooms and two others fell on the stands. Charlie Shelton decided to load his family into their car and to drive away from the city to a place of safety.

Eight-year-old Ray Brown was sheltering with his mother Ethel and brothers and sister in the half cellar at their home in Meadow Grove, next to Lady Bay Bridge. The family were frightened as their father, Frank, was not at home; he was on fire-watching duties at the London, Midland & Scottish Railway stables. The bombers seemed to be passing right over the house and when a 1,000kg parachute mine fell on the railway embankment on Meadow Lane, it shook the houses even though it did not explode. The family huddled together, as did many others as the intensity of the raid increased.

A series of loud detonations almost on top of the house were echoed by others across the river. Water thrown from the river by the blast splattered down on to the house even though it was 150 yards away. The stick of bombs that had fallen so close had destroyed five houses and a shop on Freeth Street. A garage on the corner of Holme Street had also been hit, along with an air raid shelter on the corner of Grainger Street and Freeth Street. This was the street shelter that Ray's family would normally have gone to. In the wreckage of the shelter on Freeth Street, five members of the Woolley family lay dying. Although a rescue team managed to locate them and dug them out of the rubble, they all died before they could be taken to hospital.

More incendiaries were dropped and Bitterling's offal yard opposite Ray's house burnt fiercely with all the fat from the animal carcasses. The works canteen was gutted by the fire in no time and flames began to spread to adjoining properties. "Old man Jackson", whose shop had been blasted out of existence on Freeth Street, climbed up on to the top of one of the petrol tanks by the side of the River Trent that had some incendiaries on top of it. They had failed to detonate and burn, but he was taking no chances and he kicked them into the river.

The Railway and General Stores on Meadow Lane received a high-explosive bomb and a fire developed. Boots gas mask factory, a clothing factory and the Co-op Laundry on Daleside Road were all hit,

Above: Freeth Street in 2009. Bitterlings now occupy the site where houses once stood including that of the Wooley family. Bitterlings original factory was burnt out by incendiaries during the May 1941 raid

Left: Freeth Street off Meadow Lane where houses and shops were destroyed and a street air raid shelter took a direct hit. Below: The graves of the Wooley family at Wilford Hill Cemetery. They were all killed in the shelter on Freeth Street

but it was at the Co-op Bakery on Meadow Lane where the largest loss of life in a single incident occurred. The bakery took three direct hits from high-explosive bombs while the night shift were still on the premises.

Fred Kummer and Ernie Knowles were the volunteer fire party for the Co-op bakery and they had received training from the Auxiliary Fire Service so that they could deal with incendiaries that fell on to the factory. They normally occupied a specially built observation shelter on top of the bakery during air raids and the staff at the bakery would go down to the basement shelters if it was thought necessary. Fred recalls that night.

"As things got hotter and nearer we told the night shift to go down to the shelters. Some of the bombs fell in the river. I think they were trying to hit the railway bridge." [Lady Bay Bridge]

Fred and Ernie decided that they ought to go down to the shelter too, owing to the intensity of the raid. They had only been down there a few minutes when one of the Home Guard who was based at the bakery came and told them that there was a fire on top of the confectionery building.

The men were about to leave but Fred paused for a moment to speak to Sammy Theaker, one of the bakery employees. A bomb plunged through the roof of the single-storey building at that moment and was deflected horizontally by the steel reinforcement, which caused it to pierce the floor over the air raid shelter in the cellar. Fred Kummer recalled what happened.

"It hit the floor of the shelter at an angle and skidded along the floor away from me. As it hit the ground it shook the shelter and there was a terrific flash; the blast blew me about three yards. I was up to my waist in bricks and fragments of concrete. The blast had torn away my clothes, leaving me in my pants and socks."

Another bomb had penetrated the east wall of the bread bakery block at ground level by the dough room and exploded, blowing out the retaining walls and supports. The storage rooms on the upper floors, containing tons of flour, all collapsed to ground level. The Co-op dairy and garage had been damaged too and the boot repair factory was well alight. The injured who could be reached quickly were taken to the first aid post adjacent to the factory, but it was soon decided to move them to the air raid shelter in County Road in case the fire attracted more bombs. Around twenty casualties were finally transported to hospital in lorries as there were not enough ambulances available because of other incidents.

The fire brigade were unable to make much impact on the fire at the bakery as the flames were shooting out from the gaps in the rubble like a blowtorch, fed by the fats used in the baking process. The molten fat had become like bubbling larva and a tide line was to remain on the bricks in the cellar two

Above: The site of the Co-op bakery with the River Trent behind it. The largest loss of life in one incident occurred here when two bombs struck the factory, one of which penetrated into the basement air raid shelter and then detonated

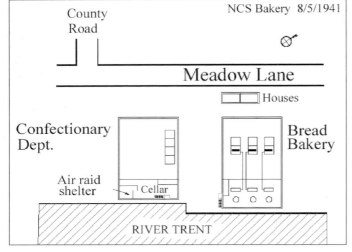

Above: Plan of the Co-op bakery site as it was in 1941

feet deep. The rescue teams faced an impossible job and it seemed unlikely that there would be any more survivors.

Further down Meadow Lane, a fire crew from Corporation Road, St Ann's were tackling a fire at the Government Stores. Their night had been hectic so far: they had started off by tackling incendiary bombs in domestic properties around St Ann's and then they had to turn their hand to putting out fires at their own station.

They were then mobilised to some shops on fire on Lower Parliament Street and from there they had been sent on to the warehouse on Meadow Lane. As they concentrated on the job of extinguishing the fire, they were unaware that an unexploded bomb that had buried itself into the ground was lying right underneath their fire appliance.

At the Nottingham LMS goods yard, 100 wagons and coaches were now on fire and the fire was still spreading. Firemen uncoupled 40 coaches that were not yet affected and helped to shunt them away from the fire. The three-wheeled vehicles that were used to move the goods about were also on fire and their petrol tanks began exploding. The same solution was applied again: they were moved to a place of relative safety. The stables at the goods yard where Ray Brown's father was on duty were being destroyed by fire and one horse was killed by falling masonry although eleven others were led to safety.

The railway goods yard and mainline LMS railway station had received a number of hits from high-explosive bombs earlier during the raid and they had been part of the stick of bombs that had struck the Boots printing works in Station Street. One of the bombs had plunged through the roof of the refreshments room between platforms 1 and 3 but then failed to detonate. The station master, Mr Davies, had to throw himself to the ground because of flying debris from one of the explosions and was lucky not to sustain any injury. A stone's throw away from where massive fires in Newark Street and Manvers Street were illuminating the night sky was Black's factory. This stood on Dakeyne Street at the bottom of Carlton Hill and had a communal air raid shelter in the basement which could hold 200 people.

It is very likely that the bomb aimer saw the fires below him and decided that it was a good moment to release the stick of bombs. The factory received a direct hit and another high-explosive bomb fell at the rear. The casualty list was not as high as it might have been because the shelter was not as crowded as usual on that particular night. The reason for this was that the night before, when the sirens sounded the

Left: Black's factory in Dakeyne Street a bomb penetrated into the basement air raid shelter and then detonated killing 22 people. The fact that many people who normally sheltered there used other shelters on the night it was hit prevented another tragedy of the same magnitude as the Co-op bakery

Below: The hedge in King Edward's Park, Dakeyne Street where the survivors sheltered in terror after the air raid shelter had been hit at Black's Factory

Black's Factory

alert, the shelter warden had not been there to unlock it. This prompted many people to make alternative arrangements on the night the shelter was hit. Fireman Edgar Sharp had been at the Dakeyne Street Boys' Club with his fire engine and crew the night the shelter was locked. The day after the raid, when he heard the shelter had been hit he said, "*I wish to God that the shelter had been locked last night instead of the night before.*"

Florence Hutchinson and her son were among those who did not use the shelter on the night it was bombed and so escaped death or injury. Hettie Callaghan and her seven-month-old baby were there, but escaped death by virtue of the baffle walls built inside the shelter to separate it into sections. It was this foresight in the shelter design that had protected them from the blast.

Tom Raven, an ex-miner who had been crippled in a pit accident years earlier, was killed along with three of his children when the shelter collapsed. One woman lost her husband and children in the explosion and six members of the Denman family all perished together. It was always this way when shelters were hit. Families cling tightly together when frightened or if a crisis threatens and these people were no exception.

Lily Hopkinson was one of the lucky ones who were able to escape. "*I squeezed through a hole in the bricks and was dragged out over the wall by two men.*"

She then went into the King Edward Park and took shelter under the hedge with others who had escaped. Her daughters, Winifred, aged 14 and Joan, aged 13 were still trapped in the wreckage. Joan was rescued alive from

The graves of Alfred and Jane Raven who normally sheltered at Dakeyne Street, but on the night of 8th / 9th May 1941 they stayed at their house in Charnwood Terrace and were killed when it was struck by a bomb. Three generations of their family were wiped out when their son and their grandchildren were killed in the Dakeyne Street shelter

the wreckage but died later that day at St Catherine's First Aid Post. Winifred's body was recovered from the debris the same day. Arthur and Nellie Stevenson and two lads from the boys' club were saved from the blast of the bomb by an extension that had recently been built on to the club.

In Dane Street, St Ann's, a bomb fell onto number 57, killing five-year-old Ramon Marvin and his father Philip. Edith Marvin was on duty as a nurse in Nottingham and when she was notified of the incident, she rushed home to find that the contents of her home had been blasted across the street, with bedding and other belongings hanging from the trees. It would be quite some time before she was able to claim the bodies as they were not intact and a lengthy process had to be gone through to ensure that the correct remains were returned to her for burial. For the firemen who had been firefighting at Liverpool, the sight of their own city burning as they returned was a real blow. From as far away as Macclesfield they could see the glow in the sky, but they could not be sure where it was that was being bombed. Then they thought that it looked like Derby; but in their hearts they knew it was Nottingham. Some of them had been to numerous cities to help with blitz firefighting during the last year, but when they were needed most at home they were miles away and it did not sit well with them.

The crews reported to their home stations and were immediately mobilised to incidents. Some of the crews had not been home for a week or a fortnight and the journey from Liverpool on poor roads in the blackout had taken several hours and had just about finished off the last of their stamina.

Frank Clay was a member of a crew that was sent to the Boots Printing works on Station Street. They set their trailer pump into the canal and began firefighting with the other firemen already there. Bombs were still falling and one landed on the canal bank, blowing up another trailer pump as it did so and dropping it into the canal. The pump operator escaped death by virtue of the odd way that blast sometimes acted. It could leave a person close by virtually unscathed and yet kill someone else further away. The pump operator had a look of complete surprise on his face. One minute he was operating a fire pump; the next there was a flash and a bang and his pump flew up in the air and landed in the canal. It can only be imagined what he said when someone from his crew came along to remonstrate with him because they had lost their firefighting water!

Frank Clay described another high-explosive bomb that fell in Station Street:

"I felt the icy blast cut across my chest like a knife. The blast pushed against you and it was impossible to resist it; it just pushed you back. The fire in the printing works had a good hold and we did not have any hopes of finding the fire-watchers alive that had been in the building when the bomb struck it."

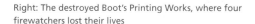

Above Left: The building prior to world war two
Above Right: The site of the Boot's Printing works in 2009

Right: The destroyed Boot's Printing Works, where four firewatchers lost their lives

Vera Anderson, a nurse with the Boots Company, tended to people injured by the bombs that had fallen on the Island Street works and also the printing works on Station Street. She was subsequently awarded the George Medal and the citation in the *London Gazette* read as follows:

"Miss Vera Anderson, Nurse, Nottingham.

Nurse Anderson was on A.R.P. duty in the basement of a building which received a direct hit. H.E. bombs continued to fall on the building and the wreckage caught fire. Nurse Anderson, who was affected by blast from an explosion, fought a way through the flames and got a casualty to safety. The raid was still in progress and she endeavoured to reach the Central Control Room. [Boots] The direct route was made impassable by flames but she made a detour of half a mile and reached there, wet through and covered by dirt, but still carrying her first aid equipment. She attended to a number of casualties but was soon forced to evacuate the post owing to fire. She arranged for the equipment to be moved to a nearby shelter and continued to deal with casualties as they arrived. Nurse Anderson showed great resource and coolness, and her heroic conduct was an example and inspiration to all around her."

Ted Cawthorne was another of the Nottingham firemen who had been tackling the Liverpool blitz for six days and he and the rest of the crew were exhausted. Regardless of this, they were needed desperately in the Lace Market and were mobilised there from Bulwell Fire Station as soon as they arrived. Henry Strickson was a full-time AFS fireman whose crew had arrived back in Nottingham

The site of the Dunlop tyre warehouse that was ablaze throughout the night of the Nottingham blitz

from Hull and they could see massive fires in and around the city. They made their way to Central Fire Station and reported in. They were sent to the Dunlop tyre warehouse which was near the ice stadium. A scene of total destruction met them when they arrived there. The "By Jingo!" pub in front of the ice stadium had received a direct hit and the tyre warehouse had obviously been hit by at least one high-explosive bomb. A fierce fire had broken out and the smoke from the burning rubber was dreadful. The men were choked and blinded by it and it was very difficult to make any progress with the fire.

Edingly Square where shops and a post office once stood. Four people were killed here when an aircraft miles from its intended target area dropped high explosive bombs onto Sherwood

The intensity of the raid was starting to ease off by this time, but to many people it seemed that it was just another lull between waves of aircraft. There appeared to be no reason why they should stop now. Other cities had coped up to this point with their own raids; it was what came after that knocked them to their knees.

Stages one, two and three of the Regional Fire Brigade Assistance Scheme had been implemented, but it would take some time for the pumps to arrive and the hard-pressed firemen did not have time on their side. If another wave of bombers came and started more fires, there would be no chance of holding out; but for the time being they were grimly hanging on.

Across the city and its suburbs, stray bombers had dropped bombs which further stretched the ARP resources. Bombs fell onto 34 Edingley Avenue, killing four people and injuring another. Michael Cousin and his mother had a lucky escape from the bomb, as Michael recalled.

"We lived at 150 Gordon Road, West Bridgford and on the night of the 9th I was with my mother at my aunt and uncle's in Sherwood. They had a grocery shop on the estate. By luck, my father phoned my mother from the phone box at the top of Gordon Road to ensure we were all right. When I heard my father's voice, I started to cry. My father said I would not settle and he came over to Sherwood and took us home.

At 5.15 the next morning the police came over to our house to take my father to Sherwood, telling him that there had been a direct hit with a bomb on the house, which was flattened, and everyone in it had been killed with the exception of his brother."

The bomb had actually hit the party wall between the grocery shop and the Post Office. Four members of the Ley family next door all escaped death as they were in their Anderson shelter at the time. In West Bridgford, AFS crews were still tackling fires involving shops and dwellings in the town. The partially built County Hall on Loughborough Road was burning unchecked, however, set alight earlier in the raid by incendiaries. Grace Webster was an auxiliary nurse at a convalescent home and she remembers how the staff and patients sat dumbstruck, watching the flames dance patterns on the wall as they shone through the windows.

Rescue workers were still digging in the rubble of numbers 32 and 34 Loughborough Road. Of the ten people still trapped, nine would be dead when rescuers found them. The tenth, fifteen year old George Gooch, held on tenaciously to life for a week before slipping away. From the top of a hill at Cotgrave, Charlie Shelton and his family looked back towards Nottingham. It appeared to be encircled by fire, and the orange and red glow lit up plumes of smoke that spiralled skywards. Would there be anything to go back to in the morning?

Above: The point on Loughborough Road where people were trapped amidst the wreckage of their homes

Left: County Hall. West Bridgford which was only partially built in May 1941. It was set on fire by incendiaries and burned all night

15. The Aftermath

At 04:58 hours the all clear sounded in Nottingham and the blackout ended officially thirty-five minutes later. The enemy bombers had carried out raids on the mainland for all but sixteen minutes of the blackout period. There had been 210 hostile aircraft over the country during the night, and 95 of them had bombed Nottingham. Many of the firemen and civil defence workers did not hear the all clear. This was partly because all their attention was directed towards their work and partly because the roar of the fires and the noise from the fire pumps drowned the sirens out.

On Fletcher Gate, Clifford McKenzie told a group of women that had gathered that they ought to go back to their shelter; they told him that the all clear had sounded. For the first time since the alert had been given, some of the civil defence workers and the firemen were able to have a drink. Some of them were scorched, some soaked, others were cut and bleeding; all were dirty and tired. The Salvation Army canteen van on South Parade in the Old Market Square was like an oasis in a desert. A cup of tea and a sandwich were of great value to the morale of the men and women who had worked so hard during the night.

The petty bureaucrats who balked at the cost of providing 600 firemen with a personal water bottle in March 1941 had caused a delay in the issue of these items so that the men did not have them when they were needed. The refusal to approve personal issue water bottles showed beyond doubt that those who sat behind desks during the day and sheltered away from the bombs at night had no concept of what a city was like during a major air raid. The situation was exactly like a battlefield and the firemen and other civil defence workers could not leave their posts to get a drink of water or something to eat any more than a soldier on a battlefield could. The bureaucrats just had no idea what conditions were like and would not listen to those who did know and told them. As the people of Nottingham emerged from their shelters a pall of smoke hung over the city and an acrid smell filled the air. Eleven-year-old Kath Price wondered if she still had a home to go to after such a heavy raid. From The Mounts at the top of Carlton Road, she looked across the city.

"I will never forget the sight of the fires burning and the devastation. But our castle and St Mary's Church were still standing, and you could see the dome of the Council House."

Iris Allsop, who was ten years old, had spent five hours in the basement with her grandmother and younger sister. During the night her grandfather, who was an ARP warden, had put out an incendiary bomb in the attic. From the window of that attic, Iris could see St Christopher's Church on Colwick Road and I. & R. Morley's factory on Manvers Street on fire. Looking towards the River Trent, she could see a red glow in the sky which she was later to discover came from all the buildings on fire on Meadow Lane.

Her house had escaped serious damage, although all the windows had been shattered by blast and there was some burning from an incendiary bomb. It was a great relief when her mother came home from the night shift at the Royal Ordnance Factory. Later on, when she was allowed out, Iris went down to Meadow Lane and saw the rubble that had been a bakery. Smoke still swirled around the fire appliances and ambulances waiting there. Rescue teams had already begun the back-breaking task of tunnelling into the rubble to recover the bodies of those still trapped. During the night, two people had been rescued from the collapsed building, but no one had any illusions about the fate of those still missing. The fire brigade continued to pump water on to the fires that were still issuing from the rubble and rafts were being organised for rescue teams to stand on while they tunnelled into the basement area from the river bank.

The Regional Tunnellers Corps undertook some of this work, working alongside the civil defence

One of the factories on Meadow Lane that was still on fire on the morning of 9th May 1941 providing a dreadful backdrop to the destruction at the Co-operative Bakery

rescue squads. Miners had been recruited into the Tunnellers Corps and fifty men from the Bestwood Associated Collieries had been sent to the Co-op Bakery incident. An agreement had been made in March 1941 that if miners were used for this type of work they would be paid one guinea (£1.1s.0d.) for an eight-hour shift. The only trouble with this arrangement was that the rescue teams who had worked all night, even at the height of the raid, were only being paid £3.3s.0d. for a week's work. The firemen who had laboured to control the massive fires would also receive the same sum for anything between 90 and 120 hours of work. This was crass insensitivity by the local politicians who approved these arrangements, not caring that they were paying one man five times the amount of another man who was working alongside him and doing the same work. Fortunately it did not seem to sour the relationship between the rescue squads, the firemen and the miners.

The fire brigade control staff began to make their way home as the day shift came in to relieve them. Group Fire Control Officer Ida Wilson stood on Mansfield Road and saw for the first time the reality of the information that she had been plotting on a map all night. The streets were empty and had an eerie feeling about them. Everywhere sparkled with broken glass and a massive pall of smoke hung over Nottingham as a testimony to the battle that had been fought against the flames. The only thing she could do now was to go home, try to get some sleep, have something to eat and come back ready to do it all again that night.

The firemen were exhausted, but they now had the fires under control and had stopped them spreading. Some fires had been put out completely, but many others would take all day to extinguish. It was now a simple race against time. The fires must be put out by nightfall, otherwise they would act as a beacon to the bombers that night as they had in other cities. Any fires not extinguished could not be allowed to show any glow that would be visible from the air. Firemen with their pumps and equipment had begun arriving from Birmingham, Wolverhampton and Manchester. Crews from the north of Nottinghamshire had arrived earlier and were already in the process of relieving city crews. During the night 272 pumps had been deployed to combat the fires, but there was no doubt that if the Luftwaffe came back again that night, the number of pumps would probably need to be doubled if the firemen were to stand any chance at all.

The city's emergency committee met on the morning of 9th May and the Deputy ARP controller, Commander Mackness, told the meeting:

". . . there have been a very large number of incidents and both major and minor fires have been caused. The casualties are severe in consequence of direct hits on at least two shelters."

During the night, 424 high-explosive bombs (139 tonnes) had fallen on the city along with 6,804 incendiaries (6.8 tonnes). In this respect the city had been remarkably lucky. Derby, which has also been raided during the night, received only 14.2 tonnes of high-explosive bombs, but 18,432 incendiaries (18.4 tonnes). If Nottingham had received similar numbers of incendiaries along with the 139 tonnes of bombs, large parts of the city centre would have been burnt out. Why the Luftwaffe did not stick to its usual tactics of massive numbers of incendiaries following high-explosive bombs remains a mystery, but the fact that they acted as they did certainly gave Nottingham a chance.

The ARP control logged 211 incidents attended within the five divisions of the city. The Leenside Division reported 148 incidents, of which 72 were fires. The City Division reported 51 incidents, 22 of them being fires. Hyson Green had six incidents which were all caused by high-explosive bombs and Bulwell reported one incident which was a fire. Radford reported five incidents; three of them were fires.

Outside the city boundary, West Bridgford had fared the worst with 37 incidents being reported to their County ARP Control at the Shire Hall. Of these incidents, ten were caused by high-explosive bombs and 27 were fires. Beeston reported twelve high-explosive bombs and Carlton reported six.

Beeston had eleven people killed during the raid and 134 injured, while Carlton reported four fatalities, four people seriously injured and eleven others slightly injured. West Bridgford received 62 high-explosive bombs, which resulted in the deaths of 46 people and injury to 201 others. Many of the casualties in West Bridgford were trapped and ten of the deaths – seven from one family – had occurred in a single incident at 32 Loughborough Road. The city area collectively had 160 people killed and 123 detained in hospitals with injuries. A further 105 people were injured but not detained in hospital. The casualty figures almost certainly do not take into account all the people who received first aid treatment only or those who were treated by family and neighbours. The names of some people who were certainly injured do not appear on any official lists, but there are statistics that show 260 people were dealt with at ten first aid posts.

Doctor Vernon Taylor of the medical service paid special tribute to the nurses at the first aid posts, "*many of whom were, for the first time in their lives, handling wounded persons.*" At one stage during the raid, there was the very real danger that there would not be enough ambulances to move the injured to first aid posts and hospitals. Of the 57 ambulances available across the five city divisions, twelve were in garages undergoing repairs on the night of the raid. Whether this weakening of the civil defence ambulance service led to long delays in reaching injured people has not been recorded in official documents or reports, but this is certainly a possibility and it may have then led to people transporting injured people in unsuitable vehicles, such as the army lorries taking casualties from the Meadow Lane incidents to hospital.

What is stated explicitly in official reports was the waste of resources caused by transporting dead bodies in ambulances to hospitals so that a doctor could certify death. There was also a problem caused by an imbalance in the numbers of casualties being taken to the two main hospitals in Nottingham, i.e. the General Hospital and the City Hospital. The lesson of evenly distributing casualties between two hospitals following the raid on Ransome & Marles in Newark had clearly not been learned by the Nottingham Casualty Service.

Of the 160 killed in the city, 93 were men, 36 women and 31 were children. The list of those injured includes 78 men, 35 women and 10 children. As planned by the civilian director of deaths, the Victoria Baths was drained of water and used as a temporary mortuary for the city's dead. The Co-op Bakery incident had resulted in 50 fatalities and 20 people being injured, while the Dakeyne Street shelter incident had resulted in 21 fatalities; there is no definitive record of the number of others injured at this incident.

A report dealing with the function of civilian services during the raid on Nottingham stated:

"Except for the fact that dead bodies were being taken to first aid posts for doctors to certify them, the arrangements worked satisfactorily."

Of all the information that was gathered together to form this report, the information on the mortuaries and the way bodies were dealt with was the most inaccurate. In fact, to state that the arrangements worked satisfactorily was untrue, and the authors of the report would have known this without any doubt at the time the report was written. Without making any slight against the hard work of individuals working in the mortuaries, the service was simply overwhelmed for between 24 and 48 hours and some dreadful errors were made that caused problems for many months afterwards.

The mortuary attendants had an unenviable job. Very few people saw their work, but many were affected by it. It was a distressing and thoroughly unpleasant task, but despite their best efforts, the mortuary attendants and those associated with dealing with war deaths were inadequately prepared and inadequately supported by the professionals who were leading them.

The city applied for permission to retain 400 soldiers who were in the Nottingham area so that they could assist with clearing debris. Military assistance was given to help with the recovery of bodies for several days after the raid. Most of the work was carried out at the site of the Co-op Bakery, but other places, such as the Boots printing works on Station Street, needed a concerted effort by large numbers of people. The Regional ARP Commissioner, Lord Trent, gave orders that the digging for casualties and the recovery of bodies was to go on 24 hours a day until everyone was accounted for. Housing in and around the city had been badly hit, along with commercial and industrial premises. Queen's Drive in Beeston was blocked and the Queen's Hotel was damaged along with 500 houses. Chilwell Ordnance Depot had been damaged and both gas and water mains in Beeston were severed through bomb damage.

West Bridgford had 34 houses destroyed and 900 others damaged; 69 of them badly. The city area had over 4,500 houses damaged: 200 of them were badly damaged, a further 250 of them were irreparable and 200 had been completely demolished. Thirty-three rest centres had been brought into operation in the city throughout the night, although only six were actually used to accommodate people. West Bridgford opened another three rest centres and both Beeston and Carlton opened one each. All through the night a steady stream of people arrived at the rest centres because they had been bombed or burned out of their homes or shelters. A total of 1,286 people passed through the rest centres and at 08:30 on the morning after the raid, there were still 801 homeless people. By midday, this total had risen again to 958, which was accounted for by some houses being declared unsafe to remain in and other people being displaced from their homes as a result of unexploded bombs.

Families who had relatives in Nottingham were told to go to them for temporary accommodation and those who had no relatives were temporarily billeted in other houses. By 19:30 hours, the two Salvation Army rest centres had closed down, which left just four operating: Blue Bell Hill School, The Bridgeway Hall, Cottesmore School and Leenside School, which between them were still accommodating 217 people. This number increased again on 10th May to 301 as more people were moved to a place of safety due to further unexploded bombs being discovered. During the time that the rest centres were in operation, 4,200 meals were served, mainly by the Woman's Voluntary Service and the Salvation Army.

Arthur Spyby was just one of the hundreds of people rendered homeless by the bombing. When he and his parents emerged from the air raid shelters in the sandstone rock underneath the Loggerheads pub in Cliff Road, the devastation was all around them. Canal Street, London Road and High Pavement all had fires burning and Arthur watched as the firemen staggered about, trying to drag their hoses over debris and bomb craters. High above them, Trivett's factory was still on fire and they were ushered away to the Canal Street Infants' School because of the danger that the factory could collapse into Cliff Road.

Places of worship had received no special favours during the raid. St John's Church on Leenside, The King's Hall Mission on St Ann's Well Road and St Christopher's on Colwick Road in Sneinton had all been burnt out. St Mary's in the Lace Market had escaped destruction by incendiaries, but had sustained serious damage to the roof of the south transept. Lenton Parish Church had been very fortunate in as much as a high-explosive bomb had crashed through the roof, leaving a gaping hole, but had failed to detonate. St Mathias Church, the Congregational Church on St Ann's Well Road, the Unitarian Chapel on Peas Hill Road, the Sacred Heart on Carlton Hill, the Church of Christ on Sherwood Street, the Methodist Church on Shakespeare Street and St Nicholas Church on Walnut Tree Lane (now Maid Marion Way) had all been damaged.

The main road between Nottingham and Grantham (the A52) had been cut by a heavy-calibre bomb blasting a huge crater in it. The Doncaster to Gainsborough railway line had similarly been affected near

Above left: The burnt out Trivett's Factory – one of the buildings where the Battle of the Flames was lost on the night of 8th – 9th May 1941 Right: An aerial view of part of the Lace Market which bears testimony to the desperate struggle against flames and high explosives

Nottingham. A crater 40 feet by 70 feet had been blown in the track and two unexploded parachute mines were on the railway embankment. Eleven other main roads in the city were blocked: Station Street, London Road, Parliament Street, Manvers Street, Woodborough Road, Middleton Boulevard, Abbey Bridge, Castle Boulevard, Victoria Embankment, Meadow Lane and Sneinton Boulevard.

Three out of four gas holders at the Eastcroft depot had been hit by high-explosive bombs and two of them had been totally destroyed. Gas supplies were interrupted to the south and south-east of the city as a result of damage to gas mains. A total of 62 gas main incidents had been reported, 50 of which were within the city area. Electricity supplies were unavailable for days after the raid in some areas due to six electrical substations and two high-tension electrical mains being damaged. A transformer at Commerce House in the city had been damaged by a high-explosive bomb which had cut off the electricity supply. Five businesses that were classed as priority industry were cut off as a result of this damage and as a consequence, electrical engineers began work at once to reinstate the supply. They had almost finished their task when an unexploded bomb was discovered close to this building and work had to stop as the electrical engineers were evacuated for their own safety.

Water mains had also been damaged in 39 separate incidents. One in particular was the 16-inch main between Burton Joyce pumping station and Carlton. This resulted in supplies to that area being completely cut off. Standpipes had to be set up in some areas to provide for 1,000 homes that were without a supply. Warnings went out to householders to boil all water as its purity could not be guaranteed and the water companies increased the chlorine in the water in an attempt to minimise the risk of disease from contaminated water. In com-

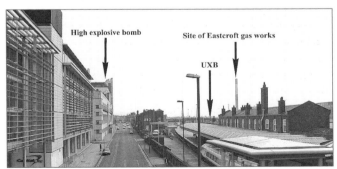

Station Street was completely blocked on the morning of 9th May 1941 and was to remain so for some time due to debris from the collapsed Boots Printing Works and also the presence of an unexploded bomb at the railway station. The site of the Eastcroft Gas Works is also marked on the photograph. The gas works was seriously damaged in the raid

mon with many other cities that had been blitzed, there was the risk that sewage had seeped into cracked water mains. Certainly there had been 19 sewers affected by high-explosive bombs.

The most serious incident involving a sewer was in Freeth Street, where a 5-foot 6-inch foul water sewer had been damaged along a length of 100 feet. Sewage went directly into the River Trent because of the damage. A 6-foot sewer in Parliament Street had been damaged along a length of 60 feet. Further out from the city centre, the 12-inch sewer in Oakdale Road had been damaged along a length of 30 feet and the city engineers estimated that repairs to the sewers would take between six and eight weeks to complete. This posed a serious threat to human health and not the least of this was the increase in the number of rats that had left the sewers and old buildings and were now being seen near to homes and food stores.

The water engineer was certainly not understating the case in terms of the water shortage. Two reservoirs, Belle Vue at Corporation Oaks and the one at Wilford Hill, were completely empty and this in conjunction with the amount of water used for firefighting during the night left the city ten million gallons short of its normal supply. The city water engineer was greatly concerned at the depletion of supplies and he informed the emergency committee on the morning of 9th May that "*An immediate recurrence* [of an air raid] *would be very serious.*"

Immediate steps were taken to try to increase the water available in reservoirs by diverting water through the network into Nottingham. The two empty reservoirs accounted for six million gallons between them. There was no immediate prospect that this shortfall in water supplies would be made up naturally as the winter and spring rains had come and gone and this water shortage came just as warmer weather was arriving and the demand for water would increase. In view of this it was decided to place notices in the papers and also to put up posters warning the public to save water. But meanwhile, the fire brigade had to pump thousands of gallons per minute on to the fires that were still burning.

The fire brigade statistics for the night showed that they had dealt with twelve serious, 40 major, 42 medium and three small fires. However, this is all relative, because even the "small" fires would need one or two main firefighting jets to extinguish them and in peacetime would have been described as "serious". In many cases where one or two crews struggled valiantly to contain a fire, in peacetime there would have been ten crews to tackle the outbreak.

No statistics exist to show how many incendiaries were dealt with by the brigade before they were overwhelmed with calls for assistance and had to restrict their response to only larger outbreaks of fire. Sadly, some homes were burnt out long before the fire brigade could even think of making a response. The firemen had a sick feeling in their gut when they saw rows of houses smouldering the next morning, knowing full well that in normal circumstances they were supposed to stop that kind of thing happening.

The ARP casualty service workers and rescue squads were sickened too; sickened by the horrific injuries sustained by some of the casualties. Some of the bodies they recovered were impossible to identify and they were placed into a coffin with just a number on it. In Roseberry Avenue, West Bridgford, demolition squads were at work on the damaged houses. They discovered a leg on the roof of one of the properties and concluded that it belonged to Constance Smith, who had been blown to pieces. Crews working on the damage at the cricket ground and on the houses on Fox Road discovered the poor girl's head.

The rescue teams had worked heroically through the height of the raid and by 04:30 on 9th May they had already rescued 90 people alive. In contrast to this, the rescue teams working at Loughborough Road in West Bridgford spent most of the day recovering one body after another, but it would take them until Monday afternoon to locate the final victim, William Gooch (69), wedged under the rafters of number 36 where he had been hurled by the blast. At Florence Road in Carlton, the rescuers finally found the remains of the person who had been missing at this incident. The blast had thrown the body into an outbuilding in a neighbouring garden. This was the reality behind newspaper headlines such as:

Above left: A row of cottages with their roofs burnt off. The Fire Brigade would have been so inundated with incidents as the raid developed that they could not attend fires in all domestic properties and had to concentrate on industrial and commercial premises for the good of the "war effort" Above right: Houses on Hound Road in West Bridgford where human body parts were found on the roofs on the morning after the raid

"Sharp raid on Midlands Town. Widespread damage."

Unexploded bombs still posed a threat to the public and during the night, 59 had been reported in the city and a further 41 in the county. The military were responsible for rendering them safe, but the police were in charge of closing off streets to ensure public safety. At 02:30 hours, while the raid was still in progress, Major McCartney of Number 3 Bomb Disposal Company, Royal Engineers, made a reconnaissance of the sites where unexploded bombs were reported. He formulated his plan of action and returned to his headquarters at 04:30 hours. At 09:00 that morning, he went to the London Midland & Scottish Railway Station and gave instructions for his men to recover a bomb that had fallen between platforms one and three. He defused the bomb himself and trains were able to use the station again by 12:30 hours. Major McCartney then went to the Boots Factory at Island Street and asked the fire brigade to pump out the basement so that he could check on the accuracy of a reported unexploded bomb there.

It was at about this time that an unexploded bomb on North Sherwood Street, near its junction with Bluecoat Street, detonated. The crater left by the impact of the bomb had become something of a spectacle and people had gone along to the site to look at it during their dinner hour. The Tomlinson sisters, Eileen (20) and Kathleen (15), who lived just around the corner at 113 Mansfield Road, were going past in the middle of the afternoon when the bomb blew up.

The blast was tremendous and it hurled the girls' bodies some distance. Jabez Johnson (41) of Waverley Terrace was killed, along with Police War Reserve Constable William Alexander. Elizabeth Bestwick (43) from Rosetta Road in Basford was missing after the explosion and her decapitated body was recovered from North Church Street. A further 28 people were injured by this blast and marks from shrapnel remained on a wall opposite for many months afterwards.

In the fire station yard at Shakespeare Street, Fireman Fred Shipley had just got back, having been relieved by an out of Nottingham crew. He heard the explosion up North Sherwood Street and a brick fell into the station yard, thrown there by the blast. Unknown to him, the lives of five more people had just been taken away.

For the ARP workers and the firemen, the daylight hours were running out too quickly. Once darkness fell that evening, the Luftwaffe would in all likelihood return and finish the job they had started. Nottingham's anti-aircraft guns had fired 254 rounds during the air raid but no aircraft had been brought down by them. An RAF night fighter had sighted and damaged a Heinkel He111 west of Nottingham at the height of the raid and another fighter had destroyed a Junkers Ju88 in the Derby area at about twenty-

Above left: The buildings at Nottingham Railway Station that were once part of the London Midland and Scottish Railway. A high explosive bomb fell onto the refreshment room but failed to detonate. The legacy of UXB's after the raid caused disruption to rail traffic and this bomb was one of those prioritised for an early attempt to defuse it Above right: The junction of North Sherwood Street and Bluecoat Street where an unexploded bomb detonated on 9th May 1941 killing and injuring people who treated the incident as a sightseeing opportunity

five past midnight. The RAF and the anti-aircraft gun crews were doing the best they could, but it was not a sufficient deterrent to the raiders.

That evening, William Joyce, infamous for his German propaganda and known by the nickname Lord Haw-Haw, came onto the wireless speaking from Germany. He said that Nottingham had been bombed heavily on the previous night and there had been widespread damage.

The darkness came again all too soon and then a bright full moon rose and reflected off the River Trent. Notting-ham waited for the bombers, but they were late. Midnight passed and then at 00:13 hours the sirens began their rising and falling warning note. Almost twenty-five minutes passed by without any sign of the raiders, but then the sound of aircraft engines were heard. It seemed that this was the lead unit who would mark the city again for the main force of

The graves of two of those killed by the North Sherwood Street bomb. The Tomlinson sisters are not buried side by side at Wilford Hill Cemetery, but are a few graves apart as originally Eileen was unidentified

bombers following. Bob Maslin was back on duty with a fire crew from St Ann's and they were damp-ing down at the Allied Paper Company fire on Fletcher Gate. All this was nothing new to Bob, as he had been in the AFS in London since the beginning of the war and had been transferred to Nottingham at the beginning of May 1941.

The crew looked skyward at the sound of the engines and were surprised to see what appeared to be an RAF Hampden Bomber approaching. In actual fact what they saw was a Dornier Do17 and these Ger-man aircraft with their slim fuselage were often mistaken for our own Hampdens.

Instead of dropping flares, the aircraft at once began to drop high-explosive bombs. If the Royal Ord-nance Factory was their target, then they were close; closer than they had been the night before. Cre-morne Street was hit, including the laundry, and two fires were started. Sarah Proctor, who was 65 years old, and her 30-year-old daughter Maisie, were killed in Wilford Road, while six others were seriously injured. Incendiaries fell in Wilford Road and it seemed that this was the start of another raid. The fire brigade and ARP services sped to the scene.

The aircraft continued to circle around, but no more high-explosive or incendiary bombs were dropped, even though the fires would have been plainly visible form the air. Suddenly the aircraft swooped low and began strafing the fire appliance on its way to the incident. The machine-gun bullets tore lumps out of the road, but none of the fire crew was injured. The aircraft made off and the expected raid did not develop.

If Nottingham had been raided on the same scale as the 8th/9th May attack, a few weeks earlier, it is

The site of where the Co-operative laundry stood on Cremorne Street, The Meadows. This area was attacked during a light raid on 10th May 1941

likely that the Luftwaffe would have made repeat visits with large numbers of bombers as they had with other cities. If the usual pattern of raids had been followed, then the Nottingham we know today would look considerably different. Entire areas of the city would have been burnt out and some of the buildings that we take for granted would have been erased by high explosives. The fact that Nottingham was not raided again on a large scale during May 1941 was due to the fact that Hitler was already fully committed to his plans for Operation Barbarossa, the invasion of Russia, in June 1941. He could no longer spare large numbers of aircraft to pound British cities by air attacks night after night. He could only keep up the impression that he would invade Britain at the end of spring or in the early summer.

The legacy of unexploded bombs in Nottingham continued to cause problems. The Assistant Chief Constable asked the Emergency Committee on the morning of 10th May 1941 if any of the unexploded bombs could be removed to relieve the traffic congestion caused by the diversions. The request seems naïve and showed that the police still had to learn the lesson of how unpredictable unexploded bombs could be, despite the deaths and injuries on North Sherwood Street as a direct result of failing to close the road when it was suspected that an unexploded bomb was in a crater there. In any case, it was Major McCartney and his men who would have to subject themselves to tremendous risk by moving the bombs. The regional ARP Commissioner told the Assistant Chief Constable firmly that this would not be done until the statutory 96 hours had elapsed. Then, and only then, would the remaining bombs be defused.

On the night of 11th May 1941, raiders carried out a small-scale bombing attack on Nottinghamshire and a German news agency claimed that a locomotive workshop in Nottingham had been damaged by direct hits. In actual fact they had bombed Cropwell Butler.

The raid began after midnight with the aircraft approaching from the south. At 00:58 hours incendiaries were dropped between the Barnstone Works and the Barnstone to Langar Road. No damage of any significance was caused and the raiders' track took them over Cropwell Butler. At Grange Farm, Samuel Parkin was woken by the noise and a bright light. He called out to his wife May, "*What do you think you are doing with the light on?*" As he became fully awake he realised that the light was from the large number of incendiaries burning outside the farmhouse. He got dressed and went outside to deal with them, along with other men from the village. His wife and the maid, 15-year-old Barbara Stewart, went outside to help deal with the threat of fire to the farm. Samuel was on the tennis courts near to the house and he was joined by a Land Army girl attached to the farm, 21-year-old Barbara Ward. At 01:15 hours, high-explosive bombs began to fall. Grange Farm was seriously damaged by the thirteen bombs that landed

Grange Farm at Cropwell Butler where May Parkin, Barbara Ward and Barbara Stewart were killed by bombs dropped on 12th May 1941. Did the bomber mistake the cow sheds at the farm for buildings at Langar Aerodrome?

nearby. Houses within a radius of 500 yards sustained damage to windows, roofs and doors. The Nottinghamshire to Derbyshire overhead power lines were brought down, water mains were damaged and the phone lines connecting the farm to Bingham were also brought down.

May Parkin and Barbara Stewart were killed by shrapnel from one of the bombs. Barbara Ward was also killed and Samuel Parkin was injured when the aircraft made a low pass over the farm. June Parker (née Parkin) was six years old at the time but recollects her father telling her that he dropped to the ground and tried to pull Barbara Ward down as well, but she was killed. June's comments raise the question as to whether it was shrapnel from a bomb or whether this was another instance of strafing by a low-flying bomber and that Barbara was perhaps actually killed by machine-gun bullets. Two other men were seriously injured and admitted to hospital for treatment as well as Samuel Parkin. One of the men, Tom Wilson, was the local postman and he lost an arm due to a shrapnel wound.

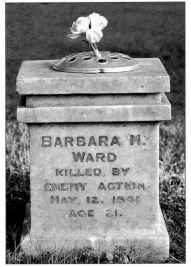

The grave of Barbara Ward in the cemetery at Cropwell Bishop. It is still tended by the villagers

June remembers sitting on the stairs of the house surrounded by glass from shattered windows and knowing that something dreadful had happened. She was eventually to learn that her mother had been killed, leaving June, her brother aged ten and a younger sister aged two to be brought up by her father.

"My father never really got over the death of Mother. We had to move out of the house because the damage was so bad and it was five years before we moved back in again. The fields were littered with craters from the bombs for years afterwards."

May Adelaide Parkin is commemorated on the memorial to the war dead in Tythby Church and Barbara Ward is buried in Cropwell Butler's cemetery.

Death and destruction being visited upon a rural farmstead seems out of place within the Luftwaffe's strategy for bombing mainland Britain, but as described earlier in this book when Laxton was bombed by mistake, bombs could fall anywhere. The bombing of Cropwell Butler is not such a major navigational error as may first appear, as its bearing and distance from Nottingham mean that navigators can conclude that Nottingham is actually Derby and therefore that the area around Cropwell Butler is Nottingham. The fact that Cropwell Butler was designated as a "Starfish Site" for decoy fires during air raids in order to fool Luftwaffe crews demonstrates that there was always the potential for bombs to fall here. June Parker also made an interesting comment about the dairy farming at Grange Farm and the fact that there were several large sheds in which the cows were kept for milking. From the air, these may have looked like aircraft hangars and the farm was perhaps mistaken for part of the nearby airfield, RAF Langar.

The two-hour visit to Nottinghamshire by the Luftwaffe on the night of 11th/12th May had been carried out with no difficulty on their part and now they felt bold enough to pay a daytime visit. At 14:20 hours on 14th May, raiders made a low-level bombing run on the Royal Ordnance Factory in a similar fashion to the raid carried out on Ransom and Marles in Newark two months previously. High-explosive bombs fell between Clifton Colliery and the gun factory and three more bombs fell inside the factory boundary. The roof of the factory was damaged but production was not disrupted. The roof was covered with tarpaulin sheets by the fire brigade so that production could continue at night during the blackout. Eight people were injured at the factory and five of them were serious enough to be admitted to hospital.

High-explosive bombs also fell on the railway leading to Wilford Power Station and the line leading to Clifton Colliery. Twenty yards of the power station's railway line and thirty yards of track belonging to the pit were destroyed. In daring fashion, one of the aircraft descended to low level in order to strafe city streets. Bill Stevenson worked on London Road at the time at a tyre distributors and he recalled seeing a Heinkel He111, with a large black cross on the fuselage, swoop over London Road at an altitude of no more than 500 feet. It headed down Station Street and then began firing its machine guns and continued to strafe vehicles and pedestrians in Canal Street. This audacious attack was reminiscent of what had occurred in West Bridgford a few months before.

During the day, another unexploded bomb was discovered at Boots' Island Street works, near London Road, a further legacy from the 8th/9th May raid. It was ascertained that it had been fitted with a long-delay fuse. Major McCartney inspected the bomb the next day and decided to leave it until the 19th.

The work of making the city safe continued on and on 18th May another unexploded bomb was discovered in the Cattle Market. Major McCartney was able to render it safe by "*sterilising*" it with a fire hose. This process involved using the high-pressure water to wash the main explosive charge out of the steel casing of the bomb. Later that night, another unexploded bomb at Colwick, that was lying adjacent to a bridge, exploded. It damaged the bridge and nearby houses and brought down telephone lines. An unexploded bomb near the railway bridge on Sneinton Dale detonated but there were no casualties because of the precautions taken by Major McCartney, who had insisted upon an evacuation of the area. The detonation of these two latest bombs served to fully vindicate the approach of Major McCartney and the ARP Commissioner in not giving in to pressure from the police to remove unexploded bombs purely on the grounds that they were disrupting traffic flow.

On 19th May, work began on the unexploded bomb still in the basement of the Boots warehouse and when Lieutenant Dunnet placed his stethoscope on the device, he realised that the long-delay fuse had begun ticking. Major McCartney had the area evacuated and arranged for the fire brigade to be called. Once he was satisfied with all the arrangements, the bomb was detonated. A serious fire resulted from this explosion and while the brigade was extinguishing it, another detonation was heard, indicating that an unexploded bomb that no one had been aware of had also been set off.

The aftermath of the 8th/9th May raid was still causing problems for the people of Nottingham, even though they were working hard to get the city back to normal. Essential as this work was, people briefly directed their attention towards burying their dead and the need to grieve the loss of their loved ones.

16. Resting in Peace?

Top: Wilford Church viewed from across the River Trent close to the site of the Wilford Power Station which was one of the targets for the Luftwaffe Middle: The graves of the Gooch family at Wilford Church

A row of graves provided by Nottingham City Council for those killed in the air raid on 8th / 9th May 1941. Right The grave of one of the unidentified victims

Wednesday 14th May was the day that most of the victims of the air raid were buried. Some of the West Bridgford victims, including seven members of the Gooch family, were interred at Wilford Church, by the River Trent. Across the river stood the power station and the gun factory that the Luftwaffe had attacked. Rumours were rife that one of the funeral processions was machine gunned by an enemy aircraft at Wilford. Forty of the Nottingham victims were buried in graves at Wilford Hill Cemetery, and each one had a headstone erected with their name on it. Even those who were unrecognisable had a stone, but theirs had the sad epitaph: "*Unidentified*".

Bishop Talbot conducted the Church of England service and Bishop McNulty conducted it on behalf of the Roman Catholics. The Methodists and Congregationalists were represented by Revd Davison-Brown and Dr Henderson.

The mass funeral was a sad scene as over 100 relatives grouped together to pay their last respects to loved ones who had been wrenched from them so brutally. Civic representatives attended the funeral along with representatives from the ARP services, the fire brigade and the police. The business of recovering bodies and human remains had been particularly unpleasant and at times had been beset by difficulties that should have been foreseen by those charged with the responsibility of putting in place adequate arrangements to deal with people killed during major air raids.

The length of time taken to recover some of the bodies and the human remains was not due to a lack of hard work on the part of the rescue parties, but when those remains were eventually recovered, they could not be dealt with in the same manner as those recovered within a few hours of death occurring. A confidential report from the department of civilian deaths commented upon the problems encountered.

> *"The first body was received at one of the mortuaries at 03:00 on 9th May and the 133rd body at 14:30 on 19th May. By this time the bodies were in such a fetid condition that it was considered impossible to accept further numbers to the mortuary."*

The largest loss of life at one incident was at the Co-op Bakery and as bodies were still being recovered from there, a mortuary superintendent was sent to the site. From 19th May onwards, he recorded the details of those recovered from the site and the bodies were placed directly into coffins for removal to the burial ground.

A key failure of the system for dealing with the air raid deaths was the lack of segregation of those identified from those unidentified. This issue alone led to some of the worst examples of bureaucracy for people trying to find out what had happened to their relatives. There was a lack of sensitivity in the process of identification that only served to compound people's grief. Examples of this at the Victoria Baths, which were used as a temporary mortuary, are typical of what happened at the time.

Interviewing relatives and claiming personal effects were carried out in the reception office of the building, which was not private, and this was a difficulty that was foreseeable and should have been planned for. Relatives who came to the mortuary were kept in a waiting room which was actually part of the room that was being used to store the personal effects of those who had died. If this was not bad enough, they then had to view their dead relative in a passageway that led from the mortuary. There is no escaping the fact that this was shoddy treatment of Nottingham's citizens; they deserved better.

The recovery of bodies continued and at the Boots printing works, the rescue squads recovered the last body from the debris. It was that of young Derek Needham and he had been missing for five days. The day he was found would have been his seventeenth birthday.

The remains of those extricated from the debris of the Co-op Bakery were placed

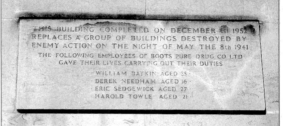

Above: Wreckage of the Boot's Printing works. Due to the amount of destruction and subsequent fire, it took some time to recover all the bodies of those killed. Inset: Memorial to the four fire watchers killed, which is still on the front wall of the building (Photograph courtesy of Nottingham City Fire Brigade archives)

Left: Grave of Frederick Bourne at Wilford Hill Cemetery. He was originally buried as unidentified

into coffins but no one could be sure in every case that the right remains were in the right coffins. Alfred Bourne recalled some very sad memories of the aftermath of the raid.

"I was a private in the Royal Army Medical Corps and was stationed in County Durham. I was told that there had been a heavy raid on Nottingham and it was feared that my father was one of the victims. I was given immediate compassionate leave to return home.

I spent a fortnight going to the Co-op Bakery every day. There were no lives for the rescue workers to save; all they could do was to move the masses of rubble. The gruesomeness of that scene is beyond my powers to depict and there was also the inevitable stench that is always present where bodies have lain for any time.

One morning I was told that my father's body had been found. I was sent to the Victoria Baths which was being used as a mortuary. Then I was told that there had been a mix-up; he had not died at the bombing, but died later of his burns. He had already been buried at Wilford Hill as an unknown casualty. We eventually established which was his grave."

The account of how Frederick Bourne was eventually identified and his family notified of his burial was not an isolated incident. Several families were to undergo additional heartache even after they knew that their loved one had died. In a letter to the Coroner dated 30th May 1941, the director of Civilian War deaths stated the following:

"I would inform you that there is now very little prospect of recovering further bodies from the wreckage of the Nottingham Co-operative Society's bakery and that the total number of records made by this department in respect of persons extricated from that site is fifty, thirty of which are identified at this date, the identity of the remaining twenty not being established."

Left: Memorial to the 49 employees killed by the bombing of the Meadow Lane Bakery. Erected by the Co-operative Society

Below Left: The memorial plaque that was originally on the wall of Co-operative Society premises; now fixed to the memorial in Wilford Hill Cemetery

Below Right: Casualty identification form. One of these should have been filled in for each fatal casualty to ensure correct identification

The letter went on to explain that an apparent discrepancy in figures between the list of identified persons and those missing was due to portions of bodies which could not at that stage be accounted for as one person or another and therefore two or more records may be connected to one person only.

The unidentified people were mainly those numbered 150 to 173 as these people had been extricated from the rubble much later than the other bodies and *"were often in such a condition that that it was impossible for the rescue or civilian deaths staff to obtain as many details as normal from them."*

On 4th June 1941 the Director of Civilian Deaths sent another letter to the Coroner with an attached list of the names of 16 men who had been buried as unidentified, but whose identities had now been established. Among the names was Frederick Bourne, aged 59, who had lived at 137 Pym Street in Nottingham. He had been buried in grave G30-1 at the Southern Cemetery (Wilford Hill).

The means by which these men were identified was the contents of a bag which bore the same number that their body had been labelled with. The bag contained items taken from the deceased person's body and it was hoped that this would enable people to make a positive identification.

Examples of the statements of identification which were based upon the items in the bags included the following:

"A leather jacket, cigarette lighter, a photograph in a locket, contribution cards, a spanner which was in my husband's possession on 8th/9th May 1941."

This was considered to be a good identification, but in most cases it was much more tenuous:

"There was part of a brown overall identified as similar to that worn by my husband."

"I recognised parts of clothing and a knife as the property my husband had in his possession on 8th/9th May 1941."

"I identified a portion of a green pullover."

"I was shown a shirt as being similar material and colour to that worn by my husband."

"I saw a shoe and a shirt that I had seen my husband wearing when he went to work on 8th May 1941."

But flimsiest of all in this list of items, through which people desperately tried to identify family members, was that which was in bag 170:

"A sock which I have identified as the property of my husband."

It does not get much sadder than this.

On 6th June 1941, the Director of Civilian Deaths had to report that two bodies buried as unidentified had now had their identities established. They were Joseph Peach of Bradfield Road, and Samuel Theaker of Fenwick Road in Broxtowe. Both men had been buried in the mass grave at the Southern Cemetery at the expense of the Nottingham Co-operative Society. One of the workers at the Co-op bakery who had been reported missing gave the authorities a real headache in trying to establish what had happened to him. His name was Joseph William Conner and he was a commercial traveller who had lived in London with his wife until the outbreak of war in 1939. In 1940 he moved to lodgings at 18 Carlisle Road in Nottingham with his wife and children and worked in the NAAFI canteen in Carlton.

In April 1941 he lost his job due to irregularities with the accounts he was in charge of. Joseph and his wife Violet, argued over this and there was much ill feeling as Conner was out of work for some weeks. He was absent from home on the night of 6th May 1941 and when he did return he said he had found a job doing night work at the bakery. He was absent on the night of 7th May and went to work as usual on 8th May. When he did not return home on 9th May, Violet Conner did not try to find him.

She eventually went to the police station at the Shire Hall on Monday 12th May, where she claims that the police told her that they could *"do nothing to help her trace her husband"*. The police claimed that Mrs

Conner gave them the impression that her husband had deserted her and that she wanted him traced for other reasons. They claimed that she did not report him as being possibly killed.

The two sides of the story leave a lot to be desired. If Violet Conner had wanted to find out whether her husband had been killed or injured in the air raid, she would have had no difficulty in doing so through the casualty lists which were widely available. Similarly, the police could easily have checked for Conner's name on those same lists and in fact it would have been advantageous to them to have done so as any information that helped reduce the numbers of those unidentified should have been welcome. Suffice it to say that neither party gave the matter their best attention.

A body that had been recovered from the Co-op bakery site at 20:30 hours on Friday 9th May was listed as number 118 and the next day was identified by Mrs Culley senior, who identified the body as that of her son, William. The body was placed into a coffin and transported to the undertakers. Two days later, Mrs Culley had second thoughts about this and said that she was wrong in her identification. She viewed the body again with another relative and said that it was not the body of her son. Nonetheless, the body was buried as William Culley and the identification form was signed by his wife, Lilley Culley. Lilley was later to state that she had signed the form without realising what it was and without seeing her husband's body. A few days later the body of the real William Culley was found in the rubble of the bakery and this presented a problem because the body in the coffin with his name on it that lay under six feet of earth in a Carlton cemetery was now unidentified and would have to be assigned a number again.

Mrs Culley had to apply to the Home Office to have the body in the family grave exhumed and this took some time. It was not until 25th June that permission was granted and by this time the Co-operative Society had provided a list of all the people who were on their premises at the time of the air raid. Joseph Conner's name was not on the list and that put paid to ideas that anyone had about it being a simple mix-up and that Conner was in Culley's coffin When body number 118 was exhumed from the Culley family grave, it was in no fit state to be identified visually and so other methods were sought. In those days before DNA identification, real difficulties surrounded attempts at identifying decomposing bodies.

Inside the coffin, officials were surprised and disconcerted to find some items of clothing. A report dealing with the investigation into identifying this body stated:

"The instructions given to those in charge of mortuaries were definite and precise, that no items of clothing or personal belongings should be buried with a body."

Two pairs of running shorts, a pair of trousers, a belt and a pair of braces were in the coffin and immediately a problem presented itself. If it was supposed that the deceased man was wearing a pair of running shorts under his trousers as underwear, what would he need two pairs for? The belt and pair of braces could be explained, as some men did wear both at the same time, but the pieces of clothing do lead to a suspicion that the items were from more than one body. Such carelessness on the part of the mortuary staff was inexcusable as their instructions were strict and inflexible on this matter. All items of clothing and personal belongings should have been placed into a bag and labelled with the same number as the body from which they had been taken. It is very easy in this case to conjure up a picture of mortuary staff discovering clothing that they could no longer account for and, rather than bag it and then be unable to give it a number, they simply disposed of it in a coffin and then put the lid on. Who would ever know?

The trousers were an item that had a story to tell as both legs were torn off, the right one above the thigh and the left one below the knee. This was a boon to those trying to establish the identity of the body as it had its left leg missing below the knee and the right leg missing above the thigh. It seemed fairly safe to say that the trousers belonged to that body.

The trousers were shown to Violet Conner, as she had described the clothing her husband had been wearing and it seemed that the material and pattern were similar. She had described his suit trousers as being "*a distinctive brown material with a red stripe*". Mrs Conner identified the trousers as belonging to her husband, but stated that the running shorts did not belong to him as he had been wearing a pair of long army pants. How much reliance can be placed upon Violet Conner's identification of a pair of torn trousers is debatable, but the fact remains that the damage to them matched the injuries on the body in the coffin and that the body was, as it would turn out, probably not that of Joseph Conner.

Mrs Conner said that her husband always carried his National Registration Card in his hip pocket but no card was found in the trouser pockets. In fact nothing at all was found in the pockets, which suggested that the items had been removed. The question was whether they had been bagged and, if so, what number bag they were in, or whether they had been disposed of in another coffin as loose items. No identity card for Joseph Conner was found at the mortuary and no personal item identifiable as belonging to him turned up either. Officials were very concerned that the identity card was not found anywhere. The discovery of such an important item would surely have been dealt with in a proper manner by mortuary staff. Nonetheless, it was never found.

The question as to whether body number 118 was Joseph Conner was answered beyond doubt by a reliable method of identification that was established before DNA testing – a person's teeth. It was known that Joseph Conner had an upper denture, but the body removed from the coffin had a full set of natural teeth and therefore it could not be Conner. The Culleys buried William in their family grave, but body number 118 remained unidentified and Joseph Conner remained missing.

The investigation to find Joseph Conner took on a different aspect altogether when the police decided to investigate Joseph Conner's ration card. In a report to the Coroner, Mr Rothera, it was stated that Conner's ration book had not been used since 8th February 1941 and in fact Joseph and Lilley's ration books had been reported missing. On 10th February, two new ration books were issued from the Carlton Food Office at a cost of two shillings, and five coupons in the book were cut out by the food office as the date for its first use was 7th January 1941. Joseph Conner's book was still in this state when examined by police, which meant that in effect Conner had not used a ration book since 8th February 1941. One of two conclusions could be drawn from this: either Conner had been dead since around 8th February and therefore had not used his ration book, or the original book was still in existence and was being used. The police had to find information to show one way or another whether Conner had been alive after 8th February 1941.

The clocking-in cards of all the employees at the Co-operative bakery were gathered together and one of them had the name Dolby on it. Over this had been written the name Conner, but the card was dated 8th March 1941. This did not tally with what Violet Conner had told police about her husband starting work at the bakery on 6th May 1941. Eventually it was established from pay records that Joseph Conner had been employed by the bakery and that he was owed £1.14s.7d. for two nights' work, i.e. 6th and 7th May. They were making some progress at last.

A foreman at the bakery, Mr Church, made a statement that he had seen Conner at the bakery on the night of 8th May and had in fact seen him go down the ladder into the basement shelter during the air raid. He described the clothing he was wearing as being a dark brown suit. He was shown a photograph of Joseph Conner which had been taken some years before. In the photograph he was wearing white flannel trousers with turn-ups, white tennis shoes, a grey sports jacket with a white handkerchief in the pocket and a white shirt with a tie. Conner appeared to be around 5' 8" or 5' 9" and had dark hair with a centre parting. The foreman identified the man he saw in the picture as being the person whom he knew as Joseph Conner. Mr Church said in his statement that he had seen Joseph Conner in the basement air raid shelter during the raid and that Conner was watching four men playing cards. Based upon this it was concluded that Conner was at the bakery on the night of 8th/9th May, that he went into the basement air raid shelter and that he was there when the bomb struck the bakery and exploded in the shelter.

The coroner accepted that the trousers in the coffin had in fact belonged to Conner and therefore his body had been at the mortuary. He went on to comment:

"... the difficulty in this particular case is due to a number of bodies never having been recovered. I have had an investigation and have been satisfied that some of them were blown to pieces. If I accept my deductions as being correct, up to the present every person has been accounted for by a body or by a verdict by myself that the body has had a direct hit.

I am satisfied taking all the evidence together and explanations as to cards and ration books etcetera, that Conner was upon the premises, that he was in the shelter when it was hit and that he is in fact killed. I therefore record a verdict that his death is due to war operations.

The body [number 118] is not a stranger of whom we have not yet heard, but it is someone already reported missing and someone has already claimed Conner's body and had it buried.

The authorities will in future take a great deal more care in how they accept the question of identification from little bits of clothing or body or some remains which never ought to have been viewed at all."

The Co-operative Society had a commemorative plaque to their employees who lost their lives at the bakery fixed to the wall of their premises. This was subsequently removed and affixed to the memorial in the cemetery at Wilford Hill, where it remains to this day.

Rescue squads were often able to identify people at the scene of operations as surviving relatives were there, or in some cases neighbours gave information that allowed positive identification. Even during the raid itself, when surrounded by the physical dangers of fires and bombs falling, the rescue workers diligently recorded this information and it would seem a simple matter to then ensure the continuity of that information at the mortuary. Sadly, there were some gross examples of where this failed.

Among those killed at the air raid shelter incident in Dakeyne Street were three members of the Widdowson family: the mother, Lavinia (25) and her two children, Christina (6) and Dennis (2). A statement made by Lavinia's brother, Edwin Powell, describes the circumstances of their identification.

"I am the uncle of Dennis Baden Widdowson. I heard that the Dakeyne Street air raid shelter had been hit and I knew that my mother, sister and members of the family sheltered there. I went to the shelter whilst bodies were being extricated. At about 5 a.m. I saw my sister Lavinia May and her son Dennis Baden, lying on the pavement in Dakeyne Street. I gave their names to the ARP rescue party and saw them make out cards and tie them to the clothing. I asked where they would be taken and the rescue party told me that they would go 'to the baths' [Victoria Baths, temporary mortuary]. I visited there on Sunday 11th May 1941 and again saw the body of Lavinia but there was no trace of Dennis."

A statement from Mary Johnson of 58 Walker Street provided vital information as to what had happened after the bodies had arrived at the mortuary.

"I was in the Dakeyne Street shelter on the 8th May. Mrs Widdowson with her two children Dennis and Christina were on one bunk when the roof fell in.

At 8 a.m. on 9th May I went to the Victoria Baths for the purpose of identifying my two children. I identified my boy, Roy, but did not see my daughter. A body was brought to me to identify as my daughter. I recognised the child as Dennis Widdowson. I told the officials that this was Mrs Widdowson's baby. At 11 a.m. the boy Dennis was again shown to me for my little girl. I told the attendant it was Mrs Widdowson's son. At 3 p.m. it was again brought to me and I again told the attendant who it was and that it was a boy, which he confirmed.

I saw the body once more when it was brought to my sister to identify as her little girl. This was about 5 p.m."

It beggars belief that these two women were at the mortuary for nine hours trying to identify their children and that they were not only repeatedly shown the wrong children, but that it was the same child over and over again. This was incompetence of the worst kind. When considering the two statements made regarding Dennis Widdowson, it is clear that it was known who he was at the incident and that at some point he was separated from his mother, most likely at the mortuary. It is known that the dead were stripped of all clothing and personal belongings at the mortuary and we can conclude that Lavinia Widdowson's clothing and belongings were properly bagged, labelled and that her body had a label attached to it because she was brought out and identified by her brother on 11ᵗʰ May. By inference, we can conclude that Dennis had no means of identification upon him and that once his clothing had been removed and with it the label bearing his name, he became just one of 26 under-14–year-olds who had died.

Wilfred Rothera, Coroner for Nottingham 1934 – 1951. He presided over the inquests into all the victims of bombing in Nottingham (Photograph courtesy of HM Coroner for Nottinghamshire)

Presenting the child to the wrong family for identification was unfortunate, but to do so three times to the same woman and then again later on to another woman was inexcusable. The child was identified the first time it was presented and a label should have been attached at that point and the child's uncle sent for to confirm the identification. The other unbelievable aspect of this mix-up was that the mortuary staff presented this child incorrectly four times as a girl instead of a boy. While some of this can be understood, as the bodies were covered with a sheet and only the head was visible, mortuary staff could easily have labelled Dennis as an "unidentified male". At least this would have narrowed down the number of options as to who he could have been. How difficult can it be for mortuary staff to segregate children by gender?

As the bodies of children were claimed by families and buried, the Widdowson family were still unable to find out where Dennis was. On 10ᵗʰ August 1941, Private Archie Widdowson, Dennis's father, who was serving in the Sherwood Foresters Regiment, wrote from Burgh Le Marsh, near Skegness, to enquire about his son. The reply was curt and merely passed him on to another department.

"I very much regret to inform you that at the present I have no news which will help you, but that the city coroner is dealing with the question of missing relatives.

W.J. Ayres
Director of Civilian War Deaths."

Three days later, a further letter was sent to Archie Widdowson and gave a more detailed and satisfactory response to his enquiry.

". . . I beg to inform you that the position respecting your child Dennis is as follows:

As you are aware, the body of Harold Denman was, by some mistake, not buried with the remainder of the family and yet the correct number of coffins were in their grave at the southern cemetery, Wilford Hill.

The general opinion is that a boy named Eric Cousins had been buried in the Denman grave and your child in the Cousins grave, as they too had the correct number of coffins, but one was described by neighbours as being too small to hold the body of Eric Cousins. When it was afterwards discovered that your child was missing it was thought Dennis was in that coffin."

On 26th June 1941 the coffin with the plate Harold Denman was exhumed and the body inside identified as Arthur Denman and not as Eric Cousins as had been expected. As a result of this, a further exhumation was carried out on 29th July 1941 of the coffin with the plate Arthur Denman on it. Upon examination of the body, it was almost certain that it was Eric Cousins, but the body was in such an advanced state of decomposition that it was impossible to say definitely. The coffin was re-buried in an "unidentified" grave. The Cousins family expressed their wish to the Department of Civilian Deaths that their family grave should not be disturbed unless absolutely necessary. Two choices were presented to the Widdowson family.

"(i) Allow the coroner to presume the death of Dennis on the basis of evidence that he had been taken to the central mortuary. On that basis a death certificate could be issued. (ii) Apply to the Home Office to have the "small" coffin in the Cousins family grave exhumed as due to its size this was believed to contain the body of Dennis."

A postscript was added to the letter to Mr Widdowson:

"Should permission be obtained from the Home Office to exhume the body it will be necessary for a member of the family to attend to identify the body. Will you please let H.M. Coroner know who that person will be?"

This was bureaucracy at its worst again. Firstly Mr Widdowson must have been emotionally exhausted by the end of July and the authorities should have taken control of the process of establishing where his child was. After all, it was their incompetence that had led to his being buried in the wrong grave.

Secondly, the postscript to the letter seems like an attempt to put him off applying for an exhumation order, knowing that if he did so, he would be faced with the task of viewing the decomposed body of his young son in an attempt to identify it. The authorities knew that visual identification would be impossible because they had failed in this regard themselves when trying to identify Eric Cousins some three weeks earlier. What chance would Mr Widdowson stand in another three or four weeks? On 23rd December 1941, the inquest into the death of Dennis Widdowson was held. The coroner, Mr W.S. Rothera, said:

"I have no hesitation in saying that the body of this child was wrongly buried. I therefore return a verdict that Dennis Baden Widdowson was killed by enemy action in May."

Above left: Grave of the Denman family at Wilford Hill Cemetery where Harold and Arthur were finally properly laid to rest
Right: The Cousins' family grave. After being interred incorrectly in the Denman's grave and then as an unidentified victim, Eric Cousins was finally laid to rest in this plot at Wilford Hill Cemetery, his mother and father are also now in the same grave

Councillor Twells represented the Widdowson family at the inquest and informed the coroner that the family wanted an exhumation of the body they believed to be Dennis Widdowson. The coroner replied that under section 30a of the Defence Regulations 1939, his duty was only to record that the child was in fact dead so that the registrar could issue a death certificate. The coroner then reiterated his point: "*I am satisfied that the body of this child has been buried as some other person.*"

Councilor Twells pressed the issue of incorrect identification, raising the point that bodies were supposed to be photographed and a disc attached to them at the mortuary. The coroner replied that he was aware of the procedure but was not prepared to say that it had been followed. Perhaps he was not in a position to say for certain whether it had been or not, but someone was and that someone should have been the Director of Civilian Deaths. Why did the coroner not call him to court and put the question directly to him, as it did have a bearing on conclusions that were being drawn about Dennis Widdowson. It is all very well saying that he was satisfied that the child had been buried as someone else, but he could have been far more helpful in establishing where Dennis was. The coroner went on to say:

"In a sudden raid it is quite likely that arrangements made beforehand just fell down."

Councillor Twells was exasperated and stated that he had made enquiries about Dennis Widdowson and that the mortuary had no record of a two-and-a-half-year-old boy despite the fact that he had been taken there and was shown to women looking for their daughters no fewer than four times.

Questions regarding this matter should have been put to the mortuary superintendent by the coroner or, at the very least, the family's representative should have had the opportunity to do so. Councillor Twells asked the coroner how the matter could be put right as the Cousins family had by that stage withdrawn their objection to an exhumation. The coroner continued to maintain his position by saying that the father would have to apply to the Home Office for an exhumation and then added: "*although the Home Office are now reluctant to grant them.*" The coroner returned a verdict on Dennis Baden Widdowson that he was "*Killed by enemy action and wrongly buried*".

The Home Office's position on these matters was perhaps unsurprising as they must by that stage of the war have realised what a mess Civilian War Deaths Departments were getting themselves into over burying bodies in the wrong grave. The coroner's comments regarding arrangements put in place just falling down were weak and there was no obvious reason why he did not require an official to explain to the Widdowson family and the public why they had failed and just as importantly why this situation had not been foreseen. After all, there were plenty of case studies to learn from based upon what other cities had been confronted with.

What the public did not know, but the coroner did, was that the catalogue of errors was worse than it appeared from the evidence given in open court. We already know about the farcical situation over Dennis's gender, and that neighbours who attended Eric Cousins' funeral stated the obvious, that the coffin was too small to contain his body. Why did this not alert officials to the fact that something was wrong with the way children were being placed into coffins? We now know that it all came to a head when it was realised that a male child's body was unclaimed and unidentified. Ross Young, Assistant Director of Civilian Deaths, had confirmed that 26 under-fourteen-year-olds had been reported as missing following the air raid in May. Twenty-five of those children had been identified and the one left was not Dennis Widdowson, but Harold Denman.

Officials may have at first thought that when the grave supposedly containing Harold Denman's body was opened, they would merely have to bury Harold in that grave and rebury Eric Cousins in his family's grave. Of course it was always going to be more complicated than that because, as the officials knew, a small coffin had been interred in the grave of Eric Cousins. Surely they must have started to realise that not one, or even two, but a whole series of mistakes had been made.

As we now know, it was Arthur Denman in that coffin and not Eric Cousins. How could the mix-up have occurred? Only through incompetence and a belief that what was being done did not matter as no one would ever find out.

Arthur Denman was 12 years old, 4 feet and 6 inches tall, weighing around 6 stones. Harold was 9 years old, 4 feet and 4 inches tall and he also weighed around 6 stones. It would perhaps have been easy to mix the two lads up, but when Arthur was placed into the coffin he did not fit. That ought to have raised enough concern to check his details, but instead he was made to fit the coffin. His knees were bent so that his legs became shorter and then he did fit – simple! The lid was then screwed down and that was the end of the matter.

It is almost certain that Eric Cousins was wrongly buried in Arthur Denman's coffin. Eric was 9 years old and as far as is known was around the same height and weight as Harold Denman. The body of Dennis Widdowson should not have been mistaken for that of Eric Cousins as he was 2 years and 8 months old and was only 2 feet and 10 inches tall, and weighed between 2 and 3 stones.

The Widdowson family did eventually succeed in gaining permission to have his body exhumed, but not until 21st April 1942. When Dennis was examined by a pathologist it was commented that he was:

". . . in a very advanced state of decomposition having been buried on 11th May 1941. The length and build of the body, limbs etc. were consistent with those of a child between two and three years."

Dennis was re-buried and at last all four boys were resting in peace.

Nottingham people gradually returned to their normal wartime lives. Life had to go on and a wedding took place in the burnt-out shell of St Christopher's Church. The bride asked for a collection to be made for the church restoration fund and £5.0s.0d. was raised by family and friends.

Clearly, the spirit of the Nottingham people was unbroken.

A church service in the burnt out shell of St. Christopher's Church (Photograph courtesy of *Nottingham Evening Post*)

17. The National Fire Service

In June 1941 Russia was not expected to stand up to the German Blitzkreig for very long and it was anticipated that the Luftwaffe would recommence heavy air raids on the United Kingdom in the autumn of 1941.

While everyone agreed that the regular fire brigades and the Auxiliary Fire Service had shown courage, skill and determination that were an example to all, there was also a voice of growing concern. It was felt that the efforts of the country's firemen were handicapped by a weakness in various local brigade organisations. Home Office officials recognised the weaknesses and were grappling with the problem of how to make 1,600 fire brigades more manageable and more able to be of national help. They wanted to establish larger units under a single command and to standardise the fire service ranks, uniforms and equipment.

Left: Cap badge and tunic button for the National Fire Service which replaced the Auxiliary Fire Service and the local authority fire brigades. Right: The new badge and tunic button for the Civil Defence organisation which replaced the Air Raid Precautions Service

At the height of the Blitz it was a common occurrence for reinforcing brigades to find that their standpipes would not fit on to the water mains in any but their own area. Sergeants and inspectors of regular brigades rubbed shoulders with Leading Firemen, Section Leaders and Patrol Officers from the Auxiliary Fire Service. In Nottingham the firemen who were on the regular brigade were issued with steel helmets that had the word "Police" on the front. The part-time firemen in the auxiliary service had "AFS" emblazoned on their helmets. The regulars in Nottingham painted out the incorrect message on the front of their helmets; they had common sense even if those running the fire brigade did not. On 5th May 1941, *The Times* newspaper commented about the firefighting situation in the country as a whole:

> *"The government should consider at once whether the army of fire-fighters should not be given a less localised organisation and status."*

The decision to take control of the country's fire brigades had already been agreed and the first set of regulations that applied to every fireman in the country were introduced on 5th August 1941. Due to an oversight by civil servants, the regulations were in use for three years before they were approved in parliament, thus making them legal.

The country was divided into a number of areas and each of those areas had its own fire force. There were 33 separate fire forces in England and Wales. Nottingham became Fire Force 8, Derbyshire became Fire Force 7, whilst Northamptonshire and Leicestershire were kept together to form Fire Force 9. Lincolnshire, who had been in the old Region 3 with Nottinghamshire, became Fire Force 10.

Within each fire force, there were subordinate levels of command. A division consisted of 100 pumping appliances and was under the command of a Divisional Officer. A column comprised 50 pumping appliances with a Column Officer in charge. Company Officers commanded ten pumps and Section Leaders were in

Above: Officers of the National Fire Service at an incident (Photograph courtesy of Nottingham City Fire Brigade)

Above: Reg Miller poses with a wry smile for a photograph with his gas mask and steel helmet with the incorrect logo 'Police' stencilled on the front (Photograph courtesy of Reg Miller ex Nottingham City Fire Brigade)

Above: National Fire Service Field telephone van for providing communications where enemy action had destroyed the public telephone network (Photograph courtesy of Nottingham City Fire Brigade archives)

Surface water main supplied from the River Trent being pressure tested before being put into service. After the air raid on Nottingham in May 1941 this was seen as essential to provide firefighting water to all parts of the city (Photograph courtesy of Nottingham City Fire Brigade archives)

charge of five pumps. It was usual for a Leading Fireman to be in charge of one pump and its crew.

Nottingham's Chief Constable had been used to doing whatever he liked with the fire brigade in the city, but now he had no authority over them whatsoever. Commander Strong was now in charge with H.C. Smith as his deputy. Shortly after the fire service had been nationalised, Chief Constable Popkess was asked to hand over a number of vehicles that had formed part of the fire division and to remove his own police vehicles from the appliance room at Central Fire Station. He complied grudgingly and with ill grace that was not befitting his position.

The National Fire Service was gradually built up until it reached its maximum strength of around 220,000 men and women in 1942. The organisation was such that if any area was so badly hit by air raids that its efficiency began to falter, then it could be replaced by another fire force from elsewhere while it was withdrawn to re-equip, rest its personnel and then recommence its duties. It was in effect the same process as withdrawing an army unit from the battle and replacing it with a fully equipped fresh unit. It was hoped that this replacement process would not be required and it was more likely that large numbers of reinforcements would be utilised from various fire forces in a similar way to that in which the regional assistance scheme had operated.

In January 1941, the Minister of Home Security was given powers to compel both men and women to undertake a maximum of 48 hours' fire prevention duty each month. In effect this was the same as the fire-watchers scheme. When the fire service was nationalised in August 1941, it was decided that "Fire Guards" should be recruited and that this would form part of the ARP Warden Service.

Supervisory roles were created in the Fire Guard scheme. A senior Fire Guard would be responsible for supervising 600 Fire Guards. Whilst it was compulsory for business premises to have a Fire Guard, in practice it was difficult to provide sufficient personnel. Up to 75 per cent of those registered for Fire Guard duties filed a claim for exemption. The message they were sending was simple – we want protection from the risks of fire from air raids, just as long as it is someone else who does it!

Each fire force area was subdivided into sectors and a Fire Guard Sector Captain was in charge. The Sector Captain could send reinforcements from one sector to another and had the ultimate decision on whether to call the National Fire Service. The ARP wardens, the police and the public were discouraged from calling the fire brigade of their own accord and were directed to report fires to the Fire Guard in the first instance.

The theory behind this may have been acceptable, but in practice it built into the system too many controls and this always led to a delay in calling professional firefighters, with obvious results. The whole weight of the National Fire Service was ready to spring into action, but one Sector Captain could hold it all back because the Fire Guards wanted to deal with the situation themselves. The Sector Captains knew that as soon as the National Fire Service arrived, they were answerable to whoever was the most senior NFS officer present. Being only human, some of them held onto their moment of glory for too long as they did not know when such a chance would come their way again. This often allowed a fire to gain a good hold and spread. The NFS would then have a considerable problem in bringing a blaze under control. If they had received a call immediately, the damage and the resources used would have been far less.

Nottingham had paid keen attention to the lessons learned in other cities about adequate water supplies for firefighting. The emergency water supplies that had been provided in 60-foot diameter wooden tanks were useful up to a point, but the heavy raid on Nottingham on 8th/9th May 1941 had shown that even greater supplies were needed in certain areas. In July 1941 it had been proposed that the flower beds in the Old Market Square should be excavated to provide open water supplies. It was estimated that the Exchange Walk and King Street corners of the square could be made to hold 50,000 gallons each. The flower beds at the Beastmarket Hill end of the square could be made to hold 100,000 gallons each.

In August of that year, a water main was finally ready for operational service that provided water directly from the River Trent for firefighting purposes. The main could provide 120,000 gallons per minute at a pressure of 100lb per square inch (7 bars pressure). This was achieved by a pumping station at Wilford drawing the water from the river and then boosting the pressure to pump it through the main. The main went along Wilford Road and on to Greyfriar Gate and then up Lister Gate to the Market Square. From there it went along Parliament Street and up Derby Road. There was a branch off the main into St Peter's Gate, Victoria Street and Goose Gate.

Arrangements were also made to be able to pump up to four million gallons from water tanks on Trent Lane to a point on Southwell Road. A fire barge was provided and equipped for firefighting purposes and this became operational along non-tidal stretches of the River Trent and the canals around the city.

Crews of the National Fire Service cooling a gasometer during a training exercise. The appliances used by these crews were very basic by modern standards, but were a huge improvement upon trailer pumps towed by under powered private cars that they had used throughout the height of the blitz (Photograph courtesy of Nottingham City Fire Brigade archives)

The first real test for the NFS came in 1942 when a series of "Terror Attacks" were ordered by Hitler as a reprisal for the RAF destroying the port of Lübeck in Germany. The undefended port was a beautiful city full of old world charm and so many fires were caused in the raid on 28th March 1942 that a firestorm developed. This caused great resentment in Germany and the retaliatory raids on Britain were deliberately aimed at places which were undefended and of great historical value and beauty. They were labelled "Baedeker Raids" as the towns and cities bombed all appeared in the Baedeker guidebook and it was rumoured that Hitler personally selected the targets from this book with the intention of destroying Britain's most beautiful cities.

Exeter was the first to receive the treatment from the Luftwaffe on 23rd April, St George's Day. Fortunately for this city the Luftwaffe crews were very inaccurate in their navigation and bomb aiming. The result was that the damage was not as great as it could have been. The following night the Luftwaffe returned and made a proper job of it. The Fire Guards in whom so much faith had been placed found that the practice of air raid firefighting differed considerably from the theory. In Exeter the narrow streets enabled a fire on the roof of one building to quickly involve another and the Fire Guards experienced difficulty in getting on to the roofs to tackle small outbreaks of fire. By the time the National Fire Service was called out, many fires involved entire roofs and were spreading rapidly. The Luftwaffe then fell back on to their old tactics and began machine gunning the Firemen and the Fire Guards on the rooftops. The Fire Guards had never experienced anything like it and unlike the firemen of the National Fire Service, who were now seasoned campaigners, they found the whole experience beyond their ability to cope with. The end result for Exeter was that two out of every three buildings that caught fire were lost.

Bath was selected as the target for the next two nights and after finding equipment not working, some Fire Guard parties not in the places they were appointed to safeguard, and poor leadership from their Fire Guard Captains, a mass exodus by the Fire Guards took place.

Norwich was attacked twice in April and again in May. Although the Fire guards did their best, they were overwhelmed by the difficulties they encountered just as their colleagues had been in Bath; again many left the city for safety. York was raided heavily and then a return visit to Exeter was made before Canterbury was raided three times. The Fire Guard in Canterbury displayed particular courage but there was no doubt that the scheme did not work in quite the way that had been envisaged. At every one of the Baedeker Raids the country was again witness to the sight of fire crews struggling against overwhelming odds to extinguish fires. Entire blocks of buildings were consumed by fire and many of them had been well alight before fire crews had even been alerted by the Fire Guard Scheme.

Pirate raids by two or three aircraft were still being carried out in the daytime and targets of opportunity were pounced on eagerly. Two Junkers Ju88 aircraft sighted a goods train in the railway sidings at Kirkby on 3rd July 1942. It was 20:15 hours, but still plenty light enough for the aircraft to make an accurate attack.

They flew from west to east at a height of only 100 feet. High-explosive bombs were dropped, which missed the train, and subsequent attacks by the aircraft were confined to machine-gun and cannon fire. A wooden signal box was damaged by the cannon fire but was not put out of action, while the locomotive was only hit by three machine-gun bullets. One entered the water tank and another penetrated the ventilator over the driver's cab. The third bullet struck the fireman in the knee. The raider made off in a north-easterly direction and swooped down to machine-gun RAF Wigsley aerodrome at 20:40 hours.

The Luftwaffe made a sharp attack on Nottingham on 24th July 1941 and it seems that the target was the railway bridge over Sneinton Dale at the Edale Road junction. There was low cloud that night and it made visual bomb aiming difficult for the Luftwaffe crews.

Five high-explosive bombs were dropped, along with incendiaries, and the Dale Cinema was damaged again, as it had been in the raid in May 1941. The Edale Road School was also damaged and a spiked railing from around the school was blasted across the road. Alfred Sabin, who was a Fire Guard, was sheltering in the doorway of the Dale Cinema and the railing struck him in the throat. He was killed instantly.

Above: Shops on Sneinton Dale damaged in the air raid of 24th July 1942 (Photograph courtesy of the heirs of Frank Stevenson)

Above: Shops at the junction of Sneinton Dale and Edale Road in 2009, which were damaged in the July 1942 air raid

Many houses in the Sneinton Dale area were damaged by the blast and the block of shops by Edale Road were hit for a second time, as they had also been damaged in the May 1941 raid. One woman who had now been bombed out twice said, "*We shall get over it and smile again.*"

Arthur England was in a shelter with his family and he commented:

"Our shelter is made of reinforced brick with two tons of concrete on top of it but it was lifted and positively rocked by the blast."

His daughter, Betty, was due to be married in September and she lost many early wedding gifts including some cut glass. A new baby grand piano was also smashed.

A mother with two young children escaped injury by sheltering under the stairs. Her husband, who was a Fire Guard, was thrown to the ground by the blast from a bomb and injured his knee. Their house was wrecked, but they were helped to safety and counted themselves lucky to all still be alive.

The casualty service and rescue parties were kept busy dealing with 25 casualties, four of whom were seriously injured. Gertrude Morton, a sixty-five-year-old from Rossington Road, managed to cling to life for over a month before she finally succumbed to her injuries on 4th September. Martha Camm, who was 66 years old and lived in Colwick Road, Sneinton, survived for a further fortnight before she died on 18th September. Rest centres opened and 150

The Dale cinema, in 2009, on Sneinton Dale. Air raid warden Alfred Sabin was in the doorway of the building during the July 1942 air raid when a piece of the railings from the Edale Road School was blasted across the road and killed him

people were given temporary accommodation in them. A civil defence official commented that people at the rest centres were extremely cheerful considering what had happened.

Three days later, Skegness and Mablethorpe – or Nottingham-on-Sea as it has euphemistically been called – received a sharp attack. Six people were killed in Skegness and twelve injured in Mablethorpe. For the small east coast towns this was not unusual as they were regularly attacked by small numbers of aircraft, sometimes just lone aircraft, as they prowled up and down the coast. In some instances they were attacked by bombers returning after failing to locate their primary target. Although the number of casualties was never large, they were just as devastating for the small communities that were affected.

The NFS introduced a duty system that was particularly arduous: 48 hours on duty and 24 hours off. This meant working a 120-hour week. If a fireman was sent away on a regional appliance, even the small amount of time free from duty would be eroded. As the tide of war began to change, the NFS firemen would find themselves having to take on new roles, which often meant sizeable sections of a fire force being moved en bloc to another part of the country. The NFS had been transferring men and women from their own city or county to various parts of the country where they were required. These transfers were usually small numbers who were transferred for months or even years into a specific post with another fire force. The wives of firemen who were left at home could not understand why people still insisted that they were all right as their husbands were at home instead of in the armed forces.

18. Deadly Butterflies

A major attack was carried out on Grimsby and Cleethorpes on the night of 13th/14th June 1943. Only four 1,000kg high-explosive bombs were dropped, along with nine smaller calibre high-explosive bombs, but the real threat in this raid came from the incendiaries and anti-personnel bombs that were dropped.

Around 6,000 incendiaries were dropped along with 44 phosphorus oil bombs and 18 "Firepots". The phosphorus oil bombs contained an oil and rubber solution, with phosphorus in glass containers inside the bomb. The glass shattered upon impact, mixing the phosphorus with the oil and rubber solution. These bombs were intended to start large fires that would quickly consume a building. They were extremely difficult for ARP workers to put out with stirrup pumps and if a building was hit by one of these incendiaries, it usually resulted in the total loss of the building.

Anti-personnel bombs were dropped in large numbers in a direct attempt to hamper firefighting and civil defence work. The Luftwaffe referred to them as Splitterbombe SD2, which was a fragmentation bomb. In the UK, they were known more imaginatively as "Butterfly Bombs" because of the way the outer casing opened out to form two wings when it was dropped. These bombs weighed two kilograms and were dropped in containers that held 23 or more of these devices. The container would be blown open at a pre-determined height by an airburst fuse and the Butterfly Bombs would then scatter over a wide area. As they fell, the outer casing was opened by the rush of the air and this formed the wings. The descent set up sufficient wind speed to rotate the whole assembly around a central wire connected to the bomb. This process ensured that the bomb was armed before it reached the ground.

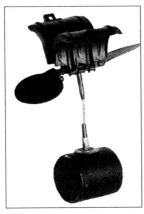

An anti personal bomb euphemistically known as a Butterfly Bomb due to the way the casing opened out like wings which was the process by which they were primed to detonate

Butterfly Bombs were about 80 millimetres long and 75 millimetres in diameter, and contained approximately 200 grams of explosive. Various fuses were used in conjunction with these bombs and this added to their effect. Some were fitted with an impact fuse, while others had an airburst fuse which had the effect of ensuring the shrapnel from the bomb sliced through the air unimpeded, and this almost always meant more casualties. Other variants included delay fuses which could vary between 30 minutes and 20 hours. A particularly nasty element to this was that many of the bombs were fitted with anti-handling fuses. The different types were always mixed in each container and so the civil defence workers never knew which type they were confronted with. The fact that one of the bombs exploded after a delay of 30 minutes would have no bearing on what the next bomb lying in the same street would do.

There was no means of defusing Butterfly Bombs and so they had to be blown up in situ. They were dangerous for the civilian population, but for the firemen and Civil Defence Personnel who had to work around and amongst them, the Butterfly Bombs were deadly. This was the reason for their use and it was just another development in the air war being waged against the United Kingdom. Some of the Butterfly Bombs were painted yellow with a red stripe, which at least enabled fairly easy identification, but the ones painted grey-green blended in with most backgrounds and it was easy to knock one without even seeing it. The outcome was frequently fatal and just for good measure it would maim a couple of your mates who were nearby.

Nottinghamshire was asked to send rescue parties to assist in Grimsby. West Bridgford and Arnold duly despatched crews to help rescue people from wrecked buildings. They were now experienced in this work

Above Left: A control unit of the National Fire Service, These vehicles were used at large incidents and also as part of mobile Fire Force Columns that were entirely self sufficient when deployed to cities outside their own area. The control operator seated is Miss Bennett (Photograph courtesy of Nottingham City Fire Brigade archives) Above Right: Damage to dockside warehouses in Grimsby after a visit by the Luftwaffe

and although there were 60 killed in Grimsby and 100 injured, in the overall view of air raids this was relatively light. Cleethorpes had 14 people killed and 23 injured.

The National Fire Service mobilised fire crews from Nottinghamshire to Grimsby, where 330 fires were burning. The docks area was the worst affected and, as in other cities, the firemen of Grimsby found themselves outnumbered. Five pumps went from the Central, Triumph Road and Bulwell fire stations in the city, and further pumps were mobilised from the county. Henry Strickson was one of the men in the Bulwell crew and he recalled the events of that night.

> "The bombers had dropped flares and it was bright enough to read a newspaper by. We went straight in rather than reporting to a marshalling point. There were so many fires that we could have had one each. The trouble was there was not enough water to extinguish the massive fires that were burning.
>
> We had to concentrate our efforts on saving the industrial parts of Grimsby and the docks, but it was very sad that we had to leave people's homes to burn. It was heartbreaking for those folk. I know that what we were doing was the right thing for the country because we were at war, but even so it is terrible to leave homes to burn; very sad.
>
> The next day there was not a single roof from the Pontoon Docks to the town centre that was intact. We found a young boy of about twelve in an Anderson Shelter and he had been killed by blast. There wasn't a mark on him and it seemed such a tragic waste of a young life. There was no one else in the shelter and no one around that may have been family; no parents or anything. We called over to a rescue party and showed them where he was.
>
> We saw a vicar climbing about on a pile of rubble and he asked us if we had seen an old lady about. We told him that we hadn't and he began pulling at spars of wood embedded in the rubble and trying to move piles of bricks. Our crew helped him to search the rubble and we found her. She was dead but we extricated her anyway. It was all very sad; the young and the old both killed, no more than a hundred yards apart."

More crews from Nottingham began arriving once it became daylight and these were the vanguard of the second wave of regional reinforcements that would continue to arrive over the next few hours. They were detailed to relieve the fire crews who had battled with the fires all night. The smoke from the fires hung over the town and as the relief crews approached it was all too familiar. The streets littered with debris, fire pumps blocking the way and hose lines criss-crossing everywhere. Firemen, dirty and tired, no longer able to hold the powerful water jets properly with their aching muscles, stared blankly at the new arrivals who had come to take over. Soon they would be as dirty as the men they had come to relieve, and it seemed to some of them that the air raids had been going on for ever. The job of clearing the Butterfly Bombs was not an easy one and ARP wardens, along with the police, tended to clear areas of bombs at ground level while the National Fire Service cleared the roofs. Moving the bombs caused them to explode, but even worse than that, it often triggered others nearby to explode, which made it extremely hazardous work. Because of this effect, wide areas had to be evacuated when the army came in to detonate one of the bombs. Henry Strickson describes one of the methods adopted by the firemen.

"We went up on to the roofs with a long stick and we flicked the bombs off with it. We ducked down as we flicked the bomb to avoid the shrapnel when it exploded."

Henry was also part of a team that was detailed to clear Dowty Road cemetery.

"We moved forward in line abreast and someone must have accidentally kicked one of the bombs in the long grass, because there was an explosion and it blew the man's leg off. Those Butterfly Bombs were nasty; they were intended to kill and maim the people who were trying to deal with the effects of an air raid."

Butterfly Bombs were still being found in Grimsby years later and a parallel can be drawn between these bombs and the legacy of landmines that are left behind after conflicts which kill and maim the innocent.

Cleethorpes was still recovering from this air raid in July and Nottingham was asked to send two rescue parties to the east coast town on 18th August to help with the ongoing task of locating and recovering those who were still missing. The National Fire Service had no sooner been built up than a series of cuts began. Personnel began to be shed from the service while, at the same time, those remaining were reorganised.

After the Baedeker Raids it was acknowledged that the biggest threat was to the towns and cities in the south where already the men and machines of war were gathering for the eventual invasion of Europe. Operation Colour Scheme involved transferring half of the full-time firefighting strength north of

Members of the National Fire Service who volunteered for "Operation Colour Scheme". Fire crews from all over the United Kingdom were formed into mobile columns to serve abroad after the liberation of occupied cities. They also provided fire cover for the huge camps of men, equipment, fuel and munitions (Photograph courtesy of Nottingham City Fire Brigade archives)

a line extending from the Wash down to the Severn, to the towns in the south. The whole operation was conducted on a large scale and 11,450 firemen and 1,240 pumps and other fire service appliances such as turntable ladders were moved.

At around the same time, 2,000 firemen were selected and organised into five self-contained firefighting units. They were given special training and equipped to serve overseas. Among the men who volunteered for the overseas contingent was Roy Wolf.

"We were transferred down to Waterlooville near Portsmouth and began our special training. Rescuing aircrew from crashed aircraft and making the aircraft safe was one of the things we learned. We also learned to lay 'Victollic' piping that could be used to pump water or fuel through. All the time we were down south we were providing fire cover for the storage dumps and the training camps for the armed forces."

Reg Miller was posted to Clacton and he recalled that they were not told where they going until they were all assembled and ready to set off from Colwick Racecourse, which was the training ground for Fire Force 8. Clifford McKenzie was posted to Portsmouth with a Fire Force 8 column and they were told to remove the badge on their fire tunic that read "NFS 8". This was so that no one would know where they were from and therefore reduced the possibility of a German spy passing on information about which parts of the country were having their fire cover reduced. The result could have been heavy air raids aimed at those areas. Fire cover was provided while the invasion exercises went on and those crews around Dover and Folkestone were sometimes involved in dealing with the aftermath of long-range shelling that the enemy indulged in from the occupied continent. Crews in the south-east of the country found that it was still the old familiar air raids that kept them busy. Reg Miller recalled some of the raids.

"An air raid began one night and several incendiaries fell in the road right outside the fire station. We went out at once and whilst we were dealing with them a civilian came up to us and asked if we would come to their house as it was on fire.

We drove round the corner and saw that the front bedroom was well alight, so we pitched a ladder and got a firefighting jet to work through the window. We had just got the fire out when an NFS dispatch rider drove up. He told us that we had to go at once to a farmhouse and buildings that had been hit by a high-explosive bomb. We had to leave the people to finish the job off themselves, which we were very upset about, but we had no choice as we had been ordered on.

The farm had been badly damaged and there were dead cattle and sheep all over. One of the firemen from another crew that were already there knocked an incendiary bomb which had not gone off and it exploded into his groin. Some of them had an exploding nose on the end and I think this must have been one of those type.

On another occasion we were firefighting with about four other crews at the Marks and Spencer's shop in Clacton, but the fire had a good hold long before we were called and the building ended up completely burnt out."

NFS firemen who had remained in Nottingham were still dealing with their share of emergencies. On 14th July 1943 an RAF Mosquito aircraft crashed into the back gardens of 52 and 54 Weardale Road off Haydn Road in Sherwood. The aircraft had been circling quite low overhead for some time before the crash and the talk at the time was that the pilot, John Grundy, was showing off to his girlfriend, who worked at the Meridian factory on Haydn Road.

The aircraft dived towards the ground but failed to pull up in time. One of the wings struck the chimney stack of a house and then it plunged down in a mass of flames. The NFS were on the scene within a few minutes but nothing could be done to save the two crewmen, who were almost certainly killed by the impact.

Despite the efforts of the firemen, the aircraft was completely burnt out, along with a garage, a car and a van. All that remained of the aircraft afterwards was the two engines. Both the houses were damaged by the fire but this damage was mainly confined to the outside. The bodies of the two airmen were recovered while the fire was still burning and were taken away in the back of a fire appliance. Two casualties, Mrs Orgill and Mrs Hood, were conveyed to hospital by ambulance.

The Germans had been developing a new weapon for some time which was capable of delivering a large high-explosive payload without any air crew being required. The V1 rocket, or "Doodlebug" as it was popularly known at the time, became a reality in June 1944. The V1 rockets were launched from various sites in France, Belgium and Holland. The Germans had developed mobile equipment for launching the rockets and these were extremely difficult to locate and attack. In effect the RAF had to catch the Germans in the act of launching in order to have any prospect of destroying the equipment. The static sites that were being used for launching rockets were at the top of the list to be overrun and captured by the ground troops fighting their way across occupied Europe.

The V1 was unreliable and many of them never even reached mainland Britain. Sussex and Kent between them received more than 60 per cent of the flying bombs launched at Britain. If a similar percentage of the rockets had landed in densely populated London, the city would have been decimated. Although the V1 rockets did not have the same effect as sustained air raids night after night on the same city, the terror that they caused among the population should not be underestimated. People who witnessed the "Doodlebugs" described the unmistakable sound of the rocket engine as it made its way across the sky. The engine

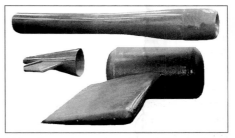

A V1 rocket used to continue the aerial bombardment of the United Kingdom when it was no longer viable for the Luftwaffe to carry out air raids

noise would suddenly stop when the fuel ran out and then there would be an ominous silence as the lethal explosive fell to the ground.

The targets were completely random and people who have described seeing and hearing the rockets have expressed a measure of guilt because they used to mentally urge the rocket noise to continue until it had passed over them. They knew that they were literally wishing for it to fall on somebody else, which is understandable and a perfectly normal response to the terror induced by these weapons. Nonetheless those people were still tinged with guilt more than fifty years later. The National Fire Service set up "Flying Columns" of three pumping appliances and a turntable ladder which turned out immediately to any incidents involving flying bombs. The speed of the NFS response often meant that they were the first disciplined service to arrive at the scene and could muster as many as twenty men as soon as they arrived.

To make the most of the available manpower, the civil defence service had begun training firemen in rescue work. The civil defence rescue teams still undertook rescue work, but the NFS was obviously a good source of additional manpower that was suitable for this kind of work.

Flying bomb incidents did not always cause a fire and where fire did break out the crews usually got it under control quickly due to the speed and weight of their initial response. The V1 rockets did not penetrate very deep into the ground and, as a result, gas mains often remained intact and that reduced the danger of further explosions caused by leaking gas building up in confined spaces and then being ignited. Domestic appliances did tend to leak following these incidents and the gas had to be cut off. The gas used then was somewhat different to the natural gas that we have become used to since the 1970s. The gas in those days was what became referred to as "town gas" or "coal gas". This was produced by heating coal to turn it into coke. The gas driven off as part of this process was high in carbon monoxide and could lead to asphyxiation if breathed in by those trapped and rescuers alike.

The breathing apparatus sets carried on some specialist fire appliances could be worn to protect the firemen against this danger. Although the oxygen breathing apparatus was still relatively scarce and only a

Above Left: A National Fire Service Crew wearing 'Salvus' oxygen breathing apparatus. These breathing apparatus sets were only carried on Emergency Tenders and were for use by specially trained firemen (Photograph courtesy of Nottingham City Fire Brigade archives) Above Right: Firemen of the National Fire Service taking part in training for rescuing people trapped underneath vehicles (Photograph courtesy of Nottingham City Fire Brigade archives)

few select personnel were trained to wear it, the equipment was extremely useful in non-fire emergencies. The NFS role evolved into one of carrying out any rescues, assisting with giving first aid to casualties, extricating people who were trapped and also carrying out salvage work such as recovering furniture and other belongings. In fact, their role became more and more what it is today.

William Chadwick was posted to Brighton with a crew from Nottingham and was later moved to Tonbridge and finally to Lewes in Sussex. While at Tonbridge and Lewes he attended flying bomb incidents and he remembered in particular going to a children's home that had been hit by one of the rockets.

Reminders of what lay in store for the country's firemen were never very far away. William Chadwick attended a house fire in Tonbridge that was not caused by enemy action. Some of the crew crawled into the smoke-filled house to try to locate the woman who was still inside. They did not have the benefit of breathing apparatus and so it was just a case of keeping as low as possible and searching quickly to try and locate the missing person before the smoke drove them back out into the street. One of the firemen found the woman and they managed to get her into the fresh air where they attempted to resuscitate her. Despite their best efforts, she died; a victim of asphyxia caused by the carbon monoxide in the smoke produced by the fire.

Column number 4 of the National Fire Service overseas contingent consisted of 540 men, mainly from East Anglia. It was this column that was selected to serve abroad and they embarked at Tilbury on 25th January 1945. One of the Nottingham firemen who had volunteered for overseas service, Roy Wolf, was disappointed that it was not his column that was chosen to go, but when he was posted back to Fire Force 8 in November 1944 he was able to hold his head high. Number 4 column reached the Rhine and was providing fire cover for the US Army as it marched into Germany. It had various stations in Frankfurt, Cologne, Namur and Verdun. Later it was transferred to the 21st Army Group, which was commanded by Field Marshal Montgomery, and served in and around Antwerp until it was posted back to Britain in July 1946. The army commanding officer under whom number 4 column had served commended the entire contingent. The final word on this subject comes from the ARP County Control Logbook. On 8th May 1945, the day that war finally ended, the controller had cheerfully written in a bold hand, "*The End*". Underneath it, someone had penned the addition: "*We hope*".

Above: A fireboat of the National Fire Service on the River Trent at Victoria Embankment. This was part of the VE Day (Victory in Europe)   Celebrations (Photograph courtesy of Steve Artinstall ex NottinghamshireFire & Rescue Service)

Left: At the end of the war, armed forces and civilian services were given the opportunity to parade through cities and towns that they had served during the conflict. The National Fire Service contingent march past the council house in Old Market Square, following them are nurses (Photograph courtesy of Nottingham City Fire Brigade archives)

19. Latter Days

In 1941, when Herbert Morrison, the Minister of Home Security, took the country's fire brigades under his control to form the National Fire Service, he promised that he would return them to local authority control after the war. He kept his promise and in 1947 the Fire Services Act received royal assent.

The brigades were returned to local authority control but some of the smaller authorities had lost their fire brigade for ever. Parish pumps and small brigades belonging to Urban District Councils were swallowed up and the 1,400 or so brigades that went into the NFS came out as 140. Nottinghamshire ended up with just two brigades: Nottingham City Fire Brigade and Nottinghamshire County Fire Brigade. The city brigade was only responsible for fire cover within the city boundary and the county brigade covered everything else. Needless to say, the two brigades did have a mutual assistance scheme.

On 1st April 1948, Gilbert Cains became the first Chief Fire Officer of Nottingham City Fire Brigade. He had joined Bristol Fire Brigade in 1925 when he was 21 years old and was involved in the firefighting following a heavy raid on 24th November 1940 when the centre of Bristol was burnt out. He was a qualified construction engineer and when the National Fire Service was formed he became the Deputy Fire Force Commander for Devon.

A ceremony took place on 5th April 1948 at Nottingham's Central Fire Station to mark the return of the fire brigade to local authority control. Among the civic dignitaries who attended were the Lord Mayor, Councillor J. Mitchell and the Chairman of the Fire Brigade Committee, Councillor Pilsworth.

The entire City Fire Brigade was on parade for inspection by the Chief Fire Officer and the Lord Mayor. After receiving a tour of the fire station, the Lord Mayor operated the turnout bells at midday and this was the signal for a series of firefighting and rescue demonstrations.

An oil fire was extinguished, followed by a demonstration in breathing apparatus. "Rescues" were effected by the fireman's lift method down a wheeled escape ladder and also with the 100-foot turntable ladder. The versatility of the turntable ladder was shown in the next drill when it was used as a water tower, directing a powerful jet of water from the monitor at the head of the ladder. Pumping appliances were put to work at the same time and an impressive water curtain was achieved by using a number of firefighting jets. The finale was a spectacular foam drill. And so the city brigade stepped forward into a new era. It now had three stations instead of the original one. The station at Triumph Road in Radford became Station Two and the station on Coventry Road in Bulwell became Station Three. There were 124 officers and men and women to crew the stations, the control room and the brigade workshops.

The appliances that they had to work with were a motley assortment and some had seen better days. There were three Pump Escapes: a 1937 Leyland which could pump 750 gallons per minute, a 1942 Ford which could pump 300 gallons per minute, and a 1943 Austin which was capable of pumping 200 gallons per minute. The brigade also had three pumps and a water tender with a 30-foot ladder on each appliance and they had a pumping capacity of between 200 and 500 gallons per minute. There was a Salvage Tender with equipment on board specifically for mitigating the effects of firefighting on goods and fixtures in the buildings affected. The Emergency Tender was a 1939 Leyland appliance which carried a range of rescue equipment as well as lighting and oxygen breathing apparatus. The two turntable ladders which had served the city so well during the war were still in use, although the 1931 Leyland was looking the worse for wear.

The brigade also had a Hose Carrier for use at larger incidents and a Chimney Tender which had been acquired in 1942. The mobile communications for the brigade was taken care of by a 1941 Wolseley mo-

Above: The funeral cortege of Divisional Officer Frank Bennett on Western Boulevard near the junction with Alpine Street (Photograph courtesy ofNottingham City Fire Brigade archives)

Right: Divisional Officer Frank Bennett of Nottingham City Fire Brigade. He was fatally injured when he fell from the roof of the Wall's ice cream factory on Castle Boulevard on the night of 5th November 1949 (Photograph courtesy of Nottinghamshire Fire & Rescue Service – Central Fire Station)

tor car which had been adapted into a wireless car. The city and county fire brigades both returned to their normal routine of peacetime firefighting with the usual busy spells. Bonfire night and the run-up to it is always a busy time for firemen and 1949 was no exception, but that particular year there was a tragedy. Divisional Officer Frank Bennett returned to Nottingham during the afternoon of 5th November after attending the Fire Service Staff College for a training course. He went on duty that night, although he could have got permission to have the night off as he had been away from home all week.

The bonfire celebrations began as soon as it got dark and in those days almost everyone with a garden had a bonfire as it was a means of disposing of garden rubbish and other items that had accumulated during the year. In some parts of Nottingham and in towns around the county, communal bonfires were organised on waste land and in some instances impromptu bonfires were lit in the street. The city brigade were kept busy that night attending bonfires that had got out of control and other fires that had been caused by sparks from bonfires or fireworks.

A call was received at the brigade control room at Shakespeare Street stating that Wall's Ice Cream Factory on Castle Boulevard was on fire. Appliances from Central Fire Station were turned out to the address, but upon arrival there were no obvious signs of fire. Frank Bennett, as officer in charge, ordered one of the crews to pitch a ladder to the flat roof of the factory so that a check could be made on the rear of the premises, which were secure. Fireman Chris Raybould accompanied Frank on to the roof and they were able to satisfy themselves that the call was a false alarm. They could not be sure, however, whether it was a malicious call made by someone who knew there was no fire, or whether the call was made with good intent by someone mistakenly thinking the building was on fire. They were about to make their way back to the head of the ladder when Frank Bennett made a fatal mistake. He accidentally stepped off the edge of the roof and crashed to the ground, landing on the base of his spine; this caused him to fracture his skull. He was rendered unconscious immediately.

The fire crew were able to get down to him as he lay in the rear yard of the factory and sent a message back to their control room that an ambulance was required at the incident. Frank was taken to Nottingham General Hospital, where he died three days later having never regained consciousness.

Chris Raybould believed that Frank made the mistake of thinking that the roof stretched further than it did. This illusion was created by the very high wall at the rear of the factory which cast a shadow over the entire roof area. In the darkness, this shadow looked solid, as if it was part of the roof.

Frank Bennett had survived firefighting in the Blitz and had escaped with minor injuries when a bomb fell directly opposite his house in Charlbury Road, but fate dealt him a cruel blow when his luck ran out attending a false alarm. Anyone who knew Frank described him as a gentleman and the firemen respected him as a very capable and fair officer. He was greatly missed by his men. Life went on, however, as it always does on the fire service. Tragedies are keenly felt but not dwelt upon as there is always someone else whose cry for help has to be answered.

The decade was drawing to close, a decade that had seen momentous changes in the fire service just as it had in all other walks of life. The firemen of Nottinghamshire, along with their comrades throughout the country, went about their daily duties just as they had before the Blitz had tested them to their limit. But, with courage, skill and tireless efforts, they had won themselves a place in the hearts of the people of Britain.

"Went the day well?
We died and never knew
But well or ill, Freedom, we died for you"

Anonymous

20. Epilogue

Ex members of the NFS who had to wait fifty years to receive their Defence Medal. Recipients at an award ceremony in 1991 at Beeston Fire Station. Left to right: Lord Lieutenant Sir Andrew Buchanan, Ida Wilson, Harry Roe, Eddie Patterson (then Chief Fire Officer of Nottinghamshire Fire & Rescue Service), George Wood, William Chadwick

During the research for 'The Battle of the Flames', David Needham found that some ex-members of the Auxiliary Fire Service had not received their Defence medal at the end of hostilities. He made enquiries to ascertain if anything could be done to rectify this oversight and was given information about how a claim could be made for the medals. The Defence Medal was awarded for three years service in Great Britain until the 8th May 1945 or six months overseas service in territories subjected to, or threatened by enemy attacks. In the case of mine and bomb disposal units the time qualification was three months.

David set about gathering the evidence required to make an application for retrospective award of the Defence medal for six people:

Ida Wilson Group Fire Control Officer Auxiliary & National Fire Service
Clifford McKenzie Fireman Auxiliary & National Fire Service
George Woods Fireman Auxiliary & National Fire Service
Albert Dobbs Dispatch Rider Auxiliary & National Fire Service
William Chadwick Fireman Auxiliary and National Fire Service
Harry Roe Fireman Auxiliary & National Fire Service

In order to prove the required length of service to qualify for the medal, David helped to find documentary evidence for each person. In the case of Ida Wilson, an Auxiliary Fire Service identification card provided a date when she was part of the service, but there was nothing to prove 3 or more years service. Finally, clothing coupons issued to her upon demobilisation from the National Fire Service were found and as the date on these was 1945, it proved that she had served at least the minimum 3 years. For Harry Roe, his call up papers to the Auxiliary Fire Service gave the first date required and a First Aid Refresher course certificate dated after 1943 proved sufficient time had been served to qualify for the medal. Similar documentary evidence was provided for each application and Eddie Patterson, Chief Fire Officer of Nottinghamshire Fire & Rescue Service at the time, endorsed the application. The six applications were eventually approved and the medals duly arrived at the Fire & Rescue Service Headquarters. The recipients were invited to a Long service Good Conduct Medal award ceremony for serving firefighters in 2001 where the Lord Lieutenant of Nottinghamshire, Sir Andrew Buchanan, presented the Defence Medal to four of those named above. The other two recipients were unable to attend for health reasons.

Each one wore their medal proudly and, as is so often said about such awards, "only the person wearing it truly knows how it was earned". In the case of the Defence Medal it is a truism and never more so than in the case of William Chadwick, who was entitled to wear a miniature silver oak leaf on the ribbon of the medal to denote that he had won a King's Commendation. In May 2001 an invitation went out to all retired fire service members to attend an open day at the Fire & Rescue Service Headquarters. Many people attended and renewed old acquaintances. Firefighters and control operators who had been part of the fire service during the war years took great delight in looking at and discussing the modern equipment used, compared to some of the heavy and cumbersome equipment they had at their disposal. They all had a glint in their eye and their modern counterparts were pleased to meet and shake hands with those who fought and won the Battle of the Flames.

Above: The Defence Medal. The ribbon is flame coloured with green edges and symbolises the air attacks and destruction on our green land. The black-out is represented by a narrow black stripe down the centre of each of the green edges. This medal was awarded for three years service in Great Britain until 8th May 1945 or six months overseas in territories subjected to, or threatened by enemy attacks. In the case of mine and bomb disposal units the time qualification was three months. In common with all other decorations and medals only the person who wears the medal knows how it was earned

Above: The author of this book David Needham – Ex Divisional Officer of Nottinghamshire Fire & Rescue Service. In 1990 he applied for the Defence Medals for five ex members of the National Fire service who had not received the award. He gathered evidence to prove their service for a minimum of three years which was the qualifying period for service in the UK

21. List of Fatal Casualties

"... To a greater degree than ever before, the 1939 – 45 War involved not merely armies, but entire nations... The names of individuals mean little save to those who knew and loved them and mourn their loss, and the number of those who mourn will dwindle as the years pass by..."

From the Introduction to the Commonwealth War Graves Commission listings

Wednesday 28th August 1940

67 Boundary Road, Beeston
Shires, Laura. Fell down cellar steps whilst going to shelter during an air raid. Died of peritonitis after a miscarriage.

Laxton, near Newark
Willis, Ruth Barbara Potter 55, of The School House, Laxton. ARP First Aid Party member

Norton Street, Radford. Hollin's Mills
Holland, William of 99 Sneinton Boulevard. Died of a heart attack whilst sheltering during air raid

84 Park Lane, Basford
Ashmore, George. Died of a heart attack associated with shock upon hearing the air raid siren.

Sneinton Dale, Sneinton
Hill, Herbert 69, of 76 Sneinton Dale. ARP Shelter Warden died next day in Nottingham General Hospital

41 Waterford Street
Warner, Elizabeth Ann. Died of a stroke whilst going to shelter during air raid

Friday 30th August 1940

6 Fairbank Crescent, Sherwood
Betts, Kevin Stuart 18 months, Died next day at Nottingham City Hospital

9 Alandine Avenue, Watnall
Lord, Mary 20, of 13 Albert Avenue, New Nuthall
Moult, John 30, of 18 Holly Road, Watnall

The Oaks, 96 Bramcote Lane; in an air raid shelter
Barks, Rebecca Mercy 76
Barks, May 47
Barks, Edna May 19
Rushin, Gertrude 49, of 38 Dulwich Road, Radford

Sunday 1st September 1940

Lowater Street, Carlton
Dainty, William Charles of No. 12. ARP Rescue Team member. Knocked down by a motor car when responding to the sirens. Died later in Nottingham General Hospital

Thursday 5th September 1940

47 Rothenay Avenue
Davis, Arthur. Fell down cellar steps whilst going to shelter upon hearing an explosion. Died in Nottingham General Hospital

Monday September 23rd 1940

Ruff's Drive, Hucknall
Evans, Albert 28
Evans, Alice 30
Evans, Ronald 8
Evans, Alice Jnr 6
Evans, John 2

Saturday 26th October 1940

7 Birch Avenue, Carlton
Owen, Mary Eliza. Fell down stairs when going to shelter during air raid warning. Died in Nottingham General Hospital of a dislocated neck.

Wednesday 13th November 1940

65 Edwin Street
Chapman, Betsy. Collapsed and died of a heart attack
during an anti aircraft barrage when an unexploded
shell onto the roof of a house in the next street

Thursday 14th November 1940

Coventry
Farndon, Clifford Richard 31, of 30 Cloister Street, Old
Lenton. Died the same day at St Cross Hospital, Rugby

Tuesday 17th December 1940

Manning Street, Nottingham
Smith, Phillip 30, of 16 Baker Street. Died of injuries
when an Auxiliary Fire Service vehicle collided with a
street air raid shelter in the blackout.

Monday 23rd December 1940

Back George Street, Manchester
Wright, Joseph Henry 31, of 24 Queen's Street, Kirkby
in Ashfield

Parker Street, Piccadilly,
Burrows, Ralph 41, of 104 Hartley Road, Kirkby in
Ashfield
Day, Alan Richard 29, of 24 Wheatley Avenue, Kirkby
in Ashfield. Died the same day at Roby Street Infirmary

Wednesday 15th January 1941

Hutton Street, Sneinton
Eggleston, Garry 3, of No. 37
Eggleston, Kenneth Michael 18 months, of No. 37
Eggleston, Patricia Maureen 10 weeks, of No. 37
Green, Gladys Edith 30, of No.27
Hopewell, John Herbert Hopewell 26, of No.33
Hopewell, Rebecca Hopewell 22, of No.33
Hopewell, Terence John Hopewell 17 months, of No.33
Marshall, Peter James 18 months, of No. 29
Marshall, Brian Herbert of 78 Miall Street, Radford
died at No 29
Stafford, George Henry 52, of No. 31
Stafford, Ada Annie 54, of No. 31
Voce, Albert 40, of No. 35
Trent Lane, Sneinton
Brewer, Arthur Malcolm 34, of 9 Taylor Close Sneinton
died at No. 21
Hughes, Evelyn 29, of 16 Pelham Crescent, Beeston
died at No. 23
Pearson, Samuel 67, of No. 27

Thursday 30th January 1941

Trent Concrete, Newark
Saxby, Joseph Norman 17, of Farndon Ferry died at
Newark Hospital
Thompson, Anthony Joseph William 16, of 2 Church
Walk, Newark died at Handley House, Northgate
Newark

Friday 7th March 1941

2 George Street Square, Newark
Cummings, Gladys 21, Died the same day in Newark
Hospital

Ransome & Marles factory
Beacon Hill, Newark
Adams, George Henry Harold 44, of 77 Millgate
Andrew, Wilfred Evelyn 39, of 48 Chestnut Avenue
Ash, Olive 31, of 14 Portland Street
Ball, Bertie Augustus 18, of 18 Belvoir Road, Balderton
Beaver, Edward 26, of 15 Rosebery Hill, Mansfield
Brown, Harold Vincent 44, of 5 Charles Street
Castle, Vivian Maud 18, of The Old Horse and Gears,
Elston
Cooper, Enid Winifred Hall 30, of 12 Pinfold Lane
Balderton. Died same day at Newark Hospital
Cottam, Edna May 19, of 27 William Street
Dixey, William Joseph 62, of 65 Bowbridge Road
Fowler, Frederick 39, of Long Street, Great Gonerby,
Lincolnshire
Godridge, George William 29, of 28 Lime Grove
Grant, Robert Barnsdale 47, of 3 Sleaford Road
Grocock, Horace 47, of 115 Millgate
Gyde, Albert Robert 42, of 60a Barnby Gate
Hall, Rose Ellen 30, of 19 Long Row, Barnby Gate
Died two days later at Newark Hospital
Hanagar, James Hazelby. 29, of 6 Cedar Avenue
Hardie, Thomas McHallam 26, of 56 Milton Street,
New Balderton
Hayden, Sybil Harriet 34, of Ivy Farm, Kirklington
Kirton, Joyce May 18, of 21 Guildhall Street
Lambert, Lily 22, of 59 Bowbridge Road
Lambley, George Felix 39, of 12 Marton Road
Makins, Edith 21, of South Collingham
Mann, Frederick William Mann 46, of 189 London
Road, Balderton
Markwell, Frederick 50, of 114 Hawton Lane,
Balderton
Martin, Claude Wark Hannah 36, ARP First Aid Party
member of 33 Bowbridge Road
Martin, Edwin 46, of 46 Newton Street
Naylor, Richard 25, of 162 Barnby Gate
Packwood, Frederick William 52, of 46 Appleton Gate
Pepper, William Thomas 18, of 7 Norwell Road,
Caunton

Richards, Frederick 32, of 104 Beacon Hill. Died next day at Newark Hospital

Ridge, Alfred Mayfield 68, of 94 Beacon Hill

Senior, Reginald William 35, of 8 Middleton Road died next day at Newark Hospital.

Swanwick, George 38, of 4 Vernon Avenue

Trueblood, Norah 34, of 42 William Street

Varney, Esther Evelyn 19, of 9 Wilson Street (missing – not found)

Warner, William 51, of 9 Grove Street, Balderton

Worrell, Arthur 31, of Chestnut Cottages, Girton

Friday 14th March 1941

92 Ribblesdale Road, Daybrook
Allcock, Hilda 44

Thursday 27th March 1941

45 Warton Road, The Wells Road
Voce, John 72

Tuesday 8th April 1941

24 Mona Street, Beeston
Cox, Sarah 64, Died the same day at Nottingham General Hospital

Friday 11th April 1941 (Good Friday)

46 Charlbury Road, Radford
Tomlinson, Maude Evelyn 39

Thursday 8th May 1941

8 Granville Grove
Wheatcroft, Frederick Thomas 53
Wheatcroft, Margaret 52

13 Morley Road, Porchester
Hayes, Sarah Anne 85
Hayes, Samuel James 52
Hayes, Mabel 52

Friday 9th May 1941

Baden Powell Road, Sneinton
Gooding, Charles Walter 49, of No. 18
Theaker, Cyril Stanley 35, ARP First Aid Party member of No. 29
Merquis, Joseph 19, Lance Corporal Royal Engineers

Bakerdale Road, Carlton
Brown, Charles Joseph 33, of No. 18
Wilson, William Jones 57, of No. 16

13 Beauchamp Street
Mosley, Arthur 59
Mosley, Gertrude 60
Mosley, Maureen 4

13 Belvoir Terrace, Bunbury Street, The Meadows
Martin, Elizabeth 74

35 Burrows Street
Parr, Henry 73
Parr, Anne Maria 70

Charnwood Terrace, Ryeland Crescent
Martin, John 71, of No. 12
Pridmore, Florence Annie 27, of No. 10
Pridmore, Shirley Lilian 5, of No. 10
Pridmore, Ann 10 months, of No. 10
Raven, Alfred 64, of No. 24
Raven, Jane 61, of No.24
Robinson, Harriet Hannah 38, of No. 8
Robinson, Douglas Harold 5, of No. 8
Sheffield, Lena 21, of No. 16
Sheffield, Pauline Ann 18 months, of No. 16

5 Colwick Crossing
Read, Amelia 66

52 Colwick Road, Sneinton
Hickling, Teresa 74, Died 19/05/41 at Nottingham General Hospital

Dakeyne Street, Sneinton. Communal air raid shelter
Coulson, Dorothy 45, Firewatcher of 67 Church Drive, Daybrook
Cousins, Eric Ernest 9, of 44 Upper Eldon Street
Cragg, Elizabeth 41, of 33 Handel St
Denman, Ada Mary 38, of 68 Henry Street, Sneinton
Denman, Kenneth George 14, of 68 Henry Street, Sneinton
Denman, Sheila Mavis 7, of 68 Henry Street, Sneinton
Denman, Gladys May 33, of 75 Walker Street, Sneinton
Denman, Harold 12, of 75 Walker Street, Sneinton
Denman, Arthur 10, of 75 Walker Street, Sneinton
Goldsbury, Brenda 21 months, of 33 Handel Street
Hopkinson, Winifred Mary 14, of 42 Henry Street, Sneinton
Hopkinson, Joan Sylvia 13, of 42 Henry Street, Sneinton. Died same day at St Catherine's First Aid Post
Johnson, Roy Alan 7, of 58 Walker Street, Sneinton
Johnson, Ursula Brenda 4, of 58 Walker Street, Sneinton
Raven, Thomas George 30, of 56 Walker Street, Sneinton
Raven, Thomas George Jnr 8, of 56 Walker Street, Sneinton

Raven, Beryl Hannah 4, of 56 Walker Street, Sneinton
Raven, Barabara May 23 Months, of 56 Walker Street, Sneinton
Stevenson, Thirza 65, of 36 Upper Eldon Street
Widdowson, Lavinia 25, of 70 Upper Eldon Street, Sneinton
Widdowson, Christina 6, of 70 Upper Eldon Street, Sneinton
Widdowson, Dennis Baden 2, of 70 Upper Eldon St Sneinton

Dale Grove
Allen, Kenneth William 19, of No. 12

57 Dane Street
Marvin, Philip George Edward 47
Marvin, Ramon Edward 5

34 Edingley Avenue, Sherwood
Cousin, Phyllis Gwyneth 36
Cousin, David 8
Jones, John David 65
Turner, Martha 45, of 77 Loughborough Road, West Bridgford

22 Elm Avenue, Beeston
Creassey, Lilian Beatrice 65

Florence Road, Thorneywood
Blackford, William David 46, ARP Warden of No. 35. Died same day at the Wells Road First Aid Post

Freeth Street, The Meadows. Communal air raid shelter
Woolley, John James 34, of 14 Freeth Street
Woolley, Elizabeth 33, of 14 Freeth Street
Woolley, Iris 9, of 14 Freeth Street. Died same day at Nottingham City Hospital
Woolley, Eric 3, of 14 Freeth Street
Woolley, Shirley 12 months, of 14 Freeth Street

Friar Lane, Moot Hall, Nottingham
Benskin, William 54, of 76 Wilford Road, Ruddington
Roberts, Samual 32, of 65 Dame Agnes Street

Huskinson Street. Black's Lace Factory
Mason, William of 117 Sherwood Street
Kentwood Road, Carlton
Walter Hinks 75, of No. 20

Kingston Street
Herbert Mills 70, of No. 58. Died same day in Nottingham City Hospital

56 Lady Bay Road, West Bridgford
Priest, Hilda May 24

6 Lees Hill Street, Sneinton
Townsend, Caroline 50
Townsend, Jean 21
Lewis Terrace, Lewis Street
Miller, Charles Frederick 40, of No. 4
Miller, Violet Alexandra Elizabeth 38, of No. 4
Miller, Alma 15, of No. 4
Miller, Charles Frederick jnr 11, of No. 4
Bethel, Alfred M.M. 45, of 23 Barnston Road, Sneinton Dale. Died at No. 6

London North Eastern Railway Goods Yard
Alcock, Harold 49, of 2 Norman Street, Netherfield

Loughborough Road, West Bridgford
Briggs, Edith Eliza 70, of No. 24
Relph, Doris Winifred 45, of No. 24, Women's Voluntary Service
Relph, Shelia Doreen 12, of No. 24
Gooch, William 69, of No. 32
Gooch, Isabella 68, of No. 32
Gooch, Ivy Eva Evelyn 36, of No. 32
Gooch, Rosetta Mary 34, of No. 32
Gooch, Lucy Ivy Edna 13, of No. 32
Gooch, Charles George 6, of No. 32
Gooch, Kenneth 4, of No. 32
Armitage, John Foster 71, of No. 34
Armitage, Clara Elizabeth 71, of No. 34
Sturt, Winifred Mary 53, of No. 34

Lower Parliament Street, Nottingham.
Nottingham City Transport
Davis, Leonard William 31, of 8 Bleasby Street
Hawton, William 37, of 60 Meeching Road, Newhaven, Sussex

34 Meadow Lane, Chilwell
Gill, Henry Thomas 43, Firewatcher. Died same day in Nottingham General Hospital

Meadow Lane, Nottingham Co-operative Bakery air raid shelter
Addis, John Joseph 30, of 94 Moore Road Carlton First Aid Party Member
Armes, Ernest Osbourne 54, of 4 Elm Tree Terrace, Spring Close, Old Lenton
Ayre, Albert Edward 61, of 52 Radford Boulevard
Bell, Charles 59, of 29 Plantaganet Street
Bilson, William 56, of 47 Bridlington Street, Hyson Green
Birch, Norman Alan 20, of 23 Denstone Road, Home Guard

Bourne, Frederick Andrew 59, of 139 Pym Street
Bream, George Samuel 37, of 78 Blake Street West
Bridgford
Brister, John George 58, of 32 Stratford Road, West
Bridgford. Died next day at Leenside First aid Post,
Kirkwhite Street.
Button, Herbert 55, of 31 Brighton Street
Chambers, Walter George Baden 19, of 61 Dennison
Street
Conner, Joseph William 47, of 18 Carlisle Road Carlton
Conway, Lewis 45, of 61 Church Drive, Daybrook
Cowlishaw Raymond 17, of 47 Mundella Road, The
Meadows
Culley, William 27, of 21 Primula Terrace, Windmill Lane
Daubney, William 64, of 17 Crosby Road. ARP Warden
Davis Harold Percy 45, of 1 Stanley Street, Blue Bell
Hill. Died 11/05/41 in Nottingham City Hospital
Gamble, Cyril Vernon 40, of 64 Goodhead Street
Hickling, Ernest 50, of 28 Barnston Road
Hill, Joseph 53, of 32 Lees Hill Street
Howman, Frank 37, of 92 Logan Street, Bulwell. ARP
Warden
Judd, Charles Philip 64, of 180 Meadow Lane
Judd, Charlotte Mary 61, of 180 Meadow Lane
Keetley, Albert 33, of 5 Lavender Street ARP Warden
Knowles, John Arthur 57, of 10 Cary Cottages,
Hawthorn Street
Levick, William Ince 65, of 82 Lees Hill Street,
Sneinton
Marshall, George William 35, of Laurie Avenue
Miller, Thomas 65, of 127 Cross Street
Morris, George Thomas 37, of 120 Rossington Road,
Sneinton Dale First Aid Party Member
Naylor, Willie 62, of 10 Rushcliffe Rise, Sherwood.
Parkes, Alfred Sydney 37, of 92 Raymede Drive
Bestwood Estate
Paul, John Samuel 64, of 70 Guthrie Street
Peach, Joseph Edward 28, of 26 Bradfield Road
Perkins, Arthur Leslie 38, of 26 Longmead Drive
Pulfree Arthur Rippin 49, of 47 St Stephen's Road,
Sneinton
Radford, William James 57, of 2 Rawson Street
Roberts, Edgar Robert 38, of 76 Hawton Crescent
Robinson, John Sanford 42, of 252 Alfreton Road,
Radford
Sands, Vernon John 54, of 5 Comery Avenue Sneinton.
Saunders, Eric Roy 15, of 51 Mundella Road.
Firewatcher
Smith, Benjamin Willis 32, of 103 Parkdale Road
Stanton, Philip 17, Home Guard, 1st Nottinghamshire
(City) Battalion
Stephenson, Frederick George 60, of 16 Dowson Street
Blue Bell Hill
Tate, Henry 61, of 41 Byron Road West Bridgford.
Died same day in Nottingham General Hospital

Taylor, Sydney Andrew 36, of 11 Bagnall Cottages, Old
Basford. Home Guard
Theaker, Samuel 29, of 1 Fenwick Road, Broxtowe
Warrener John Lowe 26, of 107 Dennison Street
Whitchurch Thomas 60, of 11 Northville Street
Woodward, John Henry 33, of 331 Foxhill Road,
Carlton

Musters Road, West Bridgford
Foster, Philip Albert Seraphis 47, of Highbeach, Sea
Terrace, Westbrook, Margate, Kent. Died at No. 10a.
Foster, Rose Helen 82, of Highbeach, Sea View Terrace,
Westbrook, Margate, Kent. Died same day at Basford
County Emergency Hospital
Hulance, Thomas Arthur 53, of No. 20
Hulance, Norah Ellen 42, of No. 20
Musson, Carrie 72, of 22a
Norris, Paul 37, of No. 24
Rushworth, Harriet 73, of No. 12
Rushworth, John Albert Swanwick 50, of No. 12
Shepperson, Olga 27, of No. 12
Souter, Albert 69, of No. 2
Souter, Mary Ann 67, of No. 2
Haylock, Joan Stewart 24, of No. 24, died at No. 28
Haylock, Kate 60, of No. 24, died at No. 28
White, William 59, of No. 20a
White, Kathleen 28, of No. 20a
White, Adeline Kathleen 6, of No. 20a
White, Stuart William 4, of No. 20a

4 Musters Road, West Bridgford
Heath, Dora Elizabeth 33, Died same day at home, 17
The Square, Bestwood Village

Port Arthur Road, Sneinton
William Edward Bush 35, of No. 63

Roseberry Avenue, West Bridgford
Smith, Constance May 24, of No. 23
Robinson, Jessie 49, of No. 25

2 Rushworth Road, West Bridgford
Berrington, Barbara Madge 9

Ryeland Crescent
Albert Frettingham 63, of No. 37
4 St Cuthbert's Road
Hitchen, Hugh Lupus 61, Died next day in Nottingham
General Hospital Hitchen, Edith May 52

St. Matthias Road
Burrows, Elizabeth Emma 70, of No. 4
Burrows, Sarah Elizabeth 77, of No. 4

Shakespeare Street, Nottingham
Patrick, Thomas Joseph 59, of No. 50 died next day in Nottingham General Hospital
Thomas, Charlotte Hannah 40, of No. 52
Boaler, Samual 65, of 51 Logan Street, Bulwell died at No. 5
Stonely, Doris Mabel 29, of No. 52

Sherwood Street
Alexander, William Frederick 37, Police War Reserve of 26 Northumberland Street
Sherwood Street, Truman's Garage
Johnson, Jabez 41, of 4 Waverley Terrace
Bestwick, Elizabeth Ellen 43, of 101 Rosetta Road, Basford
Tomlinson, Eileen Madge 20, of 113 Mansfield Road
Tomlinson, Kathleen Mary 15, of 113 Mansfield Road

Station Street, Nottingham.
Boot's Printing Works
Daykin, William 34, Firewatcher of 237 Cavendish Road, Carlton
Needham, Derek Stanley 17, of 62 The Crescent, Breaston, Derbyshire
Sedgwick, Eric 26, of 23 Cranmer Street, Long Eaton
Towle, Harold 20, of 28 Player Street

Trent Boulevard, West Bridgford
Whyte, Joan Arthurson 34, of No. 80
Thurstan, Amy 44, of No. 82
Thurstan, Isabella Grace 19, of No. 82
Thurstan, Elsie 11, of No. 82
Bowler, Arthur 68, of No. 84
Filsell, Letitia Irene 34, of No. 113. Women's Voluntary Service

6 The Crossing
Hannah Clayton 74

Trent Lane
Pearson, Samuel 67, of No. 27

30 Upper Eldon Street
Meakin, Harry 64
Meakin, David 15
Meakin, Mary 14
Meakin, Lily 11
Westwood Road
Barber, Reginald Robert William 33, of No. 34. Died the same day at Nottingham General Hospital

Saturday 10th May 1941

Wilford Road
Proctor, Sarah Ann 65
Proctor, Maisie Clara 30

Monday 12th May 1941

Grange Farm, Cropwell Butler
Parkin, May Adelaide 41, of the farm
Ward, Barbara Mary 21, of 15 Linden Grove, Beeston
Stewart, Barbara Jean 15, of Canal Cottages, Fishpond, Owthorpe

Wednesday 21st May 1941

Nottingham
Thomas, William Harrison 63, of 54 Lees Hill Road. Died at Nottingham General Hospital

Wednesday 16th July 1941

Nottingham
Clay, Arthur Bernard 33, of 40 Trent Road. Died at Nottingham General Hospital

Saturday 16th August 1941

84 London Road, Balderton
Brumpton, Geoffrey Lascelles 18
Brumpton, Joyce 14
Brumpton, Mary Elizabeth 13
Brumpton, Alan 12
Brumpton, Lucy 19
Brumpton, Sheila 6

Tuesday 4th November 1941

Southwell
Tyers, John 30, of 57 Dale Avenue, Carlton. Fireman in National Fire Service

Tuesday 11th November 1941

Nottingham
Cooke, Albert H 36, Leading Fireman National Fire Service of 124 Derby Road, Stapleford. Died as a result of injuries and illness received whilst on duty in Manchester 24/12/1940

Friday 24th July 1942

Hardstaff Road
Sabin, Alfred 39, Firewatcher of No. 18

108 Rossington Road, Sneinton Dale
Morten, Gertrude Morten 65, Died at 207 Standhill Road on 04/09/41

Woodland View, Colwick Road, Sneinton
Camm, Martha 66, Died at Annexe Hospital, Sneinton

Saturday 8th August 1942

Nottingham
Salsbury, Alfred (age unknown)

Sunday 30th March 1942

Miall Street, Radford
Bramman, John Henry Lambert 38, Firewatcher of No. 44. Died next day in Nottingham General Hospital

Wednesday 3rd March 1943

Nottingham
Jackson, William (age unknown) of 2 Snarkstone Terrace, Cardwell Street Hyson Green. Died at Nottingham General Hospital

Friday 14th May 1943

Castle Gate
Kirchin, Arthur 62, of 12 Church Street, New Lenton. Firewatcher. Died 17/05/43 at Nottingham General Hospital

Tuesday 18th May 1943

Annesley Park Road
Offler, Henry Attenborough 33, of 'Halcyon', Papplewick Lane, Linby
Leading Fireman National Fire Service

Saturday 22nd May 1943

RAF Ossington
Bell, Albert 38, of Carlton on Trent.

Monday 7th June 1943

Castle Boulevard, Nottingham
Wright, William Alexander Davidson 37, Police War Reserve of 10 Fairham Drive, Wollaton Park. Died same day at Nottingham General Hospital

Saturday 28th April 1944

Edwinstowe
Freeman, Edwin 33, Section Leader National Fire Service of 80 North Gate, Basford

Saturday 15th July 1944

Birdham, Sussex
Birch, William Clay 45, Fireman National Fire Service, of 10 Manvers Street. Died 12/02/45 at his home

Wednesday 28th May 1947

Mona Road, West Bridgford
Ross, Ronald Charles St John 58, ARP instructor of No.97. Died at his home as a result of illness contracted whilst on duty in an air raid

23rd October 1947

Kimberley Fire Station
Swanwick, Henry Howard 34, Fireman in National Fire Service of 17 Trafalgar Road, Beeston. Injured in 1946 Died in Basford County Emergency Hospital

5th November 1948

Castle Boulevard, Nottingham. Wall's Ice Cream Factory
Bennett, Frank Divisional Officer Nottingham City Fire Brigade

Index